D0392258

DATE DUE

OCT 25			
FEB 1 5 1985			
JAN 4 1988			
APR 1 1 1988			
GAYLORD			PRINTED IN U.S.A.

THE FUTURE OF VOCATIONAL EDUCATION

Edited by
Gordon I. Swanson

American Vocational Association

Staff Editor: Ruth A. Sievers

ISBN: 0-89514-034-9

Published 1981 by
The American Vocational Association, Inc.
2020 North Fourteenth Street
Arlington, Virginia 22201

CONTENTS

INTRODUCTION

Change is the way in which the future intrudes into the lives of people. As the field of vocational education sets foot in a new decade, it is important to consider the changes in conditions that surround the field and, further, to anticipate the extent to which the field will undergo adjustments that may be more or less independent of these circumstances. Both kinds of change occur. The one embraces the evolving nature of a field itself as a civilizing force in a transitional society surrounded by its institutions, values and traditions. The other involves the circumstances reflected more by current events: a leap forward in technology, an abrupt change in market conditions, structural reorganizations or influences as tenuous as a popular fad or slogan.

One cannot address the future of vocational education without reference to the two kinds of changes mentioned above, one being identified with the dynamics of the field itself and the other with the dynamics of the surrounding environment.

While the two appear inseparable, it is useful to think of them as separable: it helps in differentiating between a field's internal dynamics, dynamics generated by external forces and the influence of either or both on a view of the future. In the flow of forces affecting vocational education, internal or external, there are a number which recur with increasing frequency in discussions of the future. Mentioning them here as well as in later chapters of *The Future of Vocational Education* will highlight their importance as well as the importance of differentiating between internal and external change.

First, there is the problem of semantics and definition. Vocational education is a term that is used so widely and applied so broadly that it often escapes precise meaning. Yet it is also a term with a statutory definition, one used mainly to describe the nature of expenditures allowable under the federal statutes. A statutory definition is not very helpful in giving operational meaning to vocational education. It does not diminish the wide and growing definitional disparity that exists, for example, between the federal and local levels of government. In the federal bureaucracy, executive and legislative, vocational education has been seen largely as a remedial and compensatory activity, while at the local level it is seen more as a preventive activity. Statutory definitions notwithstanding, this mismatch in perceptions persists.

To some degree, vocational education does not describe a kind of education at all, but rather it has come to be identified with a wide range of issues and problems in society—unemployment, defense preparedness, serving the disadvantaged and helping the poor. Since vocational education occurs in many places in addition to that provided in schools, it will continue to be seen and defined by the force of external perceptions perhaps more than by the choice of internal managers.

Second, vocational education is growing controversial. The issues identified often touch the most tender sensitivities of society—income distribution, race relations, economic development, equality of opportunity and all of the other issues associated with justice. The issues also touch the proprietary sensitivities of bureaucracies—the questions of who should organize and who should govern. The controversies call attention to both the internal and the external dynamics of vocational education.

Third, vocational education concerns are relatively new on the public agenda. While the field has existed for more than a century, its theoretical and methodological bases are still primitive and much that is known about the field is frustratingly tentative. Independent, institutionalized, intellectual interventions have been slow to emerge. The field has been managed by both state and federal bureaucracies, which have consigned intellectual leadership and inquiry to themselves while being constantly immersed in the present. Although there has always been an official concern with planning, it has been less a matter of vision than a question of deterrence; after all, a bureaucracy's role is to avoid trouble, to protect prerogatives and to insure smoothness. This is not to suggest, as did Henry Kissinger*, that bureaucracy is the natural enemy of creativity and imagination; it is only to point out that it is neither its domain nor its duty. When vision does not emerge from the outside, the role of bureaucracy tends to occupy the whole scene. When concerns are expressed from the outside, vocational education suddenly appears new on the public agenda.

Fourth, vocational education concerns are always associated with, and in part a consequence of, the more general concerns of society. The issues of the 1980s are likely to reflect such associations and consequences. Issues related to jobs, poverty and training are increasingly linked with an apparent inability to deal with national economic problems. It is now uncertain whether the nation can continue to rely on the orthodoxy of economic models based on aggregate measures of economic activity such as the money supply and the unemployment rate, measures that have shed little light on questions of joblessness and inflation. It is increasingly certain, however, that more attention will be given to the unquestioned answers of the past as well as to the unanswered questions of the present.

Once again, it may be possible to expect that individual choices will not be regarded as an irrelevant factor nor as an automatic contributor to seemingly desirable *macroeconomic* ends such as high rates of economic growth and manageable inflation. Individual choices and a local community's concern for the education and training of its younger members have become disconnected from the lofty models employed in attempts to influence the nation's economic health. The need for individual choice and local community decision-making has always been an important conditioning element in vocational education. Its role in the future will depend on how the general concerns of society are reflected in the decisions that make freedoms of choice available to local jurisdictions and, likewise, to individuals.

The Future of Vocational Education addresses the foregoing concerns. They exist as an underlying influence and as a source of conjecture about the future. They increase the difficulty of looking to the future. In any volume attempting to look to the future, there are many possible directions which may be taken. One is an attempt to be predictive or at least to project what popular parlance refers to as alternative futures. This involves such factors as estimates of the number of individual available for training and employment, a consequence of present and estimated birth rates. Less clear in such estimates are the nature of required skills, the effect of legislation, the extent of migration or the employment participation rate of the sexes. Predictions or projections can be "crystal ball" guesses, a form of luxury engaged in to merely escape from the present. They may be conservative or extreme. To warn about the dangers of being extreme, someone has said that anyone with the courage to predict should do so very often!

Another direction involves a decision to reexamine the capacity of the field to look at the future. What tools, for example, are needed to be systematic in looking at the future that presumably are not needed to look at the present or the past? How much care is exercised to insure that the future is not merely relegated to the status of an afterthought, a possibility that must be awaited rather than created by efforts to develop an improved capacity to deal with the present in view of future contingencies? For vocational education, the capacity question is difficult. The field has become heavily influenced by legislation, an exercise in retrospection. Legislation is a follower of public opinion, not its generator. Public opinion never anticipates events; it merely reacts to them. Since vocational education is closely tied to legislative influence, the field is much better prepared to be reactive than proactive.

A third direction is one that often emerges in yearbooks, not as a consequence of planning but rather as visible threads in the emerging fabric, as recurrent themes or as accepted assumptions, which serve as a framework for thinking about the future. What are some of the themes that recur in this yearbook? At least five can be identified:

1. Vocational education is almost unquestioningly assumed to be a market-oriented activity. Often referred to as the labor market, the extent to which it functions as a market, as a place where buyers (employees) and sellers (unemployed workers) come together to engage in exchanges at an agreed price, is uncertain. Much that has been learned about labor markets has been in the realm of their imperfections and inadequacies as markets or marketplaces. Yet there continues to be a kind of accepted orthodoxy that such markets exist and that vocational education is, and should be, closely responsive to them.

2. Federally sponsored programs (such as ones under the Comprehensive Employment Training Act—CETA), which are tangentially related to the local and state initiated vocational education programs, will continue to exist and influence vocational education. The extent to which they will influence the future of vocational education remains, however, conjectural. Most of the federally sponsored programs are protected from concerns about the future by a preoccupation with the imperatives of the present, a present valued less for its virtues than for its distribution of benefits. The future of such programs is a significant political question, particularly in a setting where federal action emphasizes remedial and compensatory activities and local action continues to focus its main emphasis on prevention and preparation. To suggest that such programs will continue to exist is only to observe the strength of political reality.

3. Vocational education deals with a broad span of micro and macro dimensions. Its micro dimensions include the training site, the work place, the job content, literacy skills and individualized instructions. Its macro dimensions include such things as immigration, migration and affirmative action. Few fields of instruction are influenced by such a multiplicity of dimensions, each occurring vividly in every program. These dimensions become axiomatic referents in almost every discussion of present or future vocational education.

4. Vocational education is related, above all, to individual and group values. These are reflected in concerns, for example, for work satisfac-

tion, progression on an occupational ladder, the role of the family and participation in voluntary activities. For many, vocational education is an institutionalization of the Horatio Alger mentality. For some it accommodates the spirit of service to community. This theme is imbedded in the present as well as the future concepts of vocational education.

5. A final and overarching theme that transcends this yearbook is the role of vocational education as a continuing interpreter of the concepts of freedom, equality and justice. No field is more closely identified with allocating or creating opportunity, with the distribution of the rewards that attend job acquisition and advancement or with the way in which opportunities and rewards can be restricted or limited.

It is not merely the presence of these concepts that is so important; it is the recognition of their perishability, the recognition of how quickly their disuse makes them irrelevant. The theme highlighting this importance appears repeatedly in this volume, not as an injunction but as an axiom.

The Future of Vocational Education is divided into seven sections, each addressed by several authors with different perspectives. In Section I, *Lessons from History*, Robert Beck examines the sweep of vocational education through the centuries, its attachment to cultural norms and its association with the poor or charitable influences. Rejecting this as a standard of expectation ordinarily identified with an inertial view of history, Beck proposes the adoption of a "managerial" view in the future, a view that allows parity of esteem and parity of opportunity. Melvin Barlow traces the recent history of vocational education, its struggle to embrace principles and to unify goals.

In Section II, *A Capacity to Look at the Future*, Marvin Feldman, while acknowledging that attempting to predict the future can be a hazardous business, admonishes educators over their lack of willingness to accept change. He points out that placement figures can serve vocational educators effectively as a warning signal in the struggle to stay relevant. William Schoonmaker explains some of the more-commonly applied tools in futures forecasting, while Theodore Buila plays the role of an internal critic and implores his colleagues to build internal capacity to look at the future.

In Section III, *Value Dilemmas of the Future*, Katy Greenwood analyzes the value dilemmas that identify education with work, the background and the future of these dilemmas. Lowell Lerwick addresses the value dilemmas from the vantage point of existentialism while Paul Hammar calls attention to the nonsecular orientation of much that is in the domain of values.

Section IV is addressed to *Future Trends*. Richard Ruff and Bruce Shylo discuss how some of these trends might affect vocational education, offering a 1990 scenario as a basis for further discussion. David Snyder identifies the focus of a most dramatic development, the move toward a "knowledge-based" economy; Roy Amara casts up the accounts of future resources and Warren Johnson advises readers to cope with diminished resources by seeking out the new opportunities that will emerge.

With differing points of emphasis, the authors in Section V, *The Client System*, discuss the future client system. Lawrence Davenport gives much attention to the need to expand the range of the client system. Joel Galloway proposes needed changes in the present or the existing client system while George Copa emphasizes the present and future problem of dealing effectively with unemployed youth.

Section VI, *Organizational and Administrative Challenges*, shows the contrast in perspective of an outsider and an insider to the field. Samuel Halperin writing as an outsider addresses the federal influence on education as a whole, while Robert Seckendorf offers a forward look at organization finance, functional evaluation and the other tasks that require attention by those who are administrator/policy-makers.

The concluding section, *A Framework for Human Resource Development*, is addressed by three authors who share a concern with human resource policy. Sar Levitan observes that the nation has many human resource policies and that humans are better served by policy plurality than by singularity. Merle Strong acknowledges the existence of plurality in human resource policy but proposes that policies should have specifications and he recommends some for vocational education. William Conroy, Jr., calls attention to the field's limited capability for dealing with policy questions, capability to learn about it historical impact and capability to comprehend that analytical tools, though still unused, are now available to shed much light on policy options. Recognizing these capability limitations, Conroy identifies excellence and equity as policy goals as well as policy anomalies that confront the field now and will continue to do so in the future.

G.I.S.
St. Paul, Minnesota
April 1981

---

*H. Kissinger, *The Reporter*, 5 March 1959, p. 30.

SECTION I

LESSONS FROM HISTORY

Never should it be regarded as anomalous for an interest in the future to seek lessons from the past. Nor should one be casual about the importance of the lessons for seeking new ways to view the present and the future. History continues to identify the norms and the forms which are employed to express the value orientations of the groups that make up a society. Yet the forms and the norms are not displayed vividly along with such value orientations. Lessons from history do not emerge without an enormous investment of arduous intellectual labor nor without a sincere commitment to understand the destiny of the human condition.

The close connection between occupational training and the dispensing of charity, particularly during periods of high unemployment, is often seen as a solution to short-term problems. History teaches otherwise, namely, that the solution tends to expand the problem, that vocational education as an act of benevolence is destabilizing to the society.

History further clarifies the elements of individual and institutional life needing continuous regeneration and interpretation. Freedom and professionalism will die with each generation unless it is constantly exercised along with a search for its new dimensions.

These are a few of the lessons of history discussed in this section.

TOWARD A MANAGERIAL VIEW
OF HISTORY

Robert Beck

A philosopher has given us the most-frequently quoted remark about history: "Those who cannot remember the past are condemned to repeat it." Doubtless Santayana would have offered any number of instances that seemed to justify his aphorism; we will add one or two drawn from the past of vocational education. Santayana assumed that unless one knows the past—and takes steps to guard against its pitfalls—history will repeat itself. Of course history need not repeat itself; time need not run in a continuously cyclical path, which is best represented by the roll of the seasons. Men can and have intervened. Rivalry, invention, adventure and more cause the course of events to move in a most erratic way. The *erratic* course is what is to be regretted.

And history does not have to follow an erratic course. Santayana's paradigm has history evolve (sans mankind) with all the inertia of a majestic train moving steadily through curved space. When men are added to this mindless cycle they can, can but not always do, prevent the unhappy elements in this endless circling. Presumably when successful, men shunt the train of events away from accidents. The mystery remains.

THE INERTIAL AND GREAT MAN THEORIES

How humanity has managed change and can do so more effectively is not to be read out of Santayana's seductive adage. Nor can we afford to accept the notion that it should be rather easy to affect progress by avoiding missteps made by our predecessors. Progress cannot be reduced to being on guard against mistakes that have troubled our forebearers.

That is to say, vocational education has not been a series of events such that one has been followed by another with occasional progress being scored by those who have amended earlier undertakings. As things stand we are victimized by an *inertial* view of history, which assumes events follow one another in the same direction unless affected by some outside force. The lessons of vocational history call for a dynamic scene where action can be modified to almost everyone's benefit.

9

But first we must have a theory of history that stands alternative to the inertial view. It must be one that accommodates the quickened tempo of change. The inertial perspective does not. The cyclical sweep has a measure to its pace, not lively, not fast but one with a rhythm appropriate to a simple agricultural, fishing and/or hunting economy. A boy learned from his father or his father's brother and the distaff side of life had its own apprenticeship. Tomorrow was as yesterday and both lived in the character of today. This was the way for centuries. The inertial view was not circumscribed by primitive society. One has only to leaf a Book of Hours from medieval Europe. The scenes are of the season's work, the work of sowing, tending crops, harvesting, hunting. There was very little that differed from one of the earliest writings that has survived in Western literature, Hesiod's *Works and Days* of the seventh century B.C. Much of the subsequent literature offered few exceptions to the cyclical, the seasonal rhythm that seems to show a good fit between the inertial view of history and events.

There were always the great men, the celebration of whose names in the record of the sciences, letters and arts prompted another way of writing history as the story of great women and men. This great man theory of history actually only supplemented; the inertial history was not supplanted. These great men and women only came to represent those outside forces, randomly affecting the historical path. But something was happening that would lead to transforming the manner in which men's history was perceived.

Vocational Education As Charity

'Cared for' is the key phrase. This first phase of a new version of history pivoted about caring; it was a charitable vision of the poor in need of succor. In the history of education this charitable caring is venerable. There is no exact trace of efforts but surely one of the earliest developed out of German pietism and the schooling of orphans and the children of wretchedly poor parents. Here the outstanding figure is August Hermann Francke (1663-1727). Francke's fame spread through much of Western Europe but it is one of the unfortunate tricks of history that what was undertaken with the best of motives had an unhappy consequence. Education for independence because of having a marketable skill became saddled with the reputation of being charitable and its beneficiaries socially lowly.

Thus it was that Baron von Rochow, whose wealth came from farming and who was dismayed by the lot of the rural poor, in 1772 published his *School Book for Children of Country People and for the Use of Village Schools.* Other squires were in no hurry to join with Rochow but his interest did not flag and slowly Rochow won adherents to the charitable message of his first book, repeated in *Schools for the Poor: Abolition of Public Beggary.*

Franke and von Rochow might have promulgated their charitable doctrines in vain had it not been for a Swiss who always felt failure in his lifetime but whose ideas worked magic in Europe and were imported into the United States by more than one observer, whose reports were glowing endorsements of the educational philosophy of Johann Heinrich Pestalozzi (1746-1827). It did not matter to the course of educational thought that Pestalozzi's educational theory was first concealed in a romantic novel.

For 30 years Pestalozzi farmed at Neuhof only to lose everything but his homestead, which he promptly converted into an orphanage. In the orphanage lonely or abandoned waifs learned gardening, cotton spinning and housework, all in combination with reading and writing. The orphanage failed, as did a later attempt at Stanz. Yet while failure plagued the Swiss reformer's practical experiments, his novel, *Leonard and Gertrude* (1782), triumphed. Readers wept over the sentimental portrait of the good and patient Gertrude both teaching the three R's and having her children and the neighbors learn a trade by practicing housework chores, gardening, tending domestic animals and even farming in a very modest way.

Pestalozzi was furious that the novel was highly popular but the educational views neglected. He knew his readers had missed the point. Pestalozzi felt that children had to grow into having self-respect, a sense of being able to make their way in the world. He knew that if Swiss village life was to become less mean, to see less poverty and drunkenness, children had to develop character that could only come with having skills of domestic and other crafts. He knew that general education had to be changed to include what came to be thought of as vocational training.

The charity that colored the humble efforts of Pestalozzi or the better endowed workshops of Philip Emanuel von Fellenburg (1771-1844) marked a turning point in the history of vocational education. The essence of it was the hope that impoverished youngsters could learn a trade that would make them self-supporting, honest and productive however humble. Those who took it upon themselves to have these waifs taught were providing what had stood as apprenticeship longer than anyone could remember. What they did was to keep the concept of learning-by-doing alive outside the familial arrangements that had been common in apprenticeship. The vocational instruction was both elementary and provided out of a sense of charity but the beneficiaries of this charity were learning handicrafts and the elements of the three R's. The sons and daughters of those who stood higher in the social order were learning little more in privately tutored educational ventures.

What was charity for the children of one class was a fine new form of education for patrician youngsters. Not long before Pestalozzi was to feel his first failure and suffer from the misunderstanding that postponed his fame for so many years, Johann Bernhard Basedow (1724-1790) was being hailed. His *Appeal to the Friends of Mankind and to Men of Power Concerning School and Studies and their Influence on Public Welfare* (1768) resulted in money coming to Basedow from all over Europe — money with which to buy time for writing textbooks that he promised would represent a new education. The new education was to blend the three R's with training of the hand and senses! Four volumes appeared and Basedow opened his Philanthropinum in 1774. The name of the school may seem a bit pompous or, at the least, to promise a great deal with its title suggesting that its aim was to educate those who would be friends to men.

Unlike Pestalozzi's orphanages at Neuhof and Stanz, the Philanthropinum did not fail. The sons and daughters of aristocracy came to it rather than the waifs and castoffs sheltered and taught by Francke and Pestalozzi. And the thought of learning domestic and other marketable skills had nothing to do with the curriculum. True, there was attention to all that von Rochow or Pestalozzi felt important but the purpose of building vocational strength was not to taint this new vision of general education. The vision was aristocratic. Work was not sneered at; it simply was not thought of at all.

As we look back, the charity that dogs vocational education in the eighteenth and nineteenth century can leave far too much of an impression. We can be misled into thinking of vocational instruction as only for the poor or if not the under-class, passed on from generation to generation with a mindless inertia that could not make for economic progress and a higher standard of living for the masses of men. Worse yet, vocational education might become labelled something that gentlefolk do not regard as education at all. Of course, gentlefolk did not and do not think that vocational training was or is education. This is quite apparent in Europe today, at least in Western Europe and, if one gets behind such deceptive rhetoric as the Russian talk of blue collar workers as the "noble class", the invidious distinction of training and education holds for the "people's democracies."

Even educators have accepted that duality as witness the popularity of the differentiation between education and training. In no time at all, really in the next philosophic breath, educational theorists spell out their meaning of training by saying that it is a matter of acquiring techniques. These last are often talked down as "nuts and bolts." Precisely the same line of thought divides the pure or basic from the applied, theory from practice. An invidious distinction is made and it is one with historical antecedents. We have got to come to grips with that history and the thought it has transported across the centuries literally for hundreds of years—to appreciate what has to be done in clearing a way for a more promising future. 'A promising future' need not be a vague phrase, a bit of rhetoric and little more. In these pages it means that we will have adopted a *managerial view of history*. That is, history will be seen as a record that guides our action, present action, so that we can watch how our plans shape the future. In this way the past, present and future merge in a functional fashion and not simply as points on a temporal continuum.

THE GREEK CONCEPT OF WORK, RULE AND ABSTRACTION

Many of the attitudes toward work in the eighteenth and nineteenth centuries may be traced to the classic Greek or, at least, the Platonic attitude toward work. Any number of Greeks looked down on what today would be classified as unskilled and blue-collar labor. There is no reason to doubt that in the social stratification of Athenean society, craftsmen were a lower class but higher than those who did menial housework, who swept out the classroom or who tended the swine.

Plato himself honored the craftsman and time and again railed against sophists and all others who lacked true techniques, *technai*. From this review it would seem that the Greeks of classic times held conflicting views about work and workers. In Homer and only a little later in Hesiod's *Work and Days,* work and the worker are honored. So it was with Plato, at least as we have seen for the craftsman. There is no disputing the fact that Plato scourged those who felt that it was important to make money and to win the status and power that went with wealth. That was a different matter from how to look on work and the worker because it concerned what one should honor as the prime value in a life. Plato felt that above all one strove to know justice and to be just. The just, free man then would find himself happy and wise.

In the real world of the Greeks things were different, the worker was looked down upon, however skilled he might be. In the inertial view of things that always has been true. Whatever has been and continues to be said about work being good for developing and maintaining character, the conventional attitude toward work is that it is really a matter of brawn not brain, of hand not mind, for those whose collars are blue, not white, for those who may have nimble fingers and strong hands—and backs—but are not nimble of tongue nor quick of speech, for those not at home with words and such other abstractions as numbers.

It is but a step from this to the conviction that those who can work with abstractions can understand such abstractions as statements of physical principles, the "laws of nature," and such other laws as translate the rules governing grammar, logic (mathematics and statistics) and society. A small step farther allows one to greet as rulers those who can understand the rules and then, presumably, rule. These make up the aristocracy, the *aristoi*, who govern the *(hoi) poloi* grouped as the *demos* who lacking an intellectual elite and political aristocracy, would govern as a democracy.

Plato was clear in his opposition to the rule of the people. Here is the reason why the Platonic vision of man and society is significant for the history of vocational education. It has little, really nothing to do with his value of *technai*, of the skilled craftsman, the skilled worker. (He never alludes to the unskilled and we can assume that he did not think that they needed to be discussed.) It has everything to do with the concept of education as a matter of grasping and using abstractions in the analysis that leads to formulating the great values of life and the rules by which men were to live. In sum, those who could not work with the abstractions that build into laws, into rules, were uneducable. It follows that education had nothing to do with such concrete particulars as would be included in the world of work. It did not traffic with the applied, the here-and-now of the market place.

Only in the recent past has the history of science been complemented by a history of technology. In Plato's shadow would it be reasonable to have expected a history of technology? Yes and no. Yes, because Plato respected *technai* but no when one stops to think that Plato did not consider that teaching technologies or craft skills had any place in education. Surely he would have joined with everyone else who gave the matter any attention in saying that apprenticeship would take care of that "teaching." And that was the thinking that went unopposed—no more, went without consideration even of a complementary curriculum. When Aristotle said that the end of life was thought, he was endorsing Plato. Generations of historians went unopposed in describing as the Dark Ages the centuries that succeeded the so-called fall of Rome in the fifth century A.D. and preceded the Middle Ages—the lapse between the fifth and tenth centuries. It now is an old story to note that those years were said to be "dark" for only one reason: Latin was not generally known! Cultural darkness was held equivalent to not knowing Latin. The reason for that assumption was that manuscripts were in Latin and the inability to read Latin was held tantamount to living in Stygian gloom. The fact that ordinary people were developing all sorts of artifacts counted for nothing. Those inventions, those innovations may have been important for production but they did not require what Plato and Aristotle would have thought to be an education.

Bookishness

This latter belief—that without books education cannot exist—brings us to that controversial figure of the eighteenth century, Jean Jacques Rousseau (1712-1778). "I hate books," Rousseau wrote in *Emile*, "they merely teach us to talk of what we do not know." So upsetting were the ideas espoused by Rousseau in the publication of *Emile* in 1762 that at one point the author had to leave France to avoid arrest.

Rousseau strongly believed that experience was the best teacher and that "true education consists less in precept than in practice." Manual work was necessary, not as an end in itself, but for the development of intelligence. "If instead of making a child stick to his books I employ him in a workshop, his hands work for the development of his mind," he wrote in *Emile*.

Rousseau was all the rage with people of fashion but his point was almost always missed. It was not really that he was attempting to win back for men the Garden of Eden for which the eighteenth century had the more naturalistic descriptor, "the state of nature." Rousseau knew that there was no turning back to some arcadian natural state. The more likely interpretation of his recommendation was that the crafts, certainly agrarian pursuits, encouraged observation, persistence and skill—all of which well might be taken seriously by educators. That had to do with what a general education was about—its purpose and content.

UPDATING GENERAL EDUCATION

Looking to a time more recent, to the modern history of such efforts as now is summed up in the phrase "industrial arts," have we succeeded in rescuing Rousseau's vision? The harsh but true answer is that we have not, neither in preparation for work in industry, nor in that looking forward to employment in business, trade, commerce or in agriculture and agriculturally related employment. But the hope of Rousseau could be clothed in modern dress and make a brave showing as an admirable design for general education that is realistic and forward looking. That is not so much rhetoric. Our general education, even in the elementary school, could have its realism enhanced by attention to vocational life. The idea of a forward-looking general education also is not just so many words. A forward-looking general education takes into account what the future certainly will demand of those who have an adequate general education. If we do not push the future too far ahead in time, we at least can tell what stereotypes of general education are sure to be mischievous. To go the next step and to recommend additions to future models of general education is more difficult but, if we are modest in our proposals, not impossible.

As usually is the case it pays to look back to the classical period of Greek thought when reflecting on the history of education in the West. Plato accepted the standard Greek concept of an *enkuklios paideia. Paideia* translates as education but it is more than schooling. For the Greeks education was not limited to schooling. Education went on in the theater where tragedies educated. The plays were intended to teach, to raise issues about behavior which was righteous and which was not. Such ethical matters went to the heart of what the Greeks thought most important for a man or woman to acquire. The earliest literature we have in the West are the epics of Homer, whom Plato called "the educator of Hellas"—of all Greeks. The *Illiad* and *Odyssey* are replete with "lessons."

Unfortunately for education today, all this has been forgotten and the historian of education has to admit that what survived of Greek pedagogic ideals was the Platonic ideal of being governed by those most at home in abstractions, reinforced by Aristotle. Western educators even forgot that the Greeks were very interested in *musike*—a mix of the arts that made one able to play the lyre to chant and recite the store of poems that followed the Homeric. Some did remember that gymnastics were held essential to acquiring grace and for the military need for strong and enduring men. Yet, towering over all, was the precedent for the academic, that is, the bookish, the abstract against which Rousseau reacted. Education was diminished; it left out training.

What we seek is to put education back together again, a task that should not prove as formidable as restoring Humpty Dumpty. Granted, the restoration of general education is not the same in today's world as in that of ancient Greece. The education that all men should have

16

now must include much which the Greeks and their "students" would be surprised to find being considered. Let us not forget that even the most eloquent words spoken and written on behalf of democracy, those of Thomas Jefferson, did not seem to him inconsistent with the belief that general education did not go further than teaching youth a minimal literacy, the barebones of the three R's. European educators until well on in the nineteenth century took the same leaf from Plato's book. Education was schooling in abstractions. Those who learned their Platonic lessons from Jefferson, A.J. Nock for example, thought that 90 and even 95 percent of men lacked the reason, the mind that this *liberal* education required. Whether intended or not, the Latin root of "liberal" is both *liber,* translating "book" and *liber,* the "freeman", i.e., the man free from work. This man had the leisure to read books; he had no need for apprenticeship, certainly he was not an object of charity. The Greek is more direct on these matters than is the Latin. In Greek the word meaning 'leisure' is *scholia.*

Making a Start

The question is what alterations need to be made in the purpose and activities of education that will bring its contents, even the methods of instruction, into a modern and democratic world? Can these changes be guessed at from the lessons taught us by the history of vocational education? In an optimistic spirit we would answer affirmatively. Let us make a start by discarding the ideal of any vocational instruction being charitable. Not that there is anything but good to be said for charity but charity consists in a spirit of giving, an attitude toward those in need of pity and certain types of succor. It is not an act of charity to ready anyone for making a living and being productive. That is common sense and not charity. Society needs that preparation; it is not a charity to be made available only to the indigent.

Freeing vocational preparation from acts of charity comes with learning the first lesson. The second lesson to be culled from the history of vocational preparation is that apprenticeship is relevant only to a few of this world's youth. If one lives, and will live, in a pre-technological economy apprenticeship is fitting. An inertial sense of history also is apt. Carding wool, spinning, weaving, fishing, hunting and other similar activities go hand in hand with apprenticeship. There may always be room for apprenticeship in learning many trades, on farms and in homes but we now know that less and less of economic activity is to be learned via apprenticeship. That case has been made ad nauseam and need not delay us. What is worth pausing for is the danger in thoughtlessly moving from appreciating that apprenticeship is outmoded to the conclusion that contemporary vocational education is training for the technical, Plato's *technai* brought up-to-date. That conclusion would be a mistake because it would leave the age-old gap between education for the classes and training, albeit technical, for the rest of men.

Our need today is to recall Rousseau's lesson on general education and to supplement it. Very much boiled down, what Rousseau taught was that youth can learn a good deal from learning the crafts. In more recent days this has been put in terms of training the mind by learning the exactness that comes with the measuring done by the carpenter and other virtues associated with the handcrafts. There is no denying that the handcrafts call for planning, exactness in execution, patience and more. But those qualities can be practiced in many activities, not least among them in writing, sports, performing arts and so on. To improve on Rousseau's recommendations we must move well beyond his lesson.

IN CONCLUSION: A MANAGERIAL VIEW

Rousseau's aim was to learn what nature was like, what all reality was like and what one had to learn to manage it. The cue is in the *management* of our world, our environment, including that portion consisting of the interrelationships of men individually and in groups, stratified in so many ways and often overlapping in membership. Today and tomorrow an adequate general education will have to practice students in coming to know something of the dynamics of a person's life and the dynamics of groups. This essay will conclude with a few thoughts on what vocational education can teach us. It is at this point in the discussion that we turn away from the lessons of the past and confront the present with its needs—including the need to think of managing what will be.

The essence of our proposal has two parts. One is the heir of lessons first taught Western educators by the Greeks and restyled in the eighteenth century by Jean Jacques Rousseau. The other is restoration of dignity to vocational education and recognition that vocational-technical education not only is the hub of a general education fitting a new, managerial vision of history but necessary for a sense of competence. Complementing this sense of competence must be an honest ability to produce in an agricultural, industrial and business economy that has swiftly been transformed by science and technology.

The first portion of what we should have learned from the lessons of the past is that a general education must indeed be general, be a circle that can 'surround,' can include all our people. *Enkuklios paideia* we remember to be the old Greek phrase for an education that was such a circle; it encircled all citizens in the sense that each was expected to have shared in it. The content of that *paideia* may not seem relevant to us. We would not be content with what the Greeks meant by *musike*, which we remember, was literature plus the arts, all of which were to be combined with some simple arithmetic, geometry and a great deal of gymnastics. That is exactly the lesson to be learned. Today's general education should be relevant to the day. Our world is such that a vocational-technical education would be relevant as the hub of the wheel that is a general education. For the Greeks the circle was an apt enough metaphor but we must give the circle depth and the image of a wheel gives depth to the circle.

Our metaphor of the wheel, albeit promising, cannot be expected to bear too much weight. Its chief limitation is that it is too static. The hub of our general education is not something to which the several subjects of the elementary and secondary school—and even the junior college level of the educational institutions—are attached. No indeed. Our general education is a dynamic system, the hub of which is an *organizing principle*. We are making no less of a suggestion than that vocational-technical education is that organizing principle. At advanced levels, let us say in the senior grades of the secondary school and certainly at the junior college or area vocational schools, specialized courses will be listed to serve a student preparing for a career in agriculture, agribusiness, industry, commerce, office duty, service occupations and so forth.

This essay has been inspired by reflections on lessons from the past. However intriguing we cannot roam so far afield as to suggest what might be the relevance of vocational-technical education to the elementary school grades or to something beyond the counseling mission to which so many limit vocational-technical education in the secondary school grades. We rest our case for the general education of youngsters by reminding ourselves that the three R's, surely reading and arithmetic, are essential for successful adaptation to this world where science and technology live everywhere in the realm of symbols. And ours is a culture rich in symbols. If anything need be added that touches on the instruction of the adolescent, need we do more than think about the sad fate of those who lack the where-with-all to cope with the symbols that sustain our scientific-technical economy?

Even as citizens, the problems of men today cannot be divorced from vocational realities. One has only to think of the level of wages and salaries, the cost of living, productivity, the ecological implications of certain forms of production, competition at home and with foreign manufacture and on and on. To be concrete, the rate of unemployment among minorities is both a social problem and one that confronts educators as much as it does the public conscience. What more realistic, effective approach to literature, to social studies and collegiate level social science could there be than these issues in which the vocational and technical is undeniably involved?

Thirty years ago some students of the junior and senior high school curriculum advanced the phrase "the core curriculum." The melding of social studies and English literature were the conventional coupling represented by the core. We could revive that reform which perished from neglect. New life could be breathed into it, the spirit of real life, not an act of very occasional and saintly charity undertaken by a few and ignored by most. Children, youth and those not so young, but in want of a second career, would find their preparation for economic productivity moving to the center of the educational stage. And in that move no group would be omitted because of the income, sex, ethnic, religious or racial background. General and vocational-technical education would be seen hand-in-hand rather than differentiated with at best a hesitant concession that the general education was more liberal and "other than" (vocational-technical), if not "better than." For too long the general and liberal have been coupled and blessed as "better than."

If we would manage the future, create a history that will be seen in the future as managerial rather than inertial, the lesson of what has been the past of vocational education will have to be taken seriously. Else we will prove Santayana correct and be condemned to relive our mistakes.

OUR IMPORTANT PAST

Melvin L. Barlow

Vocational education has a deep, rich and abiding heritage and its basic aims have withstood the test of time. The foundations of this mammoth social and economic movement have been carefully delineated over a long period. There is no question that the design for vocational education did in fact promote the general welfare of the nation. Deeply concerned with developing the people's economic potential, it provided them opportunity in the world of work. Achievement of this potential was dedicated to raising the standards of living and educational achievements of millions of people.

In no way were the concepts of vocational education ever considered to be a band-aid to cure the stress of the moment; it was an ounce of prevention, with built-in adjustment factors to keep the program in tune with the changing social, economic and technological growth of the nation.

AN UNFAMILIARITY WITH THE PAST

Vocational education's past appears to be largely unknown to many of today's vocational educators. Consequently they are denied real knowledge of its foundations. Furthermore, when they move into proposed new ventures they are unaware whether this venture is really new or just a warmed-over reject of the past.

Forty years ago nearly all of the people in vocational education were reasonably well acquainted with its history. General practice required that practically everyone entering the field have a knowledge of its historical and philosophical background. The direction in vocational education was constantly supported by attention to basic, rather than extraneous, purposes. In recent years many people have gained positions of leadership and influence in vocational education without any knowledge of its background. Some of these fall unknowingly into the trap of promoting causes antithetical to the purposes of vocational education. What is obviously needed is a renaissance in the study of the history of vocational education.

Why Study History?

But, alas, history like algebra, is frequently dubbed as uninteresting and worthless. In part this may have happened because there are few qualified teachers of the history of vocational education—teachers who are trained and inspired to help others find the true meanings and applications of history. Although some prominent persons have referred to history as a waste of time, others have held different views.

Winston Churchill, for example, said that "the farther backward you look, the farther forward you are likely to see." The philosopher George Santayana held that "those who cannot remember the past are condemned to repeat it." The famous and oft-quoted line from Act II, Scene I of Shakespeare's *The Tempest*—"What's past is prologue"—is plainly inscribed near the entrance to the Archives of the United States in Washington, D.C.

Again, about 40 years ago there were many scholars working in the field of the history of vocational education, but today that number perhaps can be counted on the fingers of one hand. What is probably needed is a new emphasis on the study of the foundations of vocational education as a means of clarifying sound policy. Many years ago at an American Vocational Association convention a person without this background was described thus: he lost his purpose, so he doubled his effort.

A noted scholar of the nineteenth century, Sir Henry Maine, asserted that "except for the blind forces of Nature, nothing moves in this world which is not Greek in origin." Similarly some of the things in vocational education that are supposed to be new are not really new at all; the originators of the vocational education movement identified most of them. Also some new ventures in vocational education really have no bases as a part of the program. Certainly some of the new emphases are entirely unnecessary, probably because the proponents are not aware of the scope of vocational education.

It is the purpose of this chapter to trace a few basic issues in vocational education with regard for their historical origin.

VOCATIONAL EDUCATION AS A SOCIAL NEED

From the beginning one of the principal arguments for vocational education has been its social necessity. Legislation for vocational education, both in the beginning and now, has been social legislation. In theory and in fact vocational education has been concerned with an individual's turning point from economic dependence to becoming a productive member of society. The social structure changes constantly, but vocational education was intended to match this change. Social conditions have been and must continue to be the motivation for change. Because an occupation is the most occupying of all human activities, it sets the tone of social relationships. It is the major element influencing the standard of living; it is a factor in determining family solidarity; and it controls the quality and quantity of civic participation and responsibility.

Developing Citizenship

The bulletins of the National Society for the Promotion of Industrial Education, from the very first one in 1907, make it clear that the first task of vocational education is to develop citizenship, and that this concern should be ever present in vocational instruction.

One of the dramatic incidents in vocational education history is the speech made by Senator Carroll S. Page on the floor of the U.S. Senate on July 24, 1916. Senator Page declared that achieving good citizenship was among the chief purposes of vocational education and that probably there was no other way to achieve good citizenship than through vocational education. The fact that Senator Page spoke to a nearly empty Senate (only six Senators were present and Page spoke for more than three hours) does not change the fact that the social potential of vocational education was recognized and it was not a controversial issue.

Open to Everyone

Very early in the public discussions of the nature of vocational education, a 1907 bulletin of the National Society for the Promotion of Industrial Education reported a consensus that all vocational programs should be open to all; sex, creed, color or nationality should not prevent anyone from attending vocational education classes. This was not a debatable issue—it was a social necessity and recognized as a foundation of vocational education. Contemporary discussions about equity, nontraditional occupations and the like are actually unnecessary. But then so many people know so little about the historical background of vocational education that they think they have discovered something new, while in fact, their new-found concept was there all of the time.

It was no accident, for instance, that in the Vocational Education Act of 1963 the Congress indicated that vocational education was intended for all persons of all ages in all parts of the nation. The word *all* is significant—no one is left out. The social posture of vocational education had been well established, and the Congress merely emphasized the fact. The point is that social needs and concern were built into the vocational education movement in its earliest stages.

There are some limitations, however. Vocational education is concerned with people and the work they do. It was never intended that vocational education solve all of the nation's social ills, and yet some parts of the contemporary rationale seem to move in this direction. The most promising idea is that of cooperation and collaboration with a variety of social agencies for the benefit of special populations.

Concern for Special Needs Youth

During the late 1950s, vocational education leadership realized expansion was needed to include persons who were not necessarily being well served. The Panel of Consultants on Vocational Education, appointed by President Kennedy, became deeply concerned about youth with special needs. A diverse group, they included the physically handicapped, minority youth, potential dropouts, as well as youth that could be characterized as any of the following—disinterested, reluctant, disadvantaged, alienated, delinquent or culturally deprived—in short, the "social dynamite" as described by James C. Conant.

After long discussions and consultation with many persons and groups, the panel recommended to the Congress that vocational education legislation provide specifically for such persons. They would hardly be expected to retire immediately following their regular educational experience and many could profit from instruction leading to employment. This special group became a concern for vocational education.

Vocational education has always had a social flair and concern. This was seen prominently during the 1960s. The time between the report of the President's Panel of Consultants in 1963 and the President's Council on Vocational Education report in 1968 was a period of social stress—the burning of cities, revolts on college campuses, riots in Watts and other cities. The nation was embarrassed by its apparent lack of social consciousness. This social upheaval had a specific effect upon the report of the Council and upon the legislation which followed.

One hopes that some day a historian will document thoroughly how vocational education has reacted over the years to its social responsibility. Vocational education needs this kind of study in order to become aware and appreciative of its social significance. Only the most dedicated of historical researchers ever find this out and the knowledge is too important to deny it to all vocational educators.

EDUCATION AND TRAINING

Vocational education was so named for good reason. The basic intent was, and is, to combine the best of schooling with the best of practical experience. But the words education and training are often considered synonymous and have been used interchangeably throughout the history of vocational education without regard to real or imaginary difference.

The Same Principles Apply

Usage seems to indicate that education is a broader term applied to the learning process while training is applied to a narrower field. In its restricted use *training* has been used in organized learning situations where the acquisition of skill and technique is the goal. *Education* has been thought of as a process of acquiring skills, attitudes and knowledge in meeting life situations that cannot be determined specifically in advance. While training may be differentiated from education, the principles which obtain in the latter also apply to the former.

During the early years of vocational education, and to some extent continuing at present, educators tended strongly to impose traditional academic standards — time, school methods and the like — upon vocational programs. Where such standards were strictly imposed the vocational program became excessively bookish and abstract and lacked the desired technical knowledge and practical skill. Any proposal that a six-months program was appropriate for a particular vocational program was met with incredulity.

In his book *Have We Kept the Faith* (1927), Charles A. Prosser included a chapter about "the baby left on education's doorstep." The baby, of course, was vocational education. Some schools ignored the newcomer, other schools took it in but hid it from view, while still others made it a part of the family and vocational education prospered and made its contribution to the general welfare. Governor James A. Rhodes (Ohio) in his book *Alternative to a Decadent Society* (1969) pointed out that thousands of high school graduates couldn't get jobs, though jobs were plentiful. Why? Their school experience did not include the studies and practical experience that employment demanded.

"Educated Tastes"

From a study of the history of vocational education it is obvious that both education and training comprise the substance of vocational education. A decade prior to the passage of the Smith-Hughes Act (1917), the proponents of vocational education were anxious to pro-

25

mote an intellectual outlook and were aware that raising the standards of family and industrial life depended in great measure upon the educational contribution to vocational goals. In fact it was desired that "educated tastes be developed" either as a prerequisite to, or in concert with, vocational training. Obviously, competency in a variety of subjects such as spelling, writing, arithmetic, grammar, history, geography and others was essential as a background for vocational instruction, but that alone was not enough—actual instruction and practical experience leading to employment were essential.

Looking back from the vantage point of the present, we see clearly that vocational education was not narrow in its proposed scope. Those who persist in making a big issue out of the differences between education and training remind one of the very old principle of indifference—how many angels could dance on the head of a pin, for example. It really doesn't make that much difference. No one in vocational education has ever been committed to an uneducated citizenry.

Students Have Different Goals

Looking to the future, it is imperative to realize that people enrolled in vocational education have several kinds of goals. Researchers Russell Hunter and M. Stephen Sheldon identified five prototypes for persons in vocational education at the community college level: (1) the vocational career program completer, (2) the job seeker, (3) the person desiring to improve job skills, (4) the person seeking a second career and (5) the person who must return to school in order to maintain a license. Certainly they represent different emphases in the degree to which they desire or need instruction called education or training.

Perhaps the most intriguing review of this controversy was identified by philosopher Theodore M. Greene in the fifty-fourth yearbook of the National Society for the Study of Education.

> It is an everlasting pity that so sharp a dichotomy has established itself in our minds between liberal education and vocational training, with the false implication that the former is somehow higher, though useless, and the latter, useful but somehow crass and demeaning. If these two equally essential preparations for life are thus divorced, a *merely* liberal education will indeed tend to be useless, and a *merely* vocational training, crass. What is obviously needed is a truly liberal academic community in which the study of

26

art and typewriting, of philosophy and accounting, of theology and medicine, of pure and applied science are, though admittedly very different, judged to be equally honorable and valuable in their several ways. In such a community the so-called liberal disciplines would indeed be liberal because they would be studied and taught with an eye to the total enrichment of the life of responsible members of a free society; and in such a community the acquisition of the vocational skills, from the simplest to the most complex, would be equally liberal because they would be taught, not in a spirit of predatory egoism, but in a spirit of deep social concern for the needs of others and for the common good.

Only through the study of history can one find such insight as a direction for the future. Those who can read and understand the deep meaning in professor Greene's essay will be able in the future to avoid the trap of useless controversy concerning education and training.

OUR PROFESSIONAL HERITAGE

Only through the study of the history of vocational education can one develop a depth of understanding and pride in belonging to this area of education. The roots of professionalism sprouted concurrently with the development of the vocational movement in education. From the very beginning, the entire system of vocational education was based on high-level goals—for students, for teachers, for programs and for the socio-economic welfare of the nation.

In some respects professionalism in vocational education developed from two basic conditions of the nineteenth century. First, the education of craftsmen had from time immemorial been a problem that craftsmen had taken care of themselves. This was the way it had always been done; there were no problems and everyone was satisfied with the process, including the craftsmen. Societal needs for craftsmanship were being taken care of adequately.

Second, education had developed along the lines of a cultural-liberal-academic motif, and for the most part, everyone liked it that way. A storm of protest arose when educationally adventurous persons wanted to join the two educational systems—wanted in effect to place the preparation of craftsmen in the same context as cultural-liberal-academic education in general.

Those Early Supporters: A Wide Cross-Section

Our professional heritage was based upon the judgment of a vast cross-section of people whose interests in the movement were interests in and for the future welfare of America. Who were these people of vision who would see the potential of vocational education? Their names and the positions they occupied read like *Who's Who* — and like Main Street, U.S.A. At this point it is not possible to identify all of the persons involved during the formation of vocational education, because the movement was nationwide.

Yet for openers, a preview list: George W. Brown, General Manager, United Shoe Machinery Company, Boston; President Theodore Roosevelt; Henry S. Pritchett, President, National Society for the Promotion of Industrial Education (and President of the Carnegie Foundation for the Advancement of Teaching); Jane Addams, Head of Hull House, Chicago; Charles A. Prosser, Deputy Commissioner of Education, Massachusetts; Florence M. Marshall, Women's Educational and Industrial Union, Boston; Frederick P. Fish, President, American Telephone and Telegraph Company; Mary Schenck Woolman, Teachers College, Columbia University; Samuel Gompers, American Federation of Labor; James W. Van Cleve, President, National Association of Manufacturing; John A. Lapp, Secretary, Indiana State Commission on Industry and Agricultural Education; Carroll D. Wright, President of Clark College; Philander P. Claxton, Commissioner of Education; and hundreds of others. No other educational movement has ever been launched in America with such a cross-section of American thought and feeling. From the views of these people we can form ideas about our professional heritage.

From the literature of the period 1906-1917 we can find the attitudes and convictions of the founders and promoters of the vocational movement in education. This historical record, which at times seems elusive, is where you find it. Principally the record is in the publications of the National Society for the Promotion of Industrial Education and in other educational literature of the times. But one must also review the trade journals of business and industry to learn the depth of commitment for vocational education of the non-educational groups of America. It is interesting to note that despite the variety of sources, all seem to relate back to the foundation issues of the National Society for the Promotion of Industrial Education.

The Individual and Work

In the forefront of our professionalism is the primacy of the person. This concept, which is deeply embedded in vocational education, had been explored over a period of three decades by one of the tall men in vocational education, the late Franklin Keller, a man who occupies a position in the foundations of vocational education parallel to that of Charles A. Prosser. In the prologue of his book *Principles of Vocational Education,* Keller writes:

> This book is about life and education — not a segment of education, or education at any "level." It is called vocational education because vocation — what a person does to live, hunting, for instance — is conceived as a focus for many other values, as an integrating principle in a diverse life.

The prologue also sets the tone of the nature of vocational education:

Vocational education means a full, efficient, and happy life.

Vocational education assumes that life has a serious purpose, manifesting itself in a meaningful occupation.

Vocational education makes provision for the wide differences among individuals.

Vocational education assumes democracy.

Vocational education is deeply concerned with the development of the literate, the educated man.

Vocational education is concerned with every vocation.

In Keller's philosophy of education the key words were purpose, diversity, unity, democracy, service and work. And he considered that the greatest of these was work.

If it were possible to suggest an entrance examination for persons entering the field of vocational education it could well cover the ideas found in Keller's book.

The Challenge To Be Better

Historical studies alone produce abundant evidence that the highest quality of professionalism must be continuously regenerated. National, state, regional and local personnel must be better than their predecessors on every count. The educators who are the mentors of the beginning teacher must be better prepared and have a deeper and more abiding commitment to their task than ever before.

The challenge now is exactly what it was more than 70 years ago — the most important asset of this nation is not its tremendous wealth, but its ability to utilize effectively its human resources. If society is to cope with the needs of the declining years of the twentieth century and the beginning of the twenty-first, a new wave of professionalism must become impressed on the leadership of vocational education in America.

NEEDED — A RENAISSANCE

By the mid 1960s vocational education had discovered research, but practically none of the research dealt with the historical area. While few persons in vocational education were qualified to do any kind of research, even fewer were qualified to do historical research. Those who were usually were also responsible for other tasks, and ventures into the history of vocational education became of necessity a low priority. Nevertheless, some persons in vocational education did recognize the need to document developments in vocational education, and their writings became the source of most of the information about the background and purposes of vocational education. This material was used largely by teacher education programs in courses in the history and philosophy of vocational education. However, such courses seem to have the spotlight no longer, and the history of vocational education is not well known among vocational educators.

The needed renaissance is really two-fold. First is deliberate study of the background by all vocational educators. Second, and very important, is the continuation of the historical record. This seems to have fallen completely by the wayside.

The Historical Record at Three Levels

Maintenance of the historical record of vocational education should occur in at least three areas: local, state and national. The real battle of vocational education—the place where the far-reaching consequences develop—is now and always has been on the local level, but few people know about it. We need the record of successes in local activities. Every community in the nation that has or has had a vocational program in operation should record its history. Vocational educators at the local level should move rapidly to see this is done. Source material about the local history must be systematically recorded, reproduced and distributed. It is important to document the nature and extent of programs and the people involved—students and instructors, school and community cooperative efforts, as well as the social and economic impact of vocational education. The process is quite simple: the writer answers the questions—who, what, when, how, why, and where.

At the state level the process should be repeated by documenting statewide efforts in maintaining and expanding vocational education, including relationships and concerns of the state government, state boards and state agencies. A person in the state vocational agency should have the responsibility for preparing and distributing an annual descriptive report of vocational education. The people of any state should have the right to know in some detail what has happened in vocational education in their state each year.

An annual summary of vocational education at the national level is extremely important. A staff, preferably in the Department of Education, should have the responsibility for preparing an annual report — in part descriptive and in part statistical — which can be used as source material concerning the status of vocational education in the nation.

With reports from these three levels much of the history of vocational education would not become lost, and the fabulous story could reach more people. During the very early years of vocational education (1906-c1912) a record of newspaper articles and other information was kept by the National Society for the Promotion of Industrial Education and made available for review. This record is now located in the library of the American Vocational Association.

Historical Interpretation Is Important

Earlier in this chapter an issue was made of the necessity of producing competent historical researchers in vocational education. Researchers who can acquire the facts from source data and then interpret the data with full knowledge of social, economic and technological mores of the time are essential. Too often the early fact is examined in the light of contemporary situations because the researcher failed to become acquainted with the priority issues of the day.

To give an example: why was the vocational education movement so closely related to high school programs in 1906-1917? First, very few persons of high school age were in school. Second, there were so few postsecondary institutions (outside of the four-year colleges) available that it would have been folly to even project such programs for vocational education. But time changes and the movement to include vocational education in postsecondary institutions is entirely appropriate to the social, economic, educational and technological nature of recent developments. The early promoters of vocational education said little about the postsecondary level, but they most certainly would not have rejected the idea had it been feasible at the time.

Interpretive history of vocational education is imperative so to have a variety of views upon which to base projections. Some contemporary vocational educators have explored various ideas about the philosophy of vocational education arising out of the historical record. This venture must be pursued further.

On-the-Spot Reporting

Despite the value of the work of competent historians of vocational education, on-the-spot reporting by any person is imperative. This is the record that becomes lost if it is not reported immediately, and it is desirable because it gets to the fundamental purposes of vocational education. A student around 1900 wrote to the principal of a trade school indicating that before he attended the course in bricklaying his salary was 25 cents per hour. The instruction enabled him to earn 50 cents per hour from his labor. What happens to peoples' economic positions, to their self-respect, to their social positions and to their family solidarity when they improve their productive abilities? This is what vocational education is all about.

SECTION II

A CAPACITY TO
LOOK AT THE FUTURE

Will Americans be better prepared for the decade of the 1990s than they were for the 1980s? Can vocational educators become better prepared for the forces that lie ahead?

There are those who advocate the use of all the available tools for estimating or forecasting the future and, furthermore, to continue to improve the precision of the tools.

Others claim that much of the short-run future has already become available as scenarios existing in the present, ready to be assembled and studied. This is a view that claims the future has very few surprises, not because forecasting is good but because the future comes upon society in the present as scenario-based increments requiring careful observation and study.

Still others are imbued with the notion that the future is something to be created and will exist, therefore, in response to creative energies designed to yield specified future consequences.

These views are neither incompatible nor mutually exclusive. Taken together or separately, they offer clues to the extent to which a field possesses a capability for viewing its own future. This is the general theme of this section.

LOOKING AHEAD: A MATTER OF NECESSITY

Marvin Feldman

Ever since Alvin Toffler published *Future Shock* and Herman Kahn set up the Hudson Institute and the Club of Rome met to tell us, perhaps prematurely, that we would soon reach something called "the limits of growth," trying to see clearly into the future has become a popular parlor game all over the world.

The futurists have an unarguable point.

There's a tendency for the world to change faster than our perceptions of it—as the existence of the flat earth society indicates. So today's policies often deal with yesterday's realities.

If we're going to change that, if we're going to hit tomorrow's targets with today's vocational programs, we're going to have to learn, as any good skeet shooter will tell you, to lead a little.

PREDICTING IS A HAZARDOUS BUSINESS

But, as someone said, we have no facts about the future, so predicting its particulars can be a hazardous business. Recent history is littered with the shattered egos of seers whose predictions of the future turned out to be magnificently wrong.

For example, Lord Rutherford, who is usually called the father of the nuclear age, said in 1933, "The energy produced by the breaking down of the atom is a poor kind of thing; anyone who expects a source of power from the transformation of these atoms is talking moonshine."

During World War II when our Manhattan Project scientists were working frantically to make an atom bomb before the Germans did, Admiral Leahy, then chief of staff, said flatly, "The bomb will never go off, and I speak as an expert on explosives."

Early in the development of the Xerox process, a high-powered research corporation concluded that electrostatic printing was a clumsy substitute for carbon paper and could never be sold in volume. A few years later the Xerox 914 copier had become the most successful single product in history.

Not too long ago, one of the developers of computers said probably only a dozen giant companies would ever be able to use them.

Yet knowledge of the hazards of forecasting does not relieve us of the need to attempt it. For it is one of history's clearest lessons that institutional survival is not a matter of stubbornly standing pat, but of continuous, accurate adaptation to change. Everyone's favorite example is the dinosaur, staring in blank, helpless bewilderment while hordes of termites devour his legs.

Vitality is *not* a matter of learning to repeat established procedures with great and greater efficiency. It is said the inhabitants of the great twin cities of the Indian empire became so efficient at making pottery that it was the custom to use a cup once and discard it. But this once viable civilization did not survive.

A TIME OF RADICAL CHANGE

I believe we may be on the brink of a period of *categorical* change in some social elementals, changes which may not be as distinctive for their velocity as for their radicalness.

In fact, I accept as a useful model the premise of Alvin Toffler's new bestselling *The Third Wave,* in which he says we are caught up in a third historical wave as elementally important as the first two — the agricultural revolution and the industrial revolution.

Toffler says in his introduction that nothing less than a new civilization is being born

> . . . so profoundly revolutionary, that it challenges all our assumptions, old ways of thinking, old formulas, dogmas and ideologies, no matter how cherished or how useful in the past, no longer fit the facts . . . . The world that is fast emerging from the clash of new values and technologies, new geopolitical relationships, new life-styles and modes of communication, demands wholly new ideas and analogies, classifications and concepts.

If Toffler's tone is hyperbolic, his central message is essentially correct.

Mechanical Change

One massive frontier of change is mechanical. In the 1920s a Czech dramatist coined the word robot (from the Czech word for work) and wrote a play in which robots exterminated their human makers and took over the world.

Now, half a century later, more than a hundred firms are making hundreds of different types of robots, thousands of which are in place doing the work men and women used to do. These robots, carefully designed *not* to resemble people, have computers for brains.

They can handle processes with as many as a thousand steps. They don't get tired and they don't talk back. They can work in the cold and in the dark. They don't take coffee breaks. Soon they will respond to spoken orders. Already they can be retrained instantly, simply by plugging them into new software. Their use by industry is increasing at a rapid rate.

The kind of technology robots represent will arithmetically reduce the need for low and semi-skilled workers, but will geometrically increase the need for technicians. Technical education, undoubtedly, is a growth industry.

Electronics and the Cottage Industry

Another massive frontier of change is electronic.

A few years ago, a Chicago bank, goaded by an acute shortage of secretaries, began to use young mothers, retirees and handicapped people to do the bank's typing via computer hook-ups. They're calling these people "home word processing clerks."

There's a name for this arrangement. It's called "cottage industry" and it was the dominant industrial mode *before* the industrial revolution.

This is Toffler's central point. We are living in an increasingly information-intense society and we are increasing by staggering multiples the efficiency of machines that process information and the means of transmitting it. In short, soon we clearly will be able to transmit work to the people instead of transporting people to work.

A Western Electric engineer estimates that a third of the workers at one of their advanced manufacturing facilities could work at home with existing technology. A Hewlett Packard manufacturing manager figures 35 to 50 percent of his employees could work at home. A vice-president of Ortho Pharmaceutical told Toffler that "fully 75 percent (of his employees) could work at home if we provided the necessary communications technology."

For years we have been hearing about schools without walls. Now we can imagine corporations without walls. These developments are reinforcing a third massive frontier of change which is humanistic — more decentralized, re-humanized, entrepreneurial forms of industrial organization.

Norman MacRae, deputy editory of the London *Economist,* has pointed out that since the turn of the century we have increased productivity by the use of a top-down form of organization, in which

37

executives arrange how people on the assembly line work with their hands.

But this era is almost over. MacRae sees larger corporations evolving into "confederations of entrepreneurs." He believes "many of the things that have been run by some disciplined process will need to be made much more entrepreneurial."

EDUCATION AND CHANGE

If this is so, the implications for education are staggering but regrettably, even before this new deluge of change descended upon us, the American educational establishment was not known for its adaptability.

There is constant talk of change, and the press is full of breathless announcements of promising innovations in teaching technology. What has happened is the creation of an illusion of adaptability in a sector of society that has been painfully slow to adapt.

The principal illustrations of this embarrassing reality are familiar. The summer recess, which is only now beginning to disappear, is a holdover from the distant day when, as a primarily agricultural society, we needed young people to help with the harvest. The lecture method, absolutely necessary before the development of a movable type, has been logically obsolete for centuries. But it is still the basic method of information transfer in most of our educational institutions.

A Matter of Necessity

It is not much of an exaggeration to say that industry absorbs more change in a year than education absorbs in a generation.

There is a neglected reason for this. Industry accepts change, not as a matter of choice but as a matter of absolute necessity. Industry is not magically exempt from that stubborn and universal tendency to resist change; it probably fights change as fiercely as the rest of us. The difference is that industry more often loses the fight.

The inexorable competitive pressure of a free economy forces continuous innovation and its prompt, universal imitation. The changes American industry has absorbed since the great depression are absolutely staggering and there may be as much change in the next 10 years as we have seen in the last 50.

Educators must quicken the search for ways to keep pace with change—to develop internal mechanisms of their own that compensate for the lack of external discipline. And the central mechanism must make a concern for the shape of the future integral to the daily life of *all* our institutions. There must be a new awareness and acknowledgement of our inertial tendencies and continuous efforts to correct them.

Two years ago, I challenged *all* the departments at the Fashion Institute of Technology to spend a full year rethinking what our industry will require tomorrow and how we should change what we do today to meet those requirements. We are now making that process a continuing one.

Early Warnings

Vocational educators have an advantage in the struggle to stay relevant. Our placement figures constitute a distant early warning of irrelevance. If we watch them closely and search out the reasons for any change — particularly any negative change — we can keep hitting the target even as it moves faster and faster.

But an awareness that we are preparing people now for a work market that is changing more elementally than at any time since the industrial revolution has become a desperately important component in the administration of vocational programs. Thinking about the future now and adapting for it is a responsibility all vocational educators must face.

AN INTRODUCTION TO FORECASTING

William E. Schoonmaker

The serious study of the future is a relatively new development, if one equates the word *serious* with attempts to be scientific and objective. Admittedly, people have long been interested in the future; sooth-saying, tea-leaf reading and fortune-telling have been around for centuries. Only during the last few decades, however, have scientists and the formally educated decided to enter the arena of future fore-casting. Few, if any, of the newest attempts to understand the future contain the drama and the mysticism of the old ways, yet they deserve at least as much attention.

The models and methods dealt with in this article are largely untested and the subjects of continuing debate, but they represent what generally are accepted to be the most scientific and potentially productive prognosticating techniques yet to be developed.

Some confusion exists over the terminology used in the field generally known as *future studies,* and it may have arisen from mild debates in the literature. No attempt will be made here to take sides or otherwise enter the debate. However, a few comments of clarification should be made.

The term *forecasting* is used frequently. Central to most forecasting techniques is the understanding that the future does not now exist, as it might in a fortune teller's crystal ball. No one making a forecast is seriously attempting to foretell what the future will actually be like, but rather, what the future might be like. Even weather forecasters will admit, albeit sometimes reluctantly, that their forecasts represent the possible, or at best probable.

Forecasting assumes the future will be caused by the interaction of events; these events include those which have come to pass, those presently occurring and those which are about to happen. Anticipating the future involves the ability to reflect on this chain of events, to understand how each element affects the others and to see where the chain eventually may lead. Accurate hindsight, then, as well as foresight is integral to forecasting.

In some circles an attempt is made to differentiate between *quantitative* and *non-quantitative* methods for studying the future, depending upon the degree of reliance on tying the past and the present to the future (Ezell & Rogers, 1978, p. 123). Some methodologies, such as trend extrapolation, are based on an explicit understanding of prior events and are thus more quantitative. Others, for example scenario writing, are categorized as non-quantitative because they rely primarily on the intuitive judgement of individuals.

It is difficult to argue that any of the methods used, including those strongly based on intuition, do not to a substantial degree rely on an understanding of the past. Although some forecasting involves greater use of quantitative, numerical analysis than others, no true forecasting operates in a total vacuum. Forecasting is based on information and information requires knowledge.

The word *futures* is commonly used, as in *futures forecasting*. The use of the plural is not incidental. Most people involved with the study of the future accept the view than many alternative futures exist. Events, which are often the products of human endeavor, shape the outcome of the future. When one subscribes to this view of the world, it is not difficult to perceive the future as a range of possible alternatives, rather than as a single fixed outcome.

There are many different forecasting techniques in use today and many variations of specific techniques. One way of classifying forecasting into general categories is by the method employed for arriving at conclusions (Ezell). Thus, forecasting methods can be categorized as:

1. *extrapolative*—involving techniques that rely on projecting present trends into the future, usually with the assumption that a given trend will follow a predictable course;
2. *combinatory*—using strategies to related various kinds of change to one another so the interrelationships and consequences of different events can be better understood;
3. *consensus*—soliciting the opinions of different individuals, frequently an identified group of authorities, to gain a view of the future through their collective insight, and
4. *creative*—speculating about events to come, often in the distant future, which cannot realistically be projected from current trends.

On the following pages several of the most commonly utilized forecasting techniques and methods for developing general awareness of potential futures will be described. Proceed with at least two thoughts in mind. One is the observation that forecasting the future is "usually difficult, and always suspect" (Koehler, 1979, p. 200). The other is that it is realistic and desirable to believe people can actively influence their future. To adopt any other view would leave us as "passive pawns in a game whose outcome is already determined" (Rhatigan, 1972, p. 2).

FORECASTING METHODOLOGIES

Trend Extrapolation Forecasting

Probably the simplest and most frequently used method of forecasting is trend extrapolation. In nearly every phase of one's daily routine there are predictable patterns or trends. For example, it may not be difficult to predict that each Monday morning will begin with the ringing of the alarm clock, that breakfast will consist of the usual staples and that one's work day will progress as predictably (or unpredictably) as usual. Lunch will be taken at the cafe across the street from the office and the evening paper will be waiting, as usual, somewhere in the vicinity of the front porch when the day is over.

Without giving much thought to it, each of these future events will be expected to happen on the basis of observed patterns from the past; one's expectations (predictions) are based on the assumption that recent patterns will continue into the future (Collins, 1979, p. 22).

But what happens if the alarm clock fails to go off as expected or the cafe across the street burns down? Trend extrapolation relies on the probability that observed patterns will continue and is always subject to inaccuracy when unexpected, intervening events occur to alter the trend. As more time elapses, the likelihood of the unexpected increases. Because of this, trend extrapolation is usually viewed as credible for predicting events limited to the near future.

A study performed in 1968 offers a sample instance demonstrating the varying reliability of trend extrapolation (VanTil, 1979, p. 63). The study, which attempted to project the future of teacher education, took into consideration *system breaks*—possible events that contained the potential for radically altering existing trends and thus disrupting the study's projections. These included nuclear war, famine and computer domination. Although none of these breaks has occurred, the study did not consider another possibility—the women's movement —a development that has already begun to erode some of the study's projections. The substantial and fast-moving changes in the roles of women have already had a pervasive effect on employment, family life and values, which were unanticipated in 1968.

Trend analysis is used with more frequent success in the business world in matters such as stock market transactions and in anticipat-

43

ing the marketability of goods and services. By applying trend extrapolation, the broker may be able to advise when to buy low and sell high. Through analyzing recent trends in the sales of straight leg versus flair jeans, a clothing store buyer can determine the relative quantities of each to be purchased for future inventory. In either case, recent trends are used as a basis for forecasting what the future will be like.

Trend extrapolation can be divided into several subcategories, including:

1. *persistence forecasting*—assuming that the future will be the same as the past, or without substantial variation;
2. *trajectory forecasting*—assuming that, although change will occur, it will continue at a predictable rate;
3. *cyclic forecasting*—relying on the belief that cyclic patterns previously observed will continue into the future;
4. *associative forecasting*—assuming that a given event is causally associated with another event and that they will occur together, and
5. *analog forecasting*—believing that a given trend may be viewed as analagous to another trend, and that one may be used as a model for the other (Hencley & Yates, 1974, pp. 15-16).

Matrix Forecasting

In its simplest form a matrix is a rectangular grid, such as the type one might find in a teacher's gradebook in which students' names are listed in the left margin and various examinations are listed across the top margin. Each cell within this matrix would contain a grade that could be interpreted as a measure of interaction (or performance) between a given student and a given examination. Matrices typically are used to analyze interaction between several subjects, events, trends or combinations of factors.

One commonly used form of matrix forecasting is known as *cross-impact analysis* (Charlton, 1979, p. 137). In this simple type of matrix, the same factors are listed across two adjacent margins of a grid. Each intersection is analyzed separately to determine the impact one factor might have on another. For example, a cross-impact matrix might be developed to analyze the potential interaction of several events occurring simultaneously during a school's open-house day. Predominantly used for attempting to determine the effect that one event might have on another, this type of matrix forecasting does not provide answers, but it does raise questions.

44

Another form of matrix analysis may be used to clarify the relationships between various trends (McNamara, 1976, p. 153). In a typical example of *trend impact analysis,* a panel of subjects might be asked to rank a list of trends on the basis of two factors, *likelihood of occurrence* and *relative importance.* After being ranked, each trend would be placed into a cell in a matrix crossing those two factors; placement would depend on both the relative likelihood and importance assigned by the subjects. Trends ranked as less likely to occur and of lesser importance would appear near one corner of the grid, while events ranked as more likely to occur and of greater importance would appear in the opposite corner. Such a matrix would clearly show each trend's relative place in the scheme of likelihood and importance.

Matrix forecasting frequently includes the use of statistical analytic procedures, such as cross-correlation and analysis of variance. However, a matrix may also be effective simply as a means for graphically depicting a set of potential interactions for the purpose of structuring discussion and raising questions that otherwise might be overlooked.

Relevance Trees and Future Circles

Relevance trees and other similar devices such as decision trees (Charlton) are especially useful for management and goal-oriented forecasting. They usually begin with a line representing a single event or decision and then build into a more complex network representing the possible flow of events over a period of time. The development of the tree is usually from top to bottom or left to right and progresses in a constant direction until the events representing the bottom of the hierarchy are reached. The final form of the relevance tree resembles the network of branches on a tree stemming from a single trunk; hence its name.

In the case of the decision tree, the beginning point is usually an imminent or recently made decision. At each intersection a yes or no decision is labelled and identified on the resulting branch. Successive yes and no alternatives are plotted in a clear graphic format so that the likely eventual outcomes of a variety of key decisions can be predetermined, analyzed and discussed. In doing so, an individual or group can map out the probable outcome of a variety of events as an aid in decision-making. Alternate paths of action can be anticipated in the event intervening factors force a change in direction.

Not entirely unlike the relevance tree, future circles may be used to map the ramifications of a single event or issue. To begin, a circle is drawn in the middle of an area large enough to permit considerable

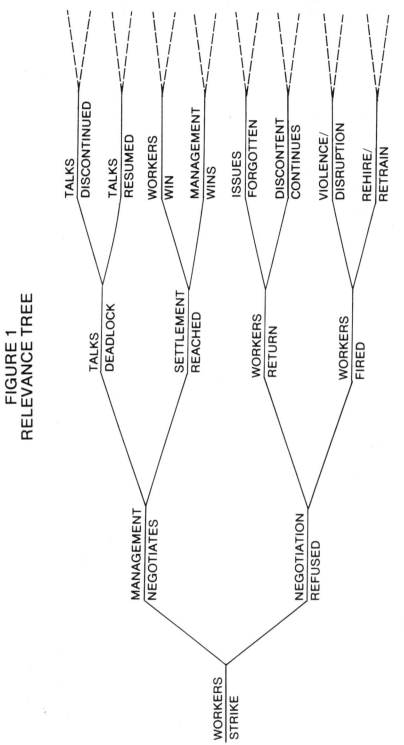

FIGURE 1
RELEVANCE TREE

WORKERS STRIKE

MANAGEMENT NEGOTIATES

NEGOTIATION REFUSED

TALKS DEADLOCK

SETTLEMENT REACHED

WORKERS RETURN

WORKERS FIRED

TALKS DISCONTINUED

TALKS RESUMED

WORKERS WIN

MANAGEMENT WINS

ISSUES FORGOTTEN

DISCONTENT CONTINUES

VIOLENCE/ DISRUPTION

REHIRE/ RETRAIN

The above represents the possible flow of events over a period of time should a given event occur (workers strike) with subsequent alternatives following. Three tiers of events are shown; additional development of various branches could be done if desired.

FIGURE 2
FUTURE CIRCLE

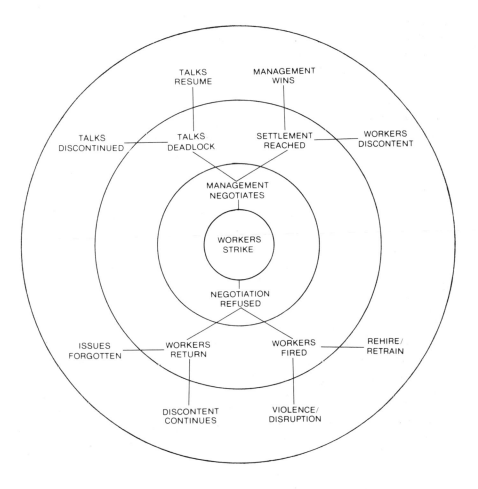

This diagram illustrates how the same event dealt with in the relevance tree (Figure 1) might be developed in the context of a future circle. The future circle is especially appropriate for identifying the potential repercussions of events where more than two alternatives exist for each event.

expansion. A lone issue or event is written within the circle, and then related or tangential ideas are placed in five or six circles surrounding the original. Third and successive layers of circles are generated and connected to their parent circles until the future circle has been expanded as far as desired. The end result may be several dozen related ideas or issues all spawned from the original central topic. The future circle provides an effective means of analyzing a wide range of repercussions that may surround a single event or decision (Charlton).

Simulation and Gaming

Both simulation and gaming involve attempts to create the setting and structure of a future or hypothetical event in order to determine in advance what might happen. The armed services occasionally engage in war games and astronauts take part in preflight simulations. In both instances, the partaicipants are helping to construct a forecast of the real-life event. These dry runs are conducted as accurately and seriously as possible in order to uncover difficulties, oversights and design flaws in anticipation of the future event. Ideally, if problems are encountered, corrective action may be taken prior to the actual event; alternative strategies can be planned.

Applications of simulation and gaming are not restricted to the military and space program. Anyone who has been in a school play has probably gone through simulation in the form of a dress rehearsal. Students who take part in mock trials or participate in formal debates on legal and social issues are gaming. Each year thousands of students take part in model United Nations programs and debate world issues while role-playing as ambassadors of member nations. Each of these examples represents an attempt to simulate a real or hypothetical situation with a focus that is usually future oriented. Rarely are the events played out as reenactments of historical events; rather, they are vignettes of the future.

Many classroom teachers effectively use gaming as a regular part of their routine (Bartling & Johnson, 1979, pp. 26-27). Temporarily removed from the constraints of the present and letting their imaginations place them somewhere in the distant future, students can be released from limiting, preconceived perceptions of how the world operates. They can assume a temporal framework that allows them to look back objectively on the world of the present and analyze, discuss and reflect upon potential solutions to problems. A problem is sometimes easier to solve if one can step away and view it with some distance; future gaming can help create that detachment necessary for objectivity.

The Delphi Technique

Much attention has been given this form of consensus forecasting since its inception nearly 30 years ago. Originally developed by Olaf Helmer and colleagues of the Rand Corporation as an experimental technique for measuring predictive ability through group consensus, the Delphi technique has been used in a wide range of applications, including many in government, business and education (Fisher, 1978, p. 64).

The Delphi technique is a multistage process with several variations. In most applications a panel, frequently composed of recognized authorities in a given field, is asked to respond to a series of three or four questionnaires; each round of questionnaires explores the same general topic in successively narrower terms until a near-concensus is reached. Panelists are often asked to project ahead several years and to give their opinions regarding the nature and time-scale estimates of future events. The following describes a typical application of the Delphi technique.

Round one begins with the initial mailing of questionnaires to the selected panelists. Although the number is not too critical, panels of fewer than 25 are usually considered too small, while panels exceeding a few hundred may be too large. The initial questions are usually open-ended enough to permit considerable latitude of response. Panelists, who remain anonymous, indicate their willingness to participate by returning the initial questionnaire before a prescribed date.

Round two begins after the researcher has analyzed the responses to round one. The second mailing contains a summary of the previous round's responses, frequently with statistical data, as well as a second, more specific questionnaire. Round two concentrates on the opinions shared by a majority from the first round and asks for more detail. Participants are encouraged either to shift toward a consensus or to provide a rationale for divergent viewpoints. Second round responses usually show a considerable narrowing of opinion.

Round three is sent out with a summary and analysis of round two responses similar to that which followed round one. Participants once again are asked to review the data and reassess their positions if they still differ significantly from the center. Rationales for divergent viewpoints are again encouraged. When the data from round three are analyzed, a decision to send out a fourth round of questionnaires may be made if further narrowing or clarification is desired. The hoped-for result is a fairly well-defined assessment of a probable future based on the collective opinions of the panelists (Brooks, 1979, pp. 377-378).

Although the Delphi technique has been used extensively and has many proponents, it has also been the subject of some controversy. Applications of the Delphi technique have been criticized for: 1) avoiding the use of standard statistical tests, including tests of significance, standard errors of estimate and correlations; 2) failing to employ replication; 3) being used for projective purposes inconsistent with the technique's original design and 4) failing to provide evidence of validity or plausibility of predictions (Fischer, pp. 69-70).

Proponents of the Delphi technique point to its economy of administration and lessening of the bandwagon effect through ensuring the anonymity of panelists and eliminating the likelihood of lengthy, persuasive arguments that could bias opinions in group conferences (Barnette, Danielson & Algozzine, 1978, p. 68).

Scenarios

A scenario is an intuitive story or play which attempts to describe a *possible* future, rather than *the* future. It may be in narrative or outline form and may be written or oral. Frequently inspired by a short, unfinished phrase such as "By the year 1995 public schools no longer existed because . . .," scenarios may take the form of the possible, the probable or the preferable (Charlton, p. 138).

Scenarios may be developed by each student in a given class or by a selected panel of two or more individuals addressing the same theme. After participants have presented their scenarios, discussion follows so that various scenarios may be criticized, defended or amended. Rarely is an attempt made to build scenarios on the basis of scientific or empirical fact; their purpose is only to describe what might be so that a free and uninhibited discussion of possible futures can ensue.

Although less quantitative and therefore more subjective than other forecasting techniques, scenarios have several advantages, including: 1) they allow a group of individuals to focus on a wider range of alternatives than might otherwise be considered; 2) participants are encouraged to consider details and dynamics that probably would be overlooked in other more quantitative exercises; 3) they may be used to explore a range of possible outcomes for past crises, had events been dealt with differently and 4) they may be used to test or demonstrate the feasibility or plausibility of a hypothetical sequence of events, either in a historical or future context (McNamara, p. 155).

CONCLUSION

The techniques briefly described in this section are those most commonly encountered in educational practice; however, they do not fully exhaust the inventory of forecasting methodologies available. There are others, many resembling each other or those already covered, the reader may want to explore. Individuals desiring more comprehensive and detailed information on futures forecasting have many sources available to them.

Future forecasting should not be viewed as an activity exclusively reserved for think-tank theoreticians or silk-robed swamis. Anyone who wonders what the future may be like is a potential futurist; anyone who attempts to anticipate the future for the sake of being better prepared is a practicing futurist. Moreover, the techniques covered in this chapter should not be viewed as the correct or the best methods. Future studies is a young discipline and there is surely ample room for the continuing improvement and development of forecasting methodologies.

The study of the future is not a science, although many of the people involved in future studies strive to be as scientific and objective as possible. The methods employed are not flawless, yet many possess proven utility as means of clarifying needs and goals, as well as serving to assist in planning and preparation.

At the very least, future studies can play a motivational role in education by helping educators and students develop a future orientation in their thinking and by inspiring them to plan ahead. At its best, future studies may provide the means for recognizing the range of alternatives available and for selecting the best future.

REFERENCES

Barnette, J.J., Danielson, L.C., & Algozzine, R.F. "Delphi Methodology: An Empirical Investigation." *Educational Research Quarterly,* 1978, *3*(1), 67-73.

Bartling, D., & Johnson, B.P. "Future Games." *Man/Society/Technology,* 1979, *38*(5), 26-27.

Brooks, K.W. "Delphi Technique: Expanding Applications." *North Central Association Quarterly,* 1979, *53*(3), 377-385.

Charlton, R.E. "Futurists in Biology: Some Techniques." *American Biology Teacher,* 1979, *41*(3), 136-139.

Collins, R.A. "Extrapolation: Going Beyond the Present." *Media Methods,* 1979, *16*(3), 22-25.

Ezell, A.S., & Rogers, J.K. "Futuring Technologies in Education," *College Student Journal,* 1978, *12*(1), 122-136.

Fischer, R.G. "The Delphi Method: A Description, Review, and Criticism." *The Journal of Academic Librarianship,* 1978, *4*(2), 64-70.

Hencley, S.P., & Yates, J.R. *Futurism in Education: Methodologies.* Berkeley, California: McCutchan Publishing Corporation, 1974.

Koehler, V. "The Future of Teacher Preparation and Research on Teaching." *Theory into Practice,* 1979, *18*(3), 200-203.

McNamara, J.F. "Trend Impact Analysis and Scenario Writing: Strategies for the Specification of Decision Alternatives in Educational Planning." *The Journal of Educational Administration,* 1976, *14*(2), 143-161.

Rhatigan, J.J. "Looking Forward to the 1980's." *NASPA Journal,* 1979, *17*(2), 2-10.

VanTil, W. "Toward the Year 2000: Teacher Education." *Journal of Teacher Education,* 1979, *30*(5), 63.

CAPACITY BUILDING IN VOCATIONAL EDUCATION

Theodore Buila

INTRODUCTION

The comments and thoughts in this essay are intended for my vocational education colleagues. It has been of great concern to me that far too many of us for far too long have been at work on the margins of vocational education—busily doing other people's work. Specifically, I refer to: (1) time and dollar resources spent away from our students to service agency regulations and in generating or storing data and (2) consulting activity, either as individuals or in a project format, that rarely goes beyond our own or someone else's response to a Request for Proposal (RFP) to produce internal lettuce to document the fact that agency staff are busy. Aside from the research and development devoted to strengthening the social integrity of vocational education, little of what poses as research and development can honestly be called a capacity-building activity.

What is most discouraging as we enter the 1980s is that we see at least some of vocational education's leadership ready to sacrifice vocational education's populist inheritance of an active commitment to full family education, excellence in craftsmanship and a continuing effort to achieve an equitable distribution of the benefits of technology. To the extent that vocational education becomes an accessory to a crib-to-grave public employment program for the culturally 'unaccepted,' we will truly have consumed our transcendence in vain.

It is imperative to remember that as recent immigrants to the intellectual community, our forebearers were never without purpose. They wanted an access to knowledge for us, their children, so even if they would not live to share the intellectual capital of humanity, their children would. The task of re-earning our inheritance and adding capital for the next generation is what capacity building, by necessity, must be. We have to push at these boundaries or vocational education will cease to be a civilizing force. The time is for self-examination and honesty. Certainly we have to agree with Shaw that "The more things a man is ashamed of, the more respectable he is." I don't think we are as respectable as we should aspire to become.

Our field gained stature wtih the problem-solving approach; we have taken pride in managing learning resources and in sharpening our ability to define as well as to solve problems. And we have a reputation of getting things done, often a little faster than some of our colleagues in education. Knowingly, we may also have been too willing to incur the deficiencies that come with "ad hocing" vocational education toward its future.

One very real result of this pattern of *reacting* to the educational and political bureaucracy has been the accumulation of a staggering amount of excess pseudointellectual baggage that exists to exhort us about what we should, and should not, be doing. I refer to labor economists, sociologists, psychologists, political scientists and other vocational education dilettantes that gadfly at the margins of the field. Most have yet to wash their first piece of vocational education laundry. The image that El Greco gives us of Christ throwing the money changers and livestock merchants out of the temple comes to mind as an essential task vocational education must undertake in restoring integrity to the profession.

There are at least four major activities in the capacity-building exercise that need to be addressed: (1) a critical assay of vocational education in terms of where it came from, where it is today and where it is heading; (2) the identification of critical elements for change and their use in programming a fuller utilization of learning resources, a step that will by necessity require some institutional restructuring; (3) identifying the particular strategies and tactics for instituting change and (4) identifying a literature that will serve as the foundation for lively dialogue and spirited discussion of our evolving field.

In this essay, I will deal with the first two activities by discussing the field from the viewpoint of the public (outsiders) and also the profession (insiders). Discussion of strategy and tactics will permeate all which remains. Its central feature will be the most important act of reform, the *full return* of vocational education operations to states and local communities, an exercise essential for recapturing the spirit and restoring the health of the field. The section on literature, the basis for foundation dialogues, is included as a direct challenge to some of the contemporary notions of what constitutes a literature for vocational education. As recent immigrants, our naturalization papers permit us to polka in the public library.

In designing an overall strategy for capacity-building in public sector vocational education, the exercise should be sensitive to the differing perceptions and expectations of its various clients. What the public *sees* vocational education as and *how the profession sees itself* are two different points of reference. This much is certain. What is less certain is whether the profession, those entrusted by the public to provide leadership and direction, is fully comprehending the public's perceptions. The leaders I refer to involve the established bureaucracies including state vocational education staff, federal Department of Education staff, professional organization staff, and private sector vocational education consultants and those who train the teachers.

There is a very real danger that such leaders could become so consumed with the tasks of internal management of educational systems that they forget that parents, above all, want their children to be literate when they finish compulsory education. The ingredients of literacy have not changed a great deal in the past 50 years: oral and written communication skills, a sense of history, and the beginnings of applied ability in science and technology and some ability to deal with society's institutions.

We must be careful that, in our zeal to strengthen vocational education from the inside out, we don't find ourselves with more students and less education. The public's expectations are to be served first. Our task then becomes a dual one: (1) to educate students of vocational education to acceptable levels of literacy—fully recognizing that the definition of literacy differs among students owing to their age, ability and background and (2) to strengthen the professional integrity that deals with the basic purpose of relating education to work.

THE PUBLIC'S VIEW OF VOCATIONAL EDUCATION

National Awareness—Vocational Education Exists

The school-to-work and work-to-school connection has become an accepted way of American life. A recent Department of Education estimate of 22 million public vocational education students coupled with at least another 5 million enrollees in private schools and government training programs represents a fair estimate of the current volume of vocational education. The reason why enrollments have grown rapidly in the past 20 years is not central to this discussion for the moment. What is, though, is that the participation rates suggest a substantial shift in the public's attitude about schools and applied education. Remember, it was only about 120 years ago in 1859 that Senator Rice from Minnesota employed educational arguments to put part of the public's case against the proposed land grant college legislation:

> If you wish to establish agricultural colleges, give to each man a college of his own in the shape of one hundred and sixty acres of land, where he and his children can learn to make it yield the fruits of the earth in the greatest abundance; but do not give lands to the states to enable them to educate the sons of the wealthy at the expense of the public. We want no fancy farmers; we want no fancy mechanics; but we do want homes for the working artisans and the cultivation of the soil.

Vocational educators should not be too anxious to conclude that America has turned the anti-intellectual corner by its vote to endorse growing attendance. Even as vocational education church-attendance figures confirm the birth of a new American educational religion, we'd best not start acting like bishops! About the only fact we need to take away from the partcipation figure (buttressed with industry training program numbers) is that we can be sure that most Americans are aware that something called vocational and technical education exists.

Public Participation

The growth in public sector vocational education enrollments in the 1970-79 period is little short of phenomenal: eight million in 1970 to an estimated 22 million in 1979. The range of course offerings covers the entire landscape. When public schools lag in course offering or know-how, the private sector is ready with an assortment of 7,500 technical schools and no one knows how many "how-to-do-it" courses are offered in studios, shops and church basements. And, remember, we have not even begun to count private industry training/management programs, trade union apprentice programs and the myriad of Department of Labor manpower programs. Americans, many at least, have become life-long vocational education activists.

The Federal Presence in Vocational Education

Local property taxes, school board elections, school band uniforms, community colleges—all of these serve as daily reminders that America's education is a local affair...well, almost.

The public's awareness of a federal involvement in vocational education probably started at the end of World War II. The training benefits of the G.I. Bill began the flow of checks from Washington,

56

D.C. Then came the Department of Labor Manpower Development and Training Act programs in the early 1960s and their successors in the 1970s along with increasing participation by workers in the retraining programs under the Trade Acts. There is no doubt that many adults are very aware that the federal government is involved somewhere in vocational education activities. Note that there have been two centuries of relatively silent federal presence in vocational education: school land legislation, seed money to establish farm and home extension service offices in 3,100 counties, and continuing support for secondary and postsecondary programs. Initially, this presence was not felt by the public. Nor was it intended to be strongly felt in the Congress. The economic depression of the 1930s and World War II, along with the emergence of the U.S. as a full member of the international community of nations seem to have *forced* a visible federal role in vocational-technical education.

A Mixed Public Image

As mentioned earlier, most people (parents, students and the public) are aware of vocational education and yet they are puzzled by it. To most, vocational education makes sense. That is, it is what school should be all about, practical and useful and not served up as educational "junk food." Some, though, make no secret of their view that vocational education is a permanent social tattoo, a type of education intended for the poor and culturally unaccepted, something to be avoided like the pox. Much of how and why Americans view vocational education the way they do, is beyond the scope of this paper. Yet some of the public's perceptions of vocational education may be within our span of control to understand and to change. For example:

Is vocational education really "for other people's children:" truants, discipline problems, mental turtles...the big family down the block?

Why is it that chemists, electrical engineers, actors, medical doctors, journalists, architects, registered nurses (the list is long) are not regarded as graduates of vocational courses?

Why are all too many vocational education students and their courses treated as devalued educational currency, often by the very educational institutions they attend (e.g., course credit, transfer value, etc.)?

Is another social class emerging from vocational education, one only fit for welfare, manpower training programs and public employment? What pox do these people carry? When are they infected?

Does indeed vocational education offer an equal or richer learning environment to students as compared to other program areas?

THE PROFESSIONAL'S VIEW OF VOCATIONAL EDUCATION

Teaching Cadre Turnover

Most vocational teacher educators acknowledge that industry is absorbing new vocational teacher-education graduates faster than they are produced. Likewise, a disturbing number of outstanding vocational education classroom teachers leave teaching each year for better paying, usually administrative, positions. Aside from the specious contention that good classroom and shop instructors make a greater professional contribution as administrators or coordinators than in classrooms, the continued rationalization that vocational education is no worse off than education in general when it comes to staff turnover rates is no answer. It is an eroding condition.

Surely a solid case can be made that the nation's commercial and technological life, military defense and the fulfillment of individual opportunity in economic and political activity is wedded to the long-term excellence of its cadre of vocational education teachers. High staff turnover rates cost dearly in terms of (1) critical local vocational education program discontinuities: subject matter skills lost between the teacher changes, students not known, local curriculum-budget-scheduling battles conceded; (2) severely limited development of community learning resources; (3) calcification in teacher training curriculum at the entry and minimum in-service needs levels and (4) professional anomie.

The Growing Bureaucracy

Mandatory reports, data collection, reports and planning documents coupled with growing numbers of state and federal guidelines and regulations are critically constraining the creative endeavors of vocational education teachers in seeking out and developing comparative learning advantages for students. During the past 20 years, there has been a gradual forced mobilization of vocational education teacher time to do paperwork and to ride agency line fences.

The administrative layering of vocational education is being supported by most vocational teacher education institutions through the almost complete orientation of graduate programs to produce vocational education administrators and data/information specialists to feed vocational education's growing administrative framework.

"Bureaucratization" can be a positive force in mobilizing resources and initiating a climate for seeking out new vocational education endeavors. However, history has taught us that bureaucracies tend to control or limit activity through regulation: the creative instructor gives way to the consensus; wild ducks either fly off or are caponized.

To the extent that the erosion of class instructional time and professional organization activity tends to serve the internal needs of agencies, students are generally the losers and the country produces less growth with its human and material resources. A bright spot in this trend is that while private vocational schools and industry training program efforts have felt the regulatory burden, they remain relatively free as compared to public vocational education.

Politization
Aside from a significant federal involvement in local vocational education classrooms in aspects of integration, sex bias and educational opportunity access for special students, local vocational education programs have remained pretty much outside federal agency disputes on how to best spend the growing federal largess targeted for education and job training. The situation is quite different at the federal level. Here we see vocational education being buffeted unmercifully and effectively by all of the single or special interest lobbies.

The politization of vocational education, particularly the area of federal-state grants for soft-money staff positions is almost complete, particularly in state and university education units. Job security and agency loyalty, not vocational education, is the issue for a growing number of individuals on vocational education payrolls.

There is another form of politization that needs mentioning. It is an effort by the professions to perpetuate an occupational-class mentality through legislative politics. For some reason carpenters and farmers need vocational education while architects, veterinarians and lawyers need professional training. Professional training costs more: oak instead of steel tubing for chairs; libraries/computer terminals instead of dog-eared magazines; smaller classes; professional training staff salaries frequently double those in the crafts.

The major point here is to openly acknowledge the existence of a socially dangerous undercurrent of occupational politics both within the occupations and between the crafts and professions.

Isolation

A type of isolation is the withdrawing of instruction *into* the school. A mixture of factors, including bureaucratization, high teacher turnover rates and financial constraints, is limiting full community learning resource mobilization in the search for comparative vocational education instructional advantage. Also nested in here is something vocational education instructors have been witness to for quite some time: *real* student-teacher contact time reduced to critically low levels in many schools.

Another, and perhaps the most socially critical type of isolation, deals with the social class segregation that somehow has become educationally acceptable in American secondary education. The comprehensive high school was by design an American answer to the European dual school system, one based on segregating students by political class. Vocational education teachers will tell you that tracking (e.g., academic, general, vocational) yields a segregated vocational education student. There is more than student-interest tracking taking place when we find vocational education students scoring one-half to one standard deviations below academic students in a cross-section of ability tests (1972 High School Longitudinal Study data).

Teacher Preparation

Teacher turnover and new teacher placement problems have been noted. The following brief list of concerns, incomplete as it is, represents a trend listing of items we may want to address in vocational education teacher education:

Occupational/craft job experience for vocational education teacher certification has been reduced to an average of two years in most states.

In-service vocational education teacher education efforts are rarely geared to providing technical updating or instruction to strengthen and upgrade particular occupational specializations.

University vocational education instructional methods course work keys more on group and technical subject matter techniques than on individual or family techniques.

Absent, for the most part, is specific methodology to develop vocational education student excellence in oral and written communication, entrepreneurial functions, group action process and work product integrity.

For some reason, vocational education teacher education programs seem to have discounted out-of-school learning resource management as a core component in undergraduate teacher preparation.

Educational Process

There are at least four dimensions to the vocational educational process that most vocational educators feel uncomfortable with, yet for some reason we are unable to make significant improvement. These areas are: (1) the underuse of out-of-school learning resources; (2) high learner-instructor ratios accompanied by growing depersonalization of the vocational education learning process; (3) an incompleteness in subject matter/learner facilitating skills development; and (4) responsibility in the process of education: school, public, learner/parent. I'll touch on each briefly:

Vocational Education Learning Resources. In-school learning environments can capture or simulate, even under the best of circumstances, a mere fragment of the occupational structure. Ninety million plus employees and employers, tens of millions uncounted out-of-the-labor-force adults, the natural and social infrastructure of a region (the human electricity generated by a society at work and rest) are physically *outside* the school. To the extent vocational education fails to demonstrate an eminent-domain mentality toward such resources, that is, through active and direct physical exploitation or mobilization, vocational education remains incomplete in process and purpose.

Learner-Instructor Ratios. A major enigma surrounds the reasons why modern educational process, particularly vocational education, continues grouping 15 to 40 students around one teacher, striving to sustain such ratios as some kind of an optimum student learning environment. The first child born to a couple has two teachers. Emile had a single tutor and the world as a school. Candide had Dr. Pangloss and Martin. The Nazarine tutored 12 and had an inner circle of three students. Almost invariably when student-teacher ratios are reduced to 1:1, all students learn. It is instructional method that separates learner and learning; subject matter rarely is the barrier. Today, vocational educators do well to exercise and amuse students for an hour or two at student-teacher ratios of 20 or 30 to 1.

Subject Matter Incompleteness. The increased use by vocational education curriculum designers of job-task and competency-based approaches tends to narrow subject matter to that necessary for the direct performance of bits or fragments of job content. The facilitating skills necessary for excellence in independent personal actions as well as those required in a given craft can be programmed in *whole work curriculums* but not when instruction is reduced to the study of production fragments.

Not only do we seem to be moving away from oral and written communication and treating excellence as neutral, we seem to be leaving out the exercises that stretch the inventive and creative capacities of learners. Most of our instruction keys on activity that will be supervised by others, not by self-directed initiative. The employee receives but a fragment of the education necessary to prepare for full economic and political freedom. A mass employee-oriented vocational education system, as it appears to be evolving in the 1980s, has a dangerous political by-product for America. It serves to feed a learner a mentality that *accepts* the notion of *limited* personal liability and responsibility to employer, government and family. Vocational educators should know better.

Educational Responsibility. The issue of responsibility in education calls for parallel and unified action based on an existing American ethic. Nothing new is required, save renewed action. As noted earlier, the public and vocational educators have a solid feeling about what should be done. Likewise, parents and students know that without their cooperation and commitment to individual excellence, little can be expected from vocational education. Industry and the trade unions have the greatest untapped learning resources for vocational education. They are aware, moreover, that their future is welded to sharing their resources for the pursuit of excellence in vocational-technical education.

Next Steps: A Quest for Substance and Function

To this point we've concerned ourselves with two perceptions of vocational education, the public's and the professional's. As indicated earlier, being successors to the problem-solving generation, there will be a strong tendency for us to isolate, define and prioritize problems and to get on with their resolution. Vocational educators can choose to approach the future on a ride across the Andalusian plain jousting with contrived bureaucratic problems. If we do choose this path, which certainly is an option, let us hope we can be clever enough to strike a Faustian bargain that denies Mephistopheles our soul.

We know, though, that history tends to treat ad hoc activity, no matter how enthusiastic, as a footnote. Perhaps, balkanized, we can cope without plans. Yet it seems inevitable that if we are ever to conceive the great plans and make the great decisions that are essential if vocational education is to achieve orderly growth, we need blueprints for our hopes.

So far, I have tried to suggest that vocational education's problems are such that only a full mobilization of the forces of spirit will see vocational education into the next century. We need to identify with an operational philosophy, one that differentiates ends and means and which is unequivocal in its pursuit of standards. Backing into the future with fashionable cliches is not a reasonable choice; it is an abject admission of individual and system bankruptcy.

In mobilizing vocational education's full resources, some "strategists" will propose that the exercise best be left to a few superordinates organized as a task force behind closed doors. Those who propose this strategy have not yet learned that unless journeymen vocational educators and their close colleagues participate in the planning, no durable capacity building can occur. This is not to deny the role of leadership, it is only to suggest that effective leadership must occur in microcosm, on a grand scale.

Fortunately there are still individuals who helped to conceive the unique American approach to vocational education. With access to this living resource, we should pursue the basis for a philosophy and not hold such exercises in contempt as something impractical.

I now turn to a literature which may be regarded as unconditionally rich in providing a basis for thinking about what is foundationally important to the field. Familiarity with it can serve as a basis for two parallel dialogues, one addressed to standards and substance and the other to questions of organization.

FOUNDATION DIALOGUES

Why Man Works

Religious, political and behavioral literature is rich with fact and speculation about why man works. Adriano Tilgher's, *Homo Faber-Work Through the Ages* is a fair primer to initiate thinking about this question.

The Nature of Work

Words such as job, work, productive/non-productive labor, play and leisure, creativity, wage equity, employment equality, social responsibility—all of these are elusive in definition and the focus of intense debate and occasionally political preference. Reisman's themes on work and play (buried in the *Lonely Crowd* and *Individualism*

Reconsidered), Illich's recent essay on the *Shadow-Work* (1980) performed by women and men in industrial societies and Serge Mallet's comments on technology and industrial labor in *Essays on the New Working Class* bring some of these definitional problems into focus.

The differential status accorded historically by governments to workers, independent artisans, peasants and non-citizen guest workers, including the right to beggary, suggests more fluidity than contemporary occupational hierarchy models contain. Laslett's *The World We Have Lost* and several chapters in Zimmern's *Greek Commonwealth* give us empirical clues of status differences in time past. Still pretty much buried are the guild documents detailing excellent craft competencies and those pertaining to one's right to rely on the alms of society for support or how to rely on the poor-house for vocational training. Some of these are included in *Vol. 1: The Process of Industrialization (Documents of European Economic History).*

And surely Adam Smith's and Ricardo's writings, classics on capitalism, the working classes and the role of the "invisible hand" in both, are instructive to vocational educators just as are Belloc's (1913) comments on minimum wages, unemployment and compulsory labor in his *The Servile State.* Rather than propagate a heresy here, we might also take another look at the traditional job-content, worker compensation model before we "technical skill" ourselves into the 1990s (see Scoville's *The Job Content of the U.S. Economy, 1940-1970).*

The Nature of Education

Observation tells us that the majority of lifetime's learning takes place outside the formal school. Experience further tells us that contemporary education continues to treat learning that takes place outside of the school as devalued educational currency. Vocational educators, parents, students and industry leaders know this, and yet the formal education myth not only survives but it is growing to worldwide proportions.

Without addressing the issue of physically *De-Schooling Society* (italicized here because it is also the title of an iconoclastic and brilliant essay by Ivan Illich), consider only how best to mobilize a society's learning resources for the act of instruction. If everything outside the school is "educationally less," one is moved toward one of two positions: (1) perpetuating a myth that is absurd or (2) co-opting society's resources and advocating lifetime schooling. Either scenario (and we have serious proponents for both) is obnoxious to the

American ethos. De-schooling becomes a serious option to be considered.

Let me suggest that, in looking to what education might be, we not start solely with the neo-rationalized system of industrial schools toward which we are now moving. Also, let us look backwards to the future. Margaret Mead encourages us to learn anew from primitive cultures of the family's capacity to educate. Alberti's *The Family in Renaissance Florence* (Book I) moves the setting to the more familiar thrifty, bourgeois civilization. Philippe Aries details not only the origins of the school class but informs us again of the educational ages of life in his *Centuries of Childhood.* Rousseau, Emile's tutor, and Candide's Dr. Pangloss teach us that the educational chain of events "in this best of possible worlds" leads us to rediscover the importance of the relationship between student and teacher. The early guilds and the modern apprentice-master ratios respect this relationship, only the modern school has ignored it.

The responsibility of a free people's school is to release individual creativity, not to limit it, as Simone de Beauvoir reminds us in her *The Ethics of Ambiguity.*

Education, by purpose, can attempt to homogenize, to build a national mentality. To the extent that citizenship or employee-level training diminishes the expression of the individual, education takes on political purposes. (See Rousseau's *Considerations on National Education to the Government of Poland.)*

One last note on modern educational purposes—more perhaps in the realm of social hopes for a best of all possible worlds. The task of placing all the nation's children in a single system of education is one kind of problem. Relating education to work and keeping America at work is quite another. To the extent that society withholds even a portion of its support to education, or expects unrealistic political results from its schools, society itself suffers. The support I have in mind is parental discipline, excellence in student performance and financial support for education. The type of unrealistic political results expected is best typified in the expectation that the school can re-machine *in a hurry* two mellenia of cultural attitudes about sex roles. Elane Pagel's chapter titled "God the Father/God the Mother" in *The Gnostic Gospels* suggests that the church may be a critical institution for political action.

Vernacular Resources

The ideal of political pluralism and individual freedom is basic to the American ethos. We also know that man is, as Pascal termed him, "a fragile thinking reed." This being the case, the concept of pluralism and freedom must be reaffirmed in each generation, to wrest man's culture and institutions from the gladitorial laws of nature. Judge Frank's chapter on the fallacy of a universal natural morality in his *A Man's Reach* is a useful introduction.

The drift toward centralism in government and economic enterprises evolves a mentality that views the vernacular as deviate behavior which the system must purge. Innovations are too frequently interpreted as irrelevant or outright threats rather than opportunities. History tells us the Confucians (under the Manchus) acted irrationally in rejecting science. Rejection may not make sense, but it is tolerable. Obliteration by force is not. It costs both the victor and vanquished alike. (Imperial Athens was never the same after she sacked Melos.) Today the ethics of modern man are being challenged through a development policy that too often obliterates. See Peter Burgers' *Pyramids of Sacrifice.*

A rich vernacularity in education thrives in both the developed and Third Worlds. To the extent that American vocational education can recognize its own vernacularity and that abroad (and cultivates both), capacity building is enhanced.

There are at least four types of Don Juanism in education (each is an essay in itself) that vocational education should become more aware of:

1. The hidden curriculum in education where institutional ritual replaces subject matter substance.
2. A form of pedagogy exported by the developed West that has a way of treating the Third World citizen and his/her culture as savage. That is, the idea that the constituents of literacy, school organization, teaching methodology, administration, school plant/equipment, etc., must be imported. Paul Friere (who is difficult to read at times) writes of this in his *Pedagogy of the Oppressed.*
3. The spiritual belief in self help that interprets any vision of humanity coming from the liberal arts as off-limits. Hofstadter provides a solid chronicle of this phenomenon in his *Anti-Intellectualism in America.*
4. The pasteurizing and homogenizing of living occupations, each quite distinct, into standard core instructional packages represents a loss in resources. Farming is different from tailoring just as data processing is different from carpentry and medicine. While there may be a common core of instructional knowledge and experience that needs sharing, each field is unique. To the

extent that federal legislation standardizes vocational education, a very rich vernacular inheritance of independence in approach and thought will be consumed.

Toward an American Vocational Education Literature

It is an almost impossible task at best to feel comfortable in the sense of being well read in the organizational foundations of American vocational education. A scattered literature exists. Why it is so scattered and unsynthesized is puzzling.

Good turn-of-the-century documentation can be found in the various works by Charles Bennett, Alfred True and Charles Prosser. The reproduction of original documentation for the *1977 Texas A&M Workshop for Interpreting Vocational Education* (e.g., Dewey, Cooley, Snedden, Prosser) shows that a foundation literature can be collected. There is also a growing modern documentary literature, e.g., Arthur Wirth and Melvin Barlow; and a growing interpretive literature characterized by the Grubb-Lazerson commentary and that in Katy Greenwood's dissertation on Prosser and his contemporaries.

The search for vocational education's literature has really yet to start. Pieces we can identify but a full literature codex is a decade or more away. Without this literature, vocational education will be hard pressed to chart a future based on anything better than random speculation.

Our task, or so it seems, is straight forward. First we need to come to some conceptual agreement as to what vocational education is. The second step is to search private and public holdings for original source material. Both steps belong to vocational educators. Contracted out to political scientists or historians, the exercise loses its internal value. Indeed an excellent codex of vocational education literature could evolve, but it would still be viewed as external.

The search may take us into new ideological territory. Differences in structural format among and between the occupational families is to be expected: technology, raw material, process, marketplace and history surely have left their imprints. This is part of vocational education's rich legacy.

The Components of Vocational Education Curriculum

Contemporary approaches in much of vocational education curriculum are identified with taking things apart, that is, a continued elaboration of task analysis routines. A fashionable new language has emerged which, upon analysis, tends to avoid any holistic approach, the role of the entrepreneur or any concern with the individual potential of students. In short, the urge to take things apart is not followed by any responsibility to teach the multiple ways of putting things together. The rush to identify the micro-job skill movements of workers has all but eliminated activity to maximize learning resources. All of the curriculum space is occupied by *means* which obliterate or serve as substitutes for *ends*. Curriculum designers merchandise their short-cut modules or competency-based instructional packages as a way to achieve a born again vocational education. Comenius utilized a variation of it for a different purpose in the 1500s in his *Didactica*. While the micro methods have the appeal of assembly-line logic, we know that *without it,* 80 percent of the work force can become reasonably well trained in three hours to 60 days of on-the-job training. Job fragmentation for teaching is an instructional method which should not be confused with curriculum. Too often it intrudes upon, or diminishes, curriculum.

The future of vocational education will be enhanced if we take the time to evolve a more generic view of curriculum. For too long our sights have been focused on ever narrowing fragments of industrial activity or the work scene. Somehow, our students have gotten in the way of vocational education. We have an ethical responsibility to conduct a functional audit of vocational education's curriculum, a search for excellence as well as opportunity. Our students are waiting.

A FINAL NOTE

If indeed, we are to build the capacity of vocational education, it is important to decide how that capacity should be used. If our goal is excellence, we should be willing to pursue it and to learn how to recognize it. Our primary effort should be internal, a recognition that the profession should begin with self-examination and a recognition of the importance of intellectual leadership. We are enslaved by a lack of clear vision of our potential to achieve and our capacity to do so. We are not unlike the superorganism Michelangelo shows emerging from the stone of antiquity in his *Awakening Slave.* We have much to do, and the public is waiting.

SECTION III

VALUE DIMENSIONS IN THE FUTURE

Vocational education is always a reflection of the prevailing values of society, reflections that are always guaranteed to reveal diversity of thought and action. It is this diversity, present and future that highlights this section.

As proponents of the important role of values in American society, and as perceptive commentators on the historical, social and educational context of the values identified with vocational education, the three authors contributing to this section offer a basis for thinking about, and inquiring into, the evolving value structure of the field.

CAN PAST VALUES GUIDE VOCATIONAL EDUCATORS IN THE FUTURE?

Katy Greenwood

We are living in times—not of future shock—but of *present* shock. We are confronted with incomprehensible change in the international scene and a convulsion of domestic indices that are unsettling and bewildering. With the erosion of established authority and a fragmented value structure, we are haunted with a sense of drift and purposelessness. We are indeed suffering from what Walter Lippman has eloquently called our loss of ancestral order.

But will attempts at ancestral ordering or reordering assist us in our attempts at steadying and positioning our directional focus for the future? Can recalling the past provide foresight to the bewildering present and uncertain future? If so, what kind of remembering will be most advantageous?

HOW TO APPROACH THE PAST?

Shall we, recognizing our lack of either productivity or stability, pay nostalgic tribute to more productive and stable times and search out signals that might reestablish such an era? Or do we turn radical, knowing that return is impossible, and blame our past by the fanatic pinpointing of past leaders and past values that led to our present state? Or do we, as true conservatives, demand a rapid return to a past core and values in an obvious retreat from the present confusion? Or do we demonstrate our new-found existentialism by pretending the past is meaningless to our present existence and close our eyes to our previous existence, while asserting that today is the first day in our remaining lives?

Or, can we make *demands* of the past—as we indeed plan to make unprecedented demands on the future? Can we call on the ideology of the past to present its vitality in directing our comprehension of the present and thus guide our choice of options for the future? This chapter heralds this particular use of the past. We must return to history to understand more clearly the nature of our confusion— neither to blame nor to lament, nor to eradicate nor to resurrect. We are in the end pragmatists who will work out the present dilemmas

71

and our future destiny, but only after we know where we are, how far we have come and for what reasons we came to the present point in our progression.

Professional fields such as vocational education must provide sponsorship and leadership in directing comprehension of the past for the institutions of work, work history, ideology of work, education for work, work benefits and value perspectives about work. This is our special mission today as it has been in the past and as it will continue to be in the future.

The Past as a Guide to the Future

Other professional fields, such as medicine, law, nursing and the broad field of education, have found history useful as an integral and necessary means of charting forward progress. Recognition of past errors as well as past contributions have guided other fields of endeavor to redirect or change focus of direction as needed. Continuity has been achieved, not through unswerving attention to straight-line direction, but through deliberate shifts in policy, a result of reassessment of the past in preparation for the future. Similarly, vocational education can utilize the past to acquire a depth perception for its forward movement.

And yet depth perception is not enough. Understanding the past as an exercise is necessary, but alone lacks the dynamism to direct the future. We are confronted with the realization that the present stands at the crossroads of value and purpose clarification. Being emancipated from tradition in the rapid reach for new dimensions of freedom has produced its own quiet terrors. Recognizing those terrors, it is the overarching function of the academic exercise to be concerned with purpose and values, to be as much concerned with the *why* of our future direction as to the *how* of technological change — to be as concerned with why we must prepare people for work as much as the preoccupation of how to design the best systems.

Influencing Change

Indeed, education, and thus vocational education more than any other process, involves an ad hoc tinkering with the margins of ignorance that has the cumulative and aggregate response of shaping the future. The challenge to education is not simply to cope with changing realities, but to influence their very content.

Exhortations about the need for direction and coherence abound on all sides. While diagnoses differ slightly in detail, there is agreement on two major points: the malaise of our time is acute and the

72

locus for our sickness is in the realm of values. In such essays dealing with our future, we uniformly invoke H. G. Wells (1961) with his warning that human history is becoming more and more a race between education and catastrophe as major elements on our philosophic landscape.

And so we direct our attention to the fundamental mission of education, and within such boundaries, the mission of vocational education. When we survey the present scene, we view a cluttered landscape of 440 academic subdivisions and some 139 technological and occupational specialities served by dedicated faculty and administrators intent on giving integrity to the lives of the 11 million students they serve. In this broad variety, it is not surprising that there is a rich diversity of view; the pluralism of institutions and missions involves the pluralism found within our value structure. The webb of tension between those values are intended to provide the tension and balance that yields both stability and growth.

But can we have confidence in the automaticity of that equilibrating mechanism? Can we expect that pluralistic mechanism to yield results consistent with the larger purpose of American society? In this context of unsettled change and unpredictable consensus, it is not only helpful but essential to re-examine some themes in the relationship of work to education, and this interface with the larger issues of national purpose and values.

Values Shape Society

We cannot for a moment depreciate the role of values in shaping the direction of our society. It is not just an article of faith to believe that the manufacture of theories, ideas, hypotheses, speculations and contentions produce the ethical systems and values that have shaped and will continue to direct human behavior. As Boulding (1973) has reminded us, it is indeed awesome that a modest carpenter in the Middle East could have created an ethical system that has guided much of the western world for nearly 20 centuries, and equally remarkable that an eccentric German professor, working in the British Museum, should construct a new philosophic system of radical protest against the abuses of contemporary industrialism that has gripped major portions of our contemporary population.

The scribblings of Keynes have shaped economic policy in western societies for three generations, and we are now in the process of an astonishing "revisionism" that finds guidelines for economic and educational policy in the writings of 19th-century classicism. The "new" supply side economics turns out, after all, to be old wine in new bottles. Once again, the ideology of the past proves its vitality in directing our comprehension of the present. What do we discover in previous value systems that help us understand the present tensions found within education, and more specifically, the tensions between liberalism and vocationalism in our present scene? While we have cast the liberalism versus vocationalism issue in terms of the global challenge to civilization itself, that larger difficulty has its counterpart, in distilled form, within the tensions continuously found within the educational scene.

PREVIOUS VALUE SYSTEMS

The arrangements that we find uniquely correct for our time, with the construction of a free society that involves parliamentary mechanisms in political decision-making, and the market mechanism in economic resource use, is a brief interlude in the parade of cultures. Some see these arrangements as increasingly fragile or vulnerable, both from internal shocks and external challenge. It is instructive to view the past to appreciate that our histories have been dominated by status rather than by market-dominated systems.

Education and Work within Status Systems

In authoritarian and status regimes, one's status is defined by religious and political authority. Surprisingly, while such arrangements are undoubtedly oppressive for individuals exposed to alternative free and mobile societies, individuals appear to have a capacity for accommodation. In some status societies, we are told of the serenity and tranquility that attaches to a well-defined role—however modest—in the culture. By contrast with present systems, one's fate is not uniquely determined by random fluctuations of impersonal market forces, but by the dictates of culture, birth, order, authority and/or religion.

Individuals living in such status systems, not trained on a dict of Horatio Alger or the "greening" of their culture, not confronted with a Penny's catalog and not expected to carve out their own destinies in an occupational structure, are capable of considerable resignation. It is not likely that a fish would be the first to discover water.

Labor, including the arduous work of early civilizations in Greece, Egypt and Rome, drew heavily on slave labor, the major rewards of military conquest. Elaborate cultures with refined epicurian as well as philosophical tastes flourished among this status system. Perhaps the historical taproot for the tensions between "thinking" and "working," between reflection and labor, between the good life and the hard life finds its origins in these early conveniences to the ruling hierarchies and priesthoods.

In these civilizations, arduous work was certainly not valued for its own sake. Education, as Aristotle acknowledged, represented the trappings of affluence. Without the foundation of wealth, provided by the physical exertions of others, there could not be the opportunity for both leisure and contemplation that sparked such a remarkable flow of philosophic observations about the nature of life and society.

In the evolution of culture and society, there were interludes that involved attention to statecraft and the practical. Montaigne noted in *Essays II* (1949) that the Romans taught their children nothing that was to be learned sitting. He later emphasized the importance of the synthesis of mind and body: "It is not a mind, it is not a body that we erect, but it is a man. We must not make him in two parts." The obligations of statecraft and guiding nations to power and influence found service in the intellectual nobility. The emergence of universities served to sanction the status hierarchy, with the priesthood in medieval Christendom serving to cultivate mastery of "pen and tongue."

Education and Work in Systems of Political Nationalism

The mercantilists were the first to evolve plans for economic development, with considerations of labor use in the production process pivotal to those plans. In 19th-century England, idleness was seen as a serious loss of human and political potential. But while concerns for full employment and the income gap involved in idleness are reminiscent of the humanitarian concerns of the Keynesian era, the mercantilists actually evolved the doctrine of "utility of poverty." In brief, subsistence or the need for survival would become the major inducement to productive labor. The purpose of education for the labor mass would be confined to the habits of industry acquired at a tender age. The concern for the development of the nation, strangely enough, involved the development of only one facet of human capability for the laboring mass. That was the work potential.

The political economy of mercantilism centered on concerns that individuals would tend, in most situations, to be as lazy as they dare be. Improvements in personal or family income would allow individuals the luxury of additional leisure. But such leisure, in the hands of the working class, would lead to debauchery, self-indulgence and a decay of work incentives. Thus, by keeping the work force on the edge of subsistence, the economy could pull a string to induce wholesome attention to work.

If subsistence required, for example, $8.00 a day and pay is at $1.00 per hour, one could be assured of an eight-hour day. If wages should increase to $2.00 an hour, individuals could afford to cut their labor force participation in half. But if, say, through the process of inflation, the buying power of the $1.00 of an hour's work should be cut in half, this would compel individuals to stretch their workday from 8 hours to 16 hours per day. By driving down real wage rates, one could then compel additional interest in honest labor.

This is the foundation for the backward sloping supply curve or what economists call the lazy S supply schedule. Subsistence was a fishing rod to fetch the labors of men. England worried it had hardly enough poor to enable it to subsist. The poverty of the masses was a precondition for its full employment. The poverty of the masses was, in this context, the precondition for the wealth and power of the nation state. We are confronted with the enigma (common to totalitarian regimes) that hard work is for the masses. The cultivation of the arts and preoccupations with statecraft properly belong to the ruling elite. It is significant that the historian who documented the brutalization of the work force in order to compel its attention to labor was John Wade. It was in Wade's elaborate detail of such history that Karl Marx began his construction of the exploitation and immiseration implicit in the industrialization process, where free markets and private property became the vehicles of such exploitation.

In this interlude of our industrial history, we have a hierarchical structure, with the universities providing education for the priesthood, lawyers and statecraft, and the barbers cum physicians dealing with physical frailities in our society. The notion of the "new" freedom found in the colonies in America was perhaps captured by one observer when he pointed out that these new countries were free of the "three scourages of mankind"—the physician, clergy and lawyer. There was little, yet to be realized, in the harmonization of the work ethic with educational values.

Education and Work in the Age of Enlightenment
The Renaissance and the Age of Enlightenment set the stage for universal suffrage and the new rationalism; it built, not on the utility of poverty, but on the "utility of utility." Private individual preferences were to represent the building blocks for cultures in the future, with individual preferences and pursuits representing, in composite, the happiness and prosperity of the nation. In a very real sense, the discovery of the printing process set the stage for the universalization of access to education. The biblical prophecy now seemed capable of

realization: "Ye shall know the truth, and the truth shall make you free."

Even here, there was a slow union between the classical and liberal education and the needs of mass education for the new enfranchised populations and the needs of the industrialization process. Even in America, there was an obvious ambivalence in viewing the influence of education on the work ethic. Some held that education would allow individuals to appreciate the rationality of capital construction and savings, investment and abstinence, as the precursor of solving the social ills of society. One must first produce what one would consume. The ethic of distributional or egalitarian concerns, involving attention to human capital and the social needs of society would follow national growth. The intelligence of the working man would allow these simple truths to be understood. The contest, then, was not between the haves and the have-nots. It was between the present and the future. An educated work force, drawn from rural and frontier settings, could readily understand (it was hoped) the risk in eating one's own seed corn.

But apart from developing an understanding of economic necessities, there was the concurrent risk that with universal suffrage, the equal influence of the artisan and employer could ignite some wild speculations about a new society, where justice could be realized through the legislative process or parliamentary reform. This was, of course, heady stuff. And employers, realizing that social protests movements were concerned with the creation of a new society in their own time, began to fear the dismantling of the economic system.

Early reforms of labor, pressing for state guardianship or universal education at public expense, were comingled with programs for the redistribution of capital (at public auction), the freedom of slaves, and perhaps least radical of all, the distribution of free lands in the west. There was a fear then that immigrant workers, particularly those from Germany and the northwest European continent, carried with them booklets in their workcoats outlining the blueprints for a new and improved society, where justice and human development would be a concommitant of education for all, and shared leisure for all.

It is within this contradiction of education (for ironically, education began to address itself to the needs of the growing society, and the discipline of manual skills in the shop), that the radical ideologues charged that the mission of higher liberal education had been preempted or co-opted by labor exploiters intent on sustaining the brutilization and exploitation of the work force. Here education that

77

centered on efficiency in the shop had the pernicious effect of increasing the opportunities for labor exploitation and diverting attention away from the "liberating" influences that permeated many of the plans for a new society.

A FOUNDATION OF VALUE TENSIONS

Vocational education emerged, then, early in this century within a context of three-way tensions. First, classical education with its attention to Latin and the traditional agenda of professional development for the very few, attempted desperately to maintain its elitist and aristocratic posture. Indeed, in the view of some, education at higher levels was threatened with abandonment, because of its inability to come to terms with the new needs of the industrializing society.

Here, it should be emphasized, the creative spark for the industrialization process was less the consequence of deductive scientists working in isolation as it was individuals tinkering with the machine process. Further, the new masters of economic development represented by the swashbuckling entreprenuers of the 19th-century (the Robber Baron in current popular literature) found little inspiration or advantage in attending the universities. Today, important elements of this tradition remain.

Fulfillment Through Employment

The second element involved a pragmatic acceptance that individuals would find fulfillment with an ample wage of income flow provided by steady employment. Thus, the fulfillment of the individual would be best realized when individuals could "fit in" to the industrialization process. This need not involve any compromise of one's ambition, the destruction of soul, or the degradation of ideals. The sturdy worker, with persistent attention to the discipline of the shop, and with reasoned responses to change, could prove his versatility on the job and the need for his services. He need not, as some charged, simply become an extension of the machine process, appearing as a badly designed single purpose machine. With high levels of productivity, he or she could expect high levels of income; and with higher levels of income, one could cultivate refinements of taste and achievement that represent the best that society had to offer.

Liberalism: The Individual as Master

The third element in the education process involved the contention that the mission of education was to liberate the individual common man from the limits of his environment and the dismal restrictions of anticipated achievement for the individual. With the fresh breeze of the new liberalism, the individual could secure a greater understanding and grasp of the complexities of contemporary life. With this insight, literacy, intelligence, perceptivity, ambition and versatility, he need not become a cog in the machine process. He could mold its focus, shape its purpose, guide its functioning. He could become master rather than slave of the industrial environment.

And even as vocational education was born of these tensions, it attempted to free itself from domination of one or more of these strains. It set itself in the peculiar position of accommodating the inherited dichotomies and at the same time asserting its uniqueness in the galaxy of the emerging educational system. It was in priding itself on the intrinsic, as well as the monetary characteristics of work, that vocational education could begin to establish itself in the educational system.

The first prerequisite for the early vocational programs was a mere *willingness* to work. The ultimate success of the earlier programs was represented in the pride and sense of accomplishment demonstrated by its participants in the marketplace. It was in their struggle to set the vocational education program apart from the inherited dichotomies that Charles Prosser and David Snedden debated John Dewey; they could not agree that "reflective thinking" as a single educational goal, without necessary survival skills, represented a balanced educational program. Neither could they embrace the American version of mercantilism—social efficiency—as a justification for vocational preparation. They fully believed that man could adapt to the industrial world and continue to maintain a satisfying perspective and control of his own destiny.

Tensions Still Present

Current criticisms of vocational education show us that remnants of those early tensions are still alive and well. The dichotomies between liberal education and vocational education are still visible and still creating tensions in education and in the society at the present time. Now, in the latter stages of this century, the classic aristocracy with attention to Grecian philosophy and Latin has indeed faded. Instead, a new professionalism has established a permanent beachhead in higher education, a vanguard of the new utilitarianism found in scientific investigation and exotic research and development.

But as one element in the triumvirate of influence is weakened, we find an increased tension between "liberalism" and "vocationalism" in education. The century-old dichotomy of cultures believing that there are contradictions built into avocations and vocations is still evident; the idea that an affluent society deserves the very best of educational experiences, often with some distance in curriculum content to any of the practicalities of the world, is still persistent. That contradiction will continue into the future and poses one of the continuing threats to the healthy development of a viable system of education for work. Attempting to alleviate these tensions is a priority goal of vocational education for the 1980s.

A CONTEMPORARY WORK ETHIC

Another critical and pivotal challenge for the future is evident from a review of past practice. A work ethic must be reestablished in the culture if the society is to prosper and continue to grow; vocational education is the most viable institution to respond to this issue in the future.

The overpowering need to redefine a suitable work ethic rests on three major compelling events of our time. First, we have a growing imbalance between our expectations for economic rewards and our capacity or willingness to produce those goods and services. The consequences of having aspirations or expectations for entitlements that run ahead of our productive impulses is reflected in inflation and unemployment. For instance, the unit labor costs of producing goods in this country is increasing at a rate of 7 percent annually. The reasons why we have a built-in reflex to pay individuals more than they are willing to produce is but another symptom of current conventions that have allowed us to break the connection between work and payment for work.

Rebuilding Our Capital Base

A second reason for establishing a contemporary work ethic is linked to the current interest in reindustrialization. The limits of capital formation, inventive activity, the decline of research and development, and the aging vintage of our capital—all are forces that compel a new look at our inventory of needs and social and economic priorities. A single conclusion exists that is of such dramatic thrust that it transcends, even in election years, political ideology. *We must rebuild our capital base.*

This creates visions of massive numbers working in the construction of railroad beds, the rebuilding of the inner cities, the rehabilitation of decaying structures found in rural America and the revitialization of the infrastructures that give strength and efficiency to our productive processes. Yet, whether or not we can count on policies that will absorb massive armies associated with the re-employment programs of the Civilian Conservation Corps (CCC) and other job development and capital growth activities of the past remains to be seen. The substitutes (e.g., automation, increasing rates of imported goods, etc.) for labor service and vocational talent have a way of popping out more frequently and at every turn.

EDUCATION AND ECONOMIC REWARDS

An additional challenge that draws on the nostalgia of the past involves the realization that the reach for ever-higher levels of educational attainment is running aground or at least striking some reefs. There appears to be a limited capacity of the economy to absorb such talent. This position is not intended to be yet another anti-intellectual or antiliberal education jab at higher education. It is simply necessary to acknowledge the warnings of a growing number of manpower specialists who anticipate that the problems of absorbing college-trained and Ph.D. talent in the future is likely to be aggravated by the nature of the future job market. In the future, from 25 percent to 50 percent of college graduates may have to accept employment in jobs that will not require college education or college graduation as an entry point for employment.

This prospect of redundancy or oversupply has reraised the options of vocational, technical and professional training, and encourages the most serious and thoughtful parents of the present generation to consider seriously academic and training paths that might allow their children the attractions of sophisticated skill-training programs that lead to rewarding (and assured) job opportunities.

To Compare: Costs, Security, Pay

The search will involve, among other things, a comparison of the high tuition of extended years in the Ivy League against the more moderate tuition of technical programs often available in one's hometown or nearby facility. There will also be a careful examination of the opportunity to secure intensive education in a craft and profession with high potential for job security and attractive pay.

The narrowing of the differentials of lifetime earnings between the college graduate and those who have completed high school and community college programs substantiates the economic rationality of this calculation. Unlike the 1950s, what is now being sought is not

81

the prospect of fraternity or sorority (i.e., group) affiliates in the classic educational mode, but the personal development available from quality vocational and professional institutes that result in job placement and the job-related justification of relatively short, intensive, single-purpose educational experiences. Obviously, the "tilt" of the income advantage of having vocational proficiency today is influenced, in part, by the soaring cost of education at all levels, concurrent with the rapidly eroding real income differentials between the socio-economic categories of the American public.

MOVEMENT TO THE FUTURE

In response to the three current realities mentioned previously, there is a need for a renewed interest in finding purpose and coherence in our life as it relates to the connection between education and work. For many, the times are now "out of joint." Every person capable of drawing or estimating indices of the major events that impinge on our personal lives indicates that, with current rates, those indices simply go off the map. Even projections to the year 2000 yield results that are either unbelievable or incomprehensible and certainly unacceptable. As every well-ordered household is now realizing, many of its best laid plans are askew. As we face the future, we are confronted with an obvious reality: "All bets are off . . ."

We have been raised in a generation of social, philosophical and ethical ferment that has done much to shatter public confidence in traditional values. We are inclined to a situation ethic, to a distilled form of pragmatism, opportunism, and, in some cases, even nihilism. In this context of a disordered scramble for resources and the protection of family and hearth, we see the dominance of the "me" or "now" value structure—the go-for-it generation—with "What's in it for me?" as the standard question posed by employers, and "What have you done for me today?" as the standard question posed with monotonous regularity by the employee. Vigilance, in this era, centers not only on attention to the work ethic, product quality and pride in one's craft. Vigilance also involves examination of the level of take-home pay, and with that, comes increasing and confused disenchantments that there are outside predators who can be blamed for insufficient pay.

Vocational Education on Center Stage

The purpose of education of all forms is to provide the rationality or understanding of not only the technique of work, but its fundamental role in sustaining the values of our society. This is not an exhortation for mindless effort, but an exhortation to appreciate that in honest labor we find the solution to many of our society's current ills. This, of course, sets the vocational education movement on center stage. It is vocational education that has the tradition of pride of craft and product. It was vocational education that initially selected its clients on the basis of willingness to work. It is vocational education that has increasingly been able to deliver its promise of rewarding employment for those who complete their programs.

Through work, and the reasoned integration of that effort with all of the liberating elements found in the educational process, we can reestablish an adhesive quality or glue that gives coherence and solidarity to our culture. In yet another metaphor, the value system that once again centers on the pride of effective and efficient performance quite literally represents the mortar of the superstructure of our postindustrial society. Without trying to convert this essay into a simple preachment, if that superstructure is decaying or crumbling, it is because of our preoccupation with rewards rather than performance, because of our distractions with consumption without the commitment to the production of that which we would consume.

Clearly, the information base of the past contains the *core values that can guide us in the future.* These quite simply involve focusing on three future thrusts: (1) easing the liberal-vocational tensions, (2) reestablishing an American work ethic that features production over consumption and (3) providing an education that is cost-efficient and relevant to current needs.

REFERENCES

Wells, Herbert G. *Outline of history, Being a Plain History of Life and Mankind.* Garden City, N.Y.: Garden City Books, 1961.

Montaigne, Michel E. *Selected Essays: The Charles Cotton—W.C. Hazlitt Translation, Revised and Edited, with an Introduction by Blanchard Bates.* The First Modern Library Edition. New York: Modern Library, 1949.

Boulding, Kenneth. "An Economist's View of the Manpower Concept." In Ahamid, B. and M. Blaug (eds.) *The Practice of Manpower Forecasting.* New York: Elsevier Scientific Publishing Company, 1973.

AN EXISTENTIAL VIEW

Lowell P. Lerwick

PREFACE

Any attempt to address values must begin with the question of
where to start. For the purposes of this particular effort July 4, 1845
and Henry Thoreau's *Walden* is as good a point of departure as any.
Thoreau opens *Walden* with an explanation of his economic values.
And in the second paragraph of "Economy" he makes this interesting
statement:

> In most books, the I, or first person, is omitted; in this
> *Walden* it will be retained; that, in respect to egotism, is
> the main difference. We commonly do not remember that
> it is, after all, always the first person that is speaking. I
> should not talk so much about myself if there were any-
> body else whom I knew as well. Unfortunately, I am con-
> fined to this theme by the narrowness of my experience.
> Moreover, I, on my side, require of every writer, first or
> last, a simple and sincere account of his own life, and not
> merely what he has heard of other men's lives . . . . (1950,
> p. 2).

Nothing expresses the existentialist preference for the personal
"I" over the imperial "we" quite as well as this statement by Thoreau.
This is precisely the position I will be taking in this chapter.

Thoreau is usually categorized as a disciple of an intellectual
movement called "New England Transcendentalism." *Walden, or
Life in the Woods* as it is otherwise known, was a singularly important work. It presented a uniquely American values perspective
and, for the first time, offered a clear alternative to old world ethical
stereotypes. It received the unilateral acclaim of Thoreau's New
England peers. His sympathizers included influential writers such as
Ralph Waldo Emerson, George Ripley and Margaret Fuller, not to
mention the ubiquitous Walt Whitman and Nathaniel Hawthorne.

Popular sympathy for New England Transcendentalism led to a
major upheaval in mid and late 19th-century society. Out of the
transcendental ideology came such communitarian experiments as

85

Brook Farm and the Mormon United Order. Its basic arguments fueled the Free Religion movement, feminism, abolitionism and the humanitarian plea. In addition, the transcendental perspective was highly supportive of innovation in educational practices and vocational choice. Its practical values are reflected in pragmatic democracy as seen by William James and John Dewey.

Transcendentalism served as the transitional value structure that marked the change from classic philosophic values to modern progressivism. Its emphasis on subjective ego may yet serve as the steppingstone to practical existentialism. Thoreau serves as a convenient and meaningful focal point. His *Walden* ties the first great American values crisis to the second great period of moral controversy.

THE EXISTENTIAL PARADIGM

Under the heading of a preface, I have digressed in order to reemphasize the values upheaval of the historic past and the recent "now." But my specific obligation is to address existentialist values and their implications for the future of vocational education. The issues of value should focus on ideological roots, rather than a complicated explanation of philosophic foundations. Yet in fairness to the reader, there is a need to recap the principal tenets of the philosophy.

Five Major Points

There are five basic premises, which when taken as a whole, serve to mark a person as an existentialist. In their simplest form, these premises are:

1. The universe is absurd rather than rational. There is no apparent justification for believing that the universe is controlled by some omnipresent inherent rationale.

2. Truth is ultimately always personally subjective. No matter how strong the testimony, one can only know what one knows and not what someone else claims to know.

3. Paradox is the central reality of human experience. Given the subjectivity of truth, there are always opposing views which are at least as valid as one's own. Values are always baseless when measured by the criteria of scientific objectivity.

4. Deep personal anxiety is the unavoidable consequence of being aware of one's own existence. Giving reason or meaning to one's existence in an otherwise absurd universe is the crux of the human dilemma.

5. Freedom is not a right to be granted by others or earned as a privilege; it is an inescapable nontransferable personal responsibility. Freedom, in the existentialist sense, begins with the recognition of the consequences of the unavoidable act of choosing. One of these consequences is the feeling of responsibility for the values generated as a result of having chosen. One is born with this freedom and the responsibility of giving existential value to one's own life.

The foregoing theses do not do justice to the complexity of existentialism. By its very nature, the philosophy is highly subjective and individualistic. But from the standpoint of an existentialist values base, this five-point package can be defended as a viable generalization.

If this is the reader's first experience with the existentialist paradigm, it is doubtful there will be any degree of immediate acceptance. My own introduction to the philosophy was as a 30-year-old toolmaker turned college freshman. The exposure came as part of the required general education sequence of courses. It was a sorry experience. I concluded that existentialism was reserved for religious apostates, weird college professors and hippies. As a group, they could be recognized by the fact that they all wore beards and had sandals made of old tire casings. They also had a preference for roll-your-own cigarettes.

My exposure to existentialism, and a two credit course called "Introduction to Logic," fostered a definite resolution. I resolved to avoid philosophy in general and existentialism in particular. That resolve was in no way inconsistent with my academic values—after all my chosen field was work education. What has philosophy to do with that? Seeing no relevance, for the next eight years I conducted myself in a manner consistent with that value judgment. It was not until an involvement, as a graduate student, in the issues of industrial and vocational education that this ethic began to be reassessed.

EXISTENTIALISM AS IDEOLOGY

About two years ago, I enlisted in a research project called "Alternative Concepts of Vocational Education" (Lerwick, 1979), sponsored by the Minnesota Research and Development Center for Vocational Education. The purpose was to define vocational education as it might be conceptualized if it were practiced from a consistent philosophical ideology. We ended up with six different "fictionalized" concepts or scenarios for vocational education. (The six categories originated with Howard Ozmon (1972) in his *Dialogue in the Philosophy of Education.)*

The old philosophic mainstays of idealism, essentialism, progressivism and reconstructionism were automatically included. In addition, so that exacting University of Minnesota standards for published weight and volume would be met, it was also decided to include behaviorism and existentialism. With the current emphasis on competency based vocational education (CBVE), behaviorism didn't present any major "fantasy" problems. There is a very clear tie between behavioral learning theory and the CBVE ideology. Existentialism, on the other hand, posed as a real challenge. In order to be accepted, good fiction, like good statistics, has to be believable. Projecting existentialism into vocational education tended to strain credibility even under poetic license.

There are several recollections that stand out in my memory of the existentialist vocational fiction. One is a reference which said something to the effect that "classicism was the philosophy of the 19th century and empiricism may be the philosophy of the 20th, but existentialism will be the philosophy of the 21st century." At the time, the claim seemed like a ridiculous overstatement. It wasn't even worthy of a recorded filing. Another, more meaningful and enduring memory, was the reading of Van Cleve Morris' *Existentialism in Education: What it Means* (1966). It was Morris' down-to-earth, practical application of existentialism as ideology that finally made it possible to write a believable scenario. And, after two years of contemplation, I have come around to his position, at least in the realm of educational values.

A Look at a World Ideology

Before getting into the question of values, it might be well to look at existentialism as a world ideology, rather than as a universal philosophy. Most readers will not be willing to concede even the first philosophic thesis, that is, that the universe is absurd. That reaction is understandable. The idea of an irrational universe is just too threatening. But even the die-hard apologist has to admit that the world is a little crazy. Ever since 1914 we (meaning Americans) have been hoping for a "return to normalcy." It hasn't happened and there is little evidence to suggest that it will. What has happened is something known variously as the death of innocence, the age of cynicism, future shock, etc. My own term, were I to coin one, would be "the apostasy from transcendentalism." Since the turn-of-the-century, and the dawn of the American scientific age, we have been hoping that our heritage of classic metaphysical reason would somehow transcend the cold logic of science. One can only repeat: it hasn't happened and there is little to suggest that it will.

The subjectivity-of-truth thesis narrows to a world view ideology similar to the absurdity theme. Again we can conclude that very few people will immediately embrace the notion of subjective truth. The idea of subjective truth, even more than the notion of relative absolutes, threatens the foundations of long-established religious and moral teachings. Yet one has to admit that knowledge, if not truth itself, has become more subjective. As education and training become increasingly specialized, fewer and fewer people are willing to speak to issues outside their respective fields. One's credibility is usually limited to a specific "subject" area. An area which is, by the way, always being systematically reduced even as overall objective knowledge expands. By absolute ratio, it is always amounting to less and less.

It is also painfully clear if there is to be reason in the world, then we have to choose to create it for and by ourselves. But the increased reliance on "subject area specialization" runs us headlong into our first paradox. That is, simultaneous with subjective specialization, there is a growing awareness of an interdependently related cognition. The result is the ever more frequent necessity of having to take someone else's word for "it" (if "it" happens to be beyond one's subjective grasp). Understandably, the whole trauma over one's ability to cope with knowledge and knowing leads to a high level of anxiety. As Thoreau (1950, p. 8) aptly observed, "The mass of men lead lives of quiet desperation." One hundred and fifty years of scientific progress doesn't seem to have invalidated Thoreau's one-line summary of the human condition.

It was also Thoreau who introduced the notion that the whole problem has something to do with the relationship between the individual and an industrialized society. The "freedom" with which this interaction occurred was a central theme in his writings. Thoreau's argument for the individual's right to march to a different drummer is basic to contemporary anti-stereotyping rhetoric. However, today's "me"-centered ideology tends to be less classically idealistic and more existential than anything suggested by Thoreau. In today's society it is perfectly acceptable to talk about the concerns of "my career." In Thoreau's day, people felt obliged to apologize for that kind of selfish ego.

WHAT MEANING TECHNOLOGY?

Up to this point, I have addressed values as if they had sprung from the ideology of a philosophy. Actually, philosophy is an anachronism; the whole presentation is functionally obsolete. Philosophy was the instrument for explaining a metaphysical universe. It was a way of implementing the "rationale" that supposedly transcended the physical world. Today, only a handful of people are seriously interested in the discussion of metaphysical reality. We live in a scientific era, and by analogy, technology becomes the instrument for effecting the "new" reality. It is more often technology, and not philosophy, that generates modern social ideology and the resulting value dilemmas.

The Logic of Computers

The 20th-century experience with technology is, in no small way, responsible for undermining the classic and pragmatic philosophies. For example, Western civilization normally assumes a definite inseparable link between logic and reason. Technology has taught us otherwise. Computers are always logical, but anyone who has argued with one will attest to their lack of rationality. Government agencies often exhibit a similar set of characteristics. We are frequently made uneasy to the extent of the similarities between human thought and computers. One is led to a disquieting suspicion of a not particularly rational, if not an irrational, world reality.

There are, of course, those who will point to the so-called "smart" technology as evidence that scientific isolation of the criteria of reason is only a matter of time. Nevertheless, one fact is all too clear: this new reason will be arbitrarily chosen and deliberately created. With respect to values, the notion of arbitrary rationales is, in itself, a serious threat to our heritage of transcendent rational certainty.

An Attack on Certitude

Technological development attacks rational certainty (or more accurately, certitude) on at least two other fronts. First, technology strains the subjective certitude of the individual. It does this by increasing the number of options and alternatives available to the individual. One is continually asked to choose between existing personal certainties and new ways of using knowledge and skills. This choosing phenomenon forces the individual, by that very fact, into the valuational mode. In effect, the valuing becomes a multiple-choice test that never ends!

Simultaneous with the attack on subjective certitude, technology makes a secondary assault on the objective certitude of the individual's peer group. Since the peer group is made up of individuals whose subjective biases have been weakened, there is a corresponding lack of objective resolve among peers. Attainment of consensus becomes more difficult. The peer group becomes less able to focus the objective pressures for central tendency or "normal" social compliance. Society tends to become timid about insisting on any given system of transcendental piety.

For an example of technology's impact on certitude, we need look no further than to vocational education itself. Throughout the past decade there has been a steady and incessant plea for some sort of national vocational policy. Yet, as more and more people join in the plea for vocational certitude, there seems to be less and less chance of any kind of consensus. This situation also serves as a good example of the existential paradox. If the individual vocational educators were sure in their own minds of the meaning of vocational education, then there would be no need for the security of a peer group definition. On the other hand, if the individual is unable to make appropriate value distinctions, what good is the opinion of others?

The dilemma of technology, like that of philosophy, always leads back to the question of freedom. In the case of technological options, the issue becomes escape from choice versus freedom to choose. Often the complaint is against the dilemma of "over choice;" there are simply too many choices that can and have to be made. But a complaint against choice restriction occurs almost as often, especially when things have boiled down to a vote. Somehow the issue is never resolved. Again one realizes the crux of the problem is subjective preference versus group objectivity.

Life in the Vocational Woods
Obviously, the strongest movement in vocational education today is toward management by objective. Terms like CBVE, PBVE, Goals, Objectives, M.B.O. and "the Five Year Plan" are almost a prescribed litany in any professional agenda. It is foolish to talk about the future of existentialist ideology without first reacting to the current trend toward objectivity. The advocates of objectivity seldom mince words on the issue of goal-directed vocational education. As one colleague argues "Vocational education without objectives is like being lost in the woods." This argument continues by suggesting that an objective is like the arrow shot by a hunter lost in the woods. Following the arrow is the only way to avoid walking in an aimless circle.

At first glance, the hunter's arrow argument sees irrefutable. But, if one happens to know something about the Chippewa, or woods

Indians, it presents a number of fallacies. To begin with, the shooting of the arrow had nothing to do with being lost. The arrow technique only served to provide an alternative to walking in a circle. Being lost or not lost is a matter of orientation. The concept of a hunter getting lost in his own element is a fallacy in itself. It is like saying a fish got lost in the ocean. True, fish get separated from their school, and a woods hunter can get separated from his tribe. But lost? No.

Long-range thinking implies a sense of subjective direction. If following the straight path of the arrow means ending up in the arms of a Sioux war party, then perhaps it is better to circle in hopes of finding kindred peoples. Which brings one to the question of choosing "good" or "bad" futures. The problem is trying to judge the future merits of certain preselected goals from facts not in evidence. Existential hope depends not on just one inescapable future, but upon the freedom to choose between several futures—one of which will be inescapable.

At this point, the management by objectives approach should be sufficiently transparent to bring the values dilemma into focus. The 19th-century entrepreneur of vocational "self" could decide everything for his or herself, but choices came from a relatively fixed inventory of ethical alternatives and options. Like our Chippewa hunters, they knew the woods. Today's entrepreneur no longer has the foundational certitude of the earlier counterpart. Value judgments have become more existentialistic and, therefore, more anxiously made. Unfortunately, today's emphasis on the normative and empirical approach actually becomes *valueless* and cybernetic when viewed from the traditional perspective. That is, values are computer generated (cybernated) from the logic of statistical input and do not, therefore, claim to be transcendentally reasonable. Such values offer very little subjective reassurance. What is exposed is a crying need for a clear statement of the role of the individual in the educational woods.

PLANNING, PROGRESS AND POLICY

There are some things about contemporary vocational education that bother me as a "born again" existentialist. For example, most states now operate under some kind of five-year objective planning. The problem, for me, is that no one seems to have given any thought to the scenario at the edge of the vocational woods. We are programmed for progress, complete with yearly short-ranged adjustment schedules, without delineating the merits of the proposed goals. Furthermore, most of today's vocational objectives are stated as anti-options; i.e., anti-stereotyping, antidiscrimination, anti-WASP bias, etc.

Even when viewed from a more positive angle these objectives don't offer much in the way of existential meaning. So Sally Suburb becomes a truck driver and George Ghetto learns to be a computer technician—so what? Granted these objectives are popular with the mainstream of today's educational thought. But leading the mainstream seems to have become a euphemism for an absurd form of social manipulation. What now seems so objectively logical as a social mandate may turn out to be subjectively unreasonable when forced upon the student, particularly if the mandate is implemented many years after the fact. Have vocational educators forgotten that the heart of the protests of the 1960s was against being "born into a world 'I' didn't create?" And yet we insist on handing our students their education is individualized preselected career packages.

It is in the drafting of policy that ideology takes shape. Policy is where notions of purpose, direction, institutional behavior, values, norms and meaningful process come together. Thus, ideology proves to be a chosen thing and the end product of hundreds of value judgments. Policy by design is value by design. Semifacetiously, it can be said that policy is equivalent to an ad hoc committee on values. Ideologically, policies become the "oughts" or ethics of vocational education, legislation becomes the strategy for the propagation of those ethics, and operations become the tactics by which ideological morality is implemented. Unfortunately, our current "objective" approach seems cybernetic and freezes us into the expediencies of norm-seeking sociopolitical mandates. The result is a static set of value priorities. Yet, values are always dynamic over time and cannot be permanently ordered either hierarchically or by priority.

A Disregard for Values

What bothers me about our present system of generating policy is not that it happens, but that it is done with such total disregard for the dynamics of values. One can only wonder how we can expect to act with a true purpose, or hope to manage a multi-echelon vocational education policy in any meaningful way, without addressing the dynamic paradox between individual and societal valuing. It also seems to me that any policy, no matter how objective, must somehow accommodate the element of *freedom,* which is so fundamental to the American dialogue on values. Current vocational policy, at least as legislated, is not particularly accommodating in this respect.

Recognition of value dynamics, or the process of valuation, seems to be the key to good policy. Long-range policy becomes an integral part of the creation of new cultural values. The decision agenda becomes the values adenda; new decisions bring new sets of values into play. The principle task of the policy-maker might well be to always think at the level of value implications. Norm-seeking value configurations (societal norms) need to be weighed against subjectively normative (personal) approaches to valuation. There is a need to consider the competition of values, that is, society's versus the individual's appraisal of desirability. The cost of values in terms of the individual as well as society needs to be considered. What gets rejected may be as important as the thing preferred, i.e., valued.

Simulation, particularly subjective role playing, could serve as an important policy planning technique. At the moment, in policy-making, we do seem to be at the crossroads of a decision between more prescriptive versus less centrally dictated control of vocational practices. If one wanted to be optimistic, this current status could be seen as promising.

EXISTENTIALISM AS PRACTICE

Based on the material just presented, the reader could easily conclude that existential ideology is categorically opposed to the establishment of educational objectives and goals. That conclusion would be premature. The issue is not about having or not having chosen outcomes, but rather, it is about who chooses the goals. Van Cleve Morris (pp. 134-135) summarizes the existential position in this way:

> Existential education assumes the responsibility of awakening each individual to the full intensity of his or her own selfhood....ideologically speaking, there are three constituent awarenesses which make up the psychological content of 'self':
>
> 1. I am a choosing agent, unable to avoid choosing my way through life.
>
> 2. I am a free agent, absolutely free to set the goals of my own life.
>
> 3. I am a responsible agent, personally accountable for my free choices as they are revealed in how I live my life.

The teacher's imperative is to arrange the learning situation in such a way as to bring home the truth of these
three propositions to every individual.

In many respects, open admission/open exit policies, encouraging students to consider programs that are for them nontraditional, and striving for open-ended vocational programs are all very
existential. Advocates of these practices are, whether they realize it
or not, advancing what are basically existential positions.

So we see that the argument for what Morris (p. 153) calls "the
policy of freedom" is not entirely new to vocational education.
There are those who are already advocating a greater freedom of
individual choice in matters of vocational selection and preparation.
And in recent years we have seen a number of innovative attempts
to increase the student's awareness of vocational "self" and the
number of occupational options available, such as, career education,
the occupational cluster concept, prevocational industrial arts programs, and so forth.

Yet to date, these efforts have been frustrated by one central
paradox: vocational education is directed toward job placement
—choices are limited to labor demands and forecasts. Thus as an
institution, vocational education has only a finite rather than an
infinite number of choices to offer its potential students. While the
students is free to choose any occupation, the institution can
responsibly offer only certain logically selected possibilities.

The Problem of Those Who Leave

From an objective economic and societal perspective, the most
important goal in vocational education is job placement. Viewed
from this perspective, accurate labor demand forecasting is the
greatest single problem in vocational education today. However, if
one were to ask the nearest vocational program director, the response
would be that placement is not the most pressing problem. Placement
is a problem, but it is not *the* problem of greatest operational
concern. The greatest problem at the operational level is those
who leave the program or, in plain English, program dropouts.
These are the students who leave for *subjective reasons* before the
societal objectives of the program are accomplished. The problem
of maintaining, what in Minnesota is called, average daily memberships (ADM's) turns out to be the true barrier to program efficiency.

And what is at the root of the dropout problem? Students are
making vocational choices (value judgments) only after they are
halfway through expensive long-term occupational programs. It is a

situation that satisfies neither the individual nor the institution. It also seems to be a costly compromise between individual freedom and societal purposes. Obviously, making choices should be a prerequisite to the consequences of having chosen. In other words, the students should become aware of the subjective value of a vocation before becoming actively engaged in the pursuit of an institutionally determined set of goals. This suggests that the best compromise between the student's existential freedom and society's need for objectivity would be if the student freely chose the same goals as the institution.

The Value of Prevocation Programs

The foregoing solution strongly indicates the need for a prevocational approach to student preparation. Prevocational programs are hardly a new idea. They have been at the center of controversy for at least a decade. The idea of prevocational education has always been seen as having some inherent merit, but so far no one has come up with a rationale that justifies funding and supporting such programs.

From an existentialist position, it is no wonder the prevocational ideal receives so little solid support. Efforts at prevocational exploration have been confused by the coining of new terminology such as career education, cluster families and prevocational industrial arts. These are all terms that require new definitions and have no *subjective* meaning to the typical vocational educator. The effect might have been much better had we been talking about trade and industrial vocational exploration, and agricultural education vocational exploration and so on through the ranks of familiar area specialties within vocational education.

Bemoaning past mistakes will not correct the basic problem—the problem being the disjuncture between the individual student's existential freedom and the sociopolitically prescribed outcomes for vocational programs. On the student side of the equation, vocational education has always been at least theoretically a completely voluntary experience. The student is free to enter any program on a first-come, first-serve basis and is also free to leave at any time. On the institutional side, vocational education has always been held accountable to a sound labor economics outcome. Again speaking theoretically, programs that do not pay off in the labor market should not be run.

The dilemma is, that over time, the theories at either end of the system have been pushed further and further toward logical perfection. What we now have is a policy of freedom at one end and fixed accountability at the other. The conflict between the values of individuality and the values of social accountability are, quite understandably, becoming unmanageable. The question is: when is the best time, and under what conditions, to address the cost of reconciling subjective and objective values? In my mind, the best time would be before the student and the school become mutually involved in a long-term program commitment. The best conditions would be participation in short-term programs with the major purpose of helping students explore vocations within *clearly established subject* areas.

THE FUTURE: AN EXISTENTIAL VIEW

Existentialism argues that existence precedes essence. I must be aware of the value of the "self" before I can determine a meaning for the future of the self. That is, I am the author of my own future; I should be aware of what I want to publish. In Maslow's psychological terms one might say: self-image determines the degree to which one becomes self-actualized. It is true that existentialism has never tried to generalize this principle to the level of a group ideology. The existential view is geared almost exclusively to the subjective reality of the individual. But, for the sake of argument, I would like to generalize this view to vocational education as an existential entity.

There are those who will argue that vocational education has no reasonable excuse for existing. It resulted as an act of historic legislation, and is nothing more than an accident of history. From an existentialist position, this argument is irrelevant. All reality is an accident, there is no rational explanation for anything's *being*. This includes the existence of the very Congress that framed the laws which created the vocational institution.

What Vocational Education Is

What does matter is that vocational education *is;* it has an identity, it has subjective meaning and a real personality to the men and women who participate in its existence. Recognizing existential paradox, one must admit that vocational education is free to become anything it chooses. As an institution, it has the freedom to completely divorce itself from any past ideal of self or to project itself toward any number of futures. However, vocational education has already established meaning for its own existence, made choices and developed a pattern of values. So it seems reasonable to analyze the identity of what is rather than what might be. So, again for the sake of argument, let us look at the existential values that will shape the future of vocational education.

The outcomes of vocational education have been dictated largely by the sociopolitical objectives of "others." The labor market objective is, in respect to other-directedness, more of a given than a value. If for some reason another prime goal were chosen, there would be little chance of implementing it as a value. Though most vocational educators endorse the employability aim, they have very little real choice in the matter. It is perhaps a good thing that most vocational educators are comfortable with the employment objective.

But there is every indication that the number of externally imposed purposes will increase over the next 20 years. The problem eventually will become one of internal reaction to the aims imposed on vocational education by outside forces. But for the moment, these external realities serve the very positive function of providing a form of world orientation. Like the sun over the woods, they give us some point of mutually shared reference or reality.

On the matter of curriculum, it is interesting to note the paradox that exists between academic and vocational education. As the so-called academic programs are becoming more conservative, vocational programs are becoming more liberally existential. Vocational educators seem to have resigned themselves to coping with the program chaos caused by technological change. We tend to hold to old ways and old definitions of work and occupations. One suspects we cling to the familiar only for purposes of orientation, for in fact, vocational programs are changing and changing rapidly. On the academic side, however, one finds a steady trend toward reintrenchment and more historic approaches toward education. This paradox is almost an ironic role reversal and it will be interesting to see how the situation unfolds.

All Things to All People

On the admissions side of the futures picture, it is plain that vocational education is bent on "being all things to all people." One questions that this goal is attainable. Yet, it is consistent with the personality of vocational education. Voluntary participation for all is probably a genuine value. From personal experience, I find that vocational educators consistently choose noncompulsory admission practices. But, as pointed out, one wonders how long we can continue to articulate this policy of freedom with strict outcome accountability. Given the number of new sociopolitical mandates that are being issued, sooner or later we are going to have to face the input-output values dilemma. We cannot continue to have laissez-faire student participation and obligatory program outcomes.

Satisfying the competition between individual freedom and societal expectations is the major challenge of the coming decades. That challenge is an issue that has been with us since Thoreau first posed it in *Walden* 130 years ago. Meeting it, to the satisfaction of all concerned, will continue to be a key item on the agenda of the future.

Who Will Shape the Future?

And who will determine that future? In my opinion, too many vocational educators are hoping for some thing or some savior, some policy or some person, which or who will relieve them of the chore of choosing. There seems to be a desire to get up in the morning without having to go through the day being responsible for value judgments. There is almost a wish to become valueless, with all the ethical questions resolved by some outside agent. And this may come to be.

But let us look at some existential facts. Most of the vocational educators who will shape, plan and determine the future of vocational education are *already on the payroll.* Barring an accident in an absurd world, we will probably start tomorrow from where we are today. The future will be built by the efforts of the people we now have. We will probably not suddenly get any brighter or more mediocre or, in some cases, any less stupid than we already are. Admittedly, this is not a very happy proposition, but it is all vocational education has going for it. That is all vocational education has ever had to give it meaning, direction and certitude. It is vocational educators themselves who are responsible for the choices which will have to be made. As people who share in the subjective meaning of vocational education, we are the free agents who will establish the values of tomorrow.

REFERENCES

Lerwick, Lowell P. *Alternative Concepts of Vocational Education.* Minneapolis: University of Minnesota, 1979.

Morris, Van Cleve. *Existentialism in Education: What It Means.* New York: Harper and Row, Publishers, 1966.

Ozmon, Howard. *Dialogue in the Philosophy of Education.* Columbus, Ohio: Charles E. Merrill, 1972.

Thoreau, Henry David. *Walden.* New York: Harper & Brothers, 1950.

A JUDEO-CHRISTIAN PERSPECTIVE

Paul L. Hammer

In approaching values as they relate to the future of vocational education, the pluralism of American culture offers insights from a variety of vantage points. The particular view as set forth in this chapter is from the discipline and perspective of a biblical scholar and teacher within the Judeo-Christian heritage, and is offered as one of many mutually enriching contributions.

The Judeo-Christian heritage in American history can be viewed as one that has influenced and continues to affect the lives of millions of our citizens, even those who may no longer have any active relationship with a synagogue or church. In other words, values from that heritage are active not only among those who still relate directly to it, but also among those who have never done so or who no longer do so.

Words from that heritage are written into some of this nation's founding documents. From the Declaration of Independence comes "all men are created equal...endowed by their Creator with certain unalienable Rights...Life, Liberty...and the pursuit of Happiness." In the Constitution we read of the purpose to "establish justice... promote the general welfare...secure the blessings of liberty." The Pledge of Allegiance emphasizes a nation created with "liberty and justice for all." My purpose here, then, is to underscore some of the values from that heritage, which relate to ways we can approach vocational education and its future.

THE INHERENT MEANING

A relevant beginning might be to look at the phrase "vocational education" itself. The terms comes from the Latin: *vocare,* to call, and *educere,* to lead out or bring forth. If we press those meanings, vocational education is not simply job training or occupational indoctrination. It views persons in terms of leading out or bringing forth their calling, their *vocatio,* as human beings, and not simply as trainees for the farm or marketplace or society's institutions.

I think here of the late George Spidel, a teacher of vocational agriculture in Waverly, Nebraska, for many years. He not only taught us animal husbandry, crops and soils and farm management. He lead out from us our calling as human beings, our potential to be not simply competent and productive farmers but cosmically sensitive and responsible persons. Thus the very words "vocational education" are packed intrinsically with values that point us to evoking the full potential of persons as responsible citizens with a particular competence to contribute to the whole of the human community.

What then are some of the specific values that we hope to lead out from persons in their calling that can serve as pillars of vocational education, no matter what particular focus it may take technically and occupationally? I want to suggest three I think flow from the Judeo-Christian heritage: 1) caring creativity, 2) liberating justice and 3) wholistic peace.

CARING CREATIVITY

The Judeo-Christian heritage affirms a caring creativity at work in the universe that undergirds all things and all persons. It sees human life as the image of that creativity, with the capacity for both reflection and participation in ways that care for nature and human beings and for the interpersonal relationships and social structures of life in the universe.

Human life then is a trust in which our inherent creativity is called forth to care with dynamic imagination for the specifics of our own particular work, as well as for the natural environment and the personal and social aspects of human existence. Therefore, for instance, I am to exercise my creativity not only as a farmer but as a member of a family, a community, a nation, a world.

Regarding such caring creativity as a value in vocational education can have significant implications in practice.

It honors the dignity of each person and sees that person not so much as a receptical for information or a mechanism for skill-development, but as a human being with a unique capacity for creative involvement both in a particular occupation and in the wider community of human responsibility.

It gives to each person a sense of identity and individuality, enhancing a sense of self-worth as a creative person within a chosen skill area, at the same time recognizing a larger creative potential—a creativity that helps prevent an individual from seeing his or her entire identity simply in terms of an occupation and its connotations.

102

It enhances a sense of self-motivation that calls forth the creative potential for a kind and quality of leadership, which in turn can honor and lead out others in the exercise of their own self-motivated creativity. Thus, the way a person experiences this value of creativity in vocational education leads not to a narrow concern for one's own creative capacity, but for living and working with others toward becoming a community of creatively caring world citizens.

LIBERATING JUSTICE

The Judeo-Christian heritage does not hold some unrealistic view of the world where all is one grand utopia of creative persons. It has a stark view of the reality of the many forms of human bondage and injustice. It sees "liberty and justice for all" not as the state of affairs, but as a hope and a task. This heritage affirms a liberating justice that meets and seeks to transform a rejection of caring creativity, a rejection that causes all kinds of distortion in the relationships among people, as well as in relationships to nature and to society's institutions. Such examples include exploitation of the earth; problems of human sexuality; jealousy, hatred, and murder; violence, corruption, injustice and deceit in the social fabric; self-centered human idolatry that seeks to exalt and secure itself but ends in human confusion and the breakdown of human community. (These examples are drawn partly from the Hebrew commentary on the human condition in the stories of Adam and Eve, Cain and Abel, Noah and the Flood, and the Tower of Babel in Genesis 1-11.)

A concern for the value of liberating justice works toward overcoming the personal and social, economic and political enslavements and injustices that are the opposite of creative caring and caring creativity. The spiritual, "Go down, Moses, tell old Pharaoh to let my people go," celebrates both the ancient and contemporary call for liberating justice. The American Revolution with its concern for "liberty," "rights," "just powers" and appeals "to the Supreme Judge of the world for the rectitude of our intentions. . . with a firm reliance on the Protection of Divine Providence" (from the Declaration of Independence) also articulates something of that heritage.

Seeing such liberating justice as a value in vocational education, I think, also has definite implications in practice.

In a culture that awards a high degree of technical competence, it is easy to become so engrossed in "our trade" that we can become blind to much that goes on around us and not even care or be aware of the potential social impact of our own work. A student said to me: "My experience of the geology department is that all they care about is geology, and they don't give a damn for its social implications." Liberating justice calls for a concern to lift the sights of students to the wider community and to the reality of the exploitation of persons and of the earth; of the terrible starvation and poverty that inflict so much of the human race; of the need for economic and political, criminal and racial justice; of the cries of people for freedom from the personal and social bondages that enslave them.

It calls for taking a hard look at the impact of our own area of work and for asking whether or not we are sensitive to the ways in which it either promotes or hinders liberating justice. This includes a concern for the personal relationships and the economic circumstances of those with whom we are immediately involved, as well as for the impact of our trade on the wider concerns of the environment and of the social impact on the wider human community.

It calls for challenging persons to discover ways in which we may involve ourselves beyond our immediate jobs in seeking to work and fight for greater justice and against exploitation and dehumanizing forces in our local communities, as well as aligning ourselves with and supporting the efforts toward greater justice and freedom elsewhere in our country and throughout the world.

WHOLISTIC PEACE

The Judeo-Christian heritage affirms that the values of caring creativity and liberating justice are joined to the value of wholistic peace: peace in the sense of the Hebrew *shalom*. It means wholeness, harmony, health. Thus it means a concern for whole persons in a whole society in a whole universe. This involves a healing or whole-making or wholistic process that seeks the integration and interdependence of persons and society and environment in healthy harmony. It seeks to meet the breakdown and fragmentation of human personality and social structures, as well as the misuse and abuse of earth, atmosphere and outer space, with healing *shalom,* with wholistic peace.

This means a concern for the whole person — what we think, feel, are and do, mind, heart, soul and strength. The American Youth Foundation articulates a fourfold understanding of personal wholeness in terms of the physical, mental, social and religious. In whatever terms we may express it, wholistic peace seeks the healthy interrelationship of all facets of a person's life.

Further, such wholistic concern for the individual cannot be separated from the multiple social structures of which persons are a part: familial, economic, political, educational, racial, cultural, etc. Therefore, wholistic peace—the healthy interdependence and harmony of the multiple facets of society and the human community —is essential to any comprehensive understanding of human wholeness.

Finally, the concern for personal and social wholistic peace, of necessity, calls for a healthy relationship to the earth and universe that is our temporal home. An earth marred more and more and an atmosphere polluted more and more finally would leave us homeless. Therefore, the need to include a concern for ecological health in all its ramifications is essential to a complete approach to wholistic peace, to a global sense of *shalom.*

The Practical Applications

If we regard such wholistic peace as a value in vocational education, it has, I think, some practical implications.

Our approach to any technical competence will understand that a whole person is involved. Thus, that competence is part of the development of the rich facets of the entire human personality: the being and doing, the cognitive and the affective—the left and right hemispheres of the brain. Highly competent "robots" who are unbalanced and fragmented persons are not the goal of vocational education. Whole persons, competent in their chosen focus of work, are. Therefore, we need to ask what is happening to the whole person in the process of vocational education.

Further, the value of wholistic peace will recognize that our particular vocational education is part of a much larger social whole. It means we need to ask whether what we do in this process furthers or hinders the movement toward a whole and healthy interdependence and interrelationships of the multiple social structures of human life. It means asking whether the people involved are becoming sensitively concerned and active in seeking the wholistic peace of society.

Finally, the value of wholistic peace will help us see that vocational education not only affects the whole person and the whole social structure; it affects also the approach we take to the environment and the universe. This means that our goals in vocational education need to include an ecological concern for the effect of our life and work upon the earth and its resources—of air and water, the inland and oceanic; upon the concern for sources of energy and for the mineral deposits of the earth; upon our approach to the use of space and the atmosphere; upon our development of weapons of destruction that can destroy both human life and the environment of earth. The value of wholistic peace calls for seeing ourselves as citizens, responsible citizens of the universe.

As I look back over what I have written, I am very much aware how the concerns for caring creativity, liberating justice and wholistic peace overlap. They are all part of one piece. One without the others is incomplete and they do interpenetrate one another. In relating them to vocational education it means we need to keep all three of these values in mind simultaneously as we seek to pursue the shaping of the future of vocational education. The values I have enunciated point to a quite overwhelming task, but (to paraphrase a poet) our reach must exceed our grasp.

SECTION IV

FUTURE TRENDS

Many of the conditions, states and events of the future already exist in the sense that tomorrow's work force is already born. Barring catastrophe, we are thus safe in associating a relatively high order of certainty with the demographic expectations of the next 10 to 20 years.

At the same time, however, quantitative representations of the future tend to create illusions of certainty that can be problematic in a number of ways. First, there may be changes in, or different intensities of, the referent value structure as expressed in the previous section. Second, the forecasts of the future often become the self-fulfilling prophecies of the future when resources are matched to limited expectations rather than to expanding realities. Finally, it is difficult to anticipate the extent to which the anticipated problems of the future may offer avenues for new opportunities.

These illusions are thoughtfully considered by the authors of this section as they attempt to offer a view of the trends of the future.

THE 1980s:
A WINDOW IN TIME

Richard Ruff and Bruce Shylo

Only rarely in a social system does a period of time occur in which a need and an opportunity for significant change coexist, a period when significant change is not only a possibility, but a necessity. Such times are seldom since the major forces at play in social systems tend to reinforce the momentum of the status quo. As a result, isolated changes and innovations proliferate, but major reformulations and reforms are mollified. Because of the convergence of a set of powerful social, economic and political trends, the 1980s appear to represent such a unique period in our history—a decade that will require and create new leadership, new alliances and the fundamental reformulation of ideas.

If the 1980s are such a period in time, vocational education has the potential to experience an era of significant growth, perhaps a growth unprecedented in its history. To note just one case for this potential, industry and labor unions will be seeking assistance in the 1980s to meet the retraining needs of the workers being displaced by the fundamental and permanent shifts occurring in the manufacturing industries. In addition the avalanche of high technology will create a pervasive requirement for upgrading the skills of incumbent industrial workers.

The need to retrain and upgrade displaced and incumbent workers will be a major economic issue in the 1980s. While all segments of vocational education may not be in equal positions to respond to these types of challenges, the overall vocational education enterprise possesses the talent and the existing infrastructure not only to respond, but to respond with an effort of high quality.

The challenge, however, will be difficult. Significant changes will be required to achieve the new responsiveness. A snapshot taken of vocational education in 1990 may bear only a family resemblance to the one in the present album. A new set of varied and complex issues will have to be addressed and qualitative changes will be required. It will be necessary to develop not only new approaches for addressing the existing set of goals but also to develop approaches for responding to a new set of goals, which as yet are not even within the defined mainstream responsibility of vocational education.

In meeting these challenges, two considerations are superordinate. First, it is important to envision the next 10 years as a truly unique period of time—a period in which significant changes can be instituted that normally would encounter insurmountable barriers and one where opportunities once lost cannot be regained. Moreover, it will be a time in which substantial changes will be required in order for significant growth to occur. As Florence Hood (1980, p. 46) relates, "The winds of educational change have been blowing for several decades, frequently at hurricane force, as public, private and technological demands for a quality product different than that of traditional schools have increased noticeably."

The second consideration relates to developing an understanding of the social, economic and political forces that will shape society and hence will be the contextual forces influencing vocational education. At no time in its long history has it been more important for the vocational education establishment to avoid dialogues related solely to the issues inherent to vocational education. It is critically important that vocational education concern itself with the issues and challenges derived from the social and economic needs of society at large. As Dan Dunham (1980, p. 12) recently urged, vocational education will achieve its "long-sought greatness" when it becomes a key variable in the larger social and economic systems that make this country work.

The suggestion that vocational education has the potential to experience a significant period of growth during the 1980s is brought forth in the recognition that some feel vocational education is at a low ebb. There are some vocational educators who feel the last decade was a period of misdirection and some external critics simply have written off vocational education as an expensive failure. This perspective suggests the 1980s will be a period of further decline. Although this latter forecast does represent a possible alternative scenario and one which should not be lightly dismissed, it appears to be based on the assumption that the vocational community lacks the flexibility and creativity to be responsive in times requiring qualitative change. Although the 1980s will prove challenging for vocational education, no other aspect of education is in a better position to respond to the demands of the 1980s than vocational education—the assumed lack of flexibility and creativity is fallacious. As Daniel B. Taylor (1980, p. 10) recently emphasized, "It is my firm belief that we in vocational education can make a major contribution in the revitalization of America."

The first part of this chapter posed the idea that the 1980s will be a unique period in our history, a period in which vocational education can experience significant growth. It was emphasized, however, that the proposed growth was not guaranteed. The critical importance of focusing vocational education's energy on the issues and challenges derived from the needs of society at large was emphasized. The remaining sections of this chapter are devoted to delineating a set of social and economic trends likely to influence vocational education and to describing a 1990 scenario responsive to the dynamics generated by these trends.

TRENDS OF THE 1980s

Christopher Dede, a leading educational futurist, recently noted. "It is vital that we as educators become proactive rather than reactive in shaping education's relationship to the rest of society" (Dede, 1980, p. 16). If vocational educators are to meet this challenge, it is critical to develop an understanding of the trends that will drive the events of the 1980s. In this section, four societal trends are discussed which are particularly important for vocational education.

High Technology

In his recent book, *The Third Wave,* Alvin Toffler (1981, p. 140) stated, "Today, four clusters of related industries are poised for major growth and are likely to become the backbone industries of the third wave era, bringing with them major shifts in economic power and in social and political alignments." These four clusters of industries—electronics, space-based, ocean-based and genetics—all rely on advanced technologies. Commenting in a recent article in the *Futurist* on just the impact of microelectronics, Colin Norman (1981, p. 30) noted that "the advances in microelectronic technology have touched off a Second Industrial Revolution."

The major impact of high technology on the job market and on training requirements has yet to occur. Advances in technology, coupled with the proposed investment and tax policies of the Reagan administration, should create a boom period for new technologies. In addition to creating new skilled positions, the expansion of high technology will force the upgrading of existing occupations, transforming previously routine positions into ones with higher skill demands. Moreover, a number of displaced workers will require retraining in order to be employable.

It is difficult to envision the total magnitude of the influence that the wide-scale introduction of high technology will have on vocational education. Forecasting that item would seem similar to judging the impact of the airplane on modern society by observing the happenings at Kitty Hawk, North Carolina in 1903. The scope is difficult to envision since it will influence not only the type of training vocational education will be called upon to deliver, but also the methods employed to deliver that training.

Demographics

The dominant source of demographic change in the 1980s will be the continuing influence of the baby boom generation born between the years 1945 and 1963. As that group ages, it will have a direct and indirect influence on the labor force and hence on vocational education.

The most critical change in demographics for vocational education will be the sharp decline in the absolute number of the 16- to 24-year-old age group. This decline will affect vocational education in several different ways. For example, the number of students enrolled in high school, grades 9 to 12, is projected to drop from 15 million in 1980 to approximately 12.5 million in 1990 (Lewis and Russell, 1980, p. 125). In reference to labor market in participation, the number of entrants from this age group is projected to decline by 14 percent from 1977 to 1990. The labor market decline in the number of 16- to 19-year-olds will be evident by 1985; the decline in 20- to 24-year-olds will be felt in the late 1980s.

Although the number of 16- to 24-year-olds will decrease in the coming decade, there will be a sharp increase in the 35- to 44-year-old age group. This group will experience a 33 percent increase between 1977 and 1985. In addition, the number of women in this age group who will enter or reenter the work force is projected to increase sharply from 60 percent in 1977 to 75 percent in 1995 (Lewis and Russell, 1980, p. 143).

The importance of demographics for planning and policy formulation in vocational education extends beyond the shifts in the relative number of individuals in different age groups. The minority mix of the population is one additional important consideration. For example, although the number of individuals in the 16- to 24-year-old age group is declining, the percentage of minority group members in that age group is increasing. By the late 1980s, it is projected that approximately 30 percent of all new labor force entrants will be minority group members (Lewis and Russell, 1980, p. 108). In selected parts of the country, such as the southwest and in certain large urban areas, this percentage will be even higher.

The educational and training implications of the loss of traditional clients and the rise in importance of new populations is a trend to which vocational education must be extremely sensitive during the 1980s.

Economics

If the decade of the 1960s was the Age of Aquarius, the 1980s may well be the Age of Economics. Never before has economics been more talked about and never before have so many different opinions been voiced. Although the discussion has just begun, the critical consideration for the vocational education community is the recognition that the 1980s will not be business as usual when it comes to economic issues.

Although the opinions of economists tend to differ, most do agree that a fundamental change is needed in our present economic policy. Amitai Etzioni (1980, p. 1818) recently noted, "All agree that something is more amiss in the American economy than an unduly high reading on some indicators, poor productivity growth and low savings—the problem is more severe than just one more downturn of the age-old business cycle." This need for substantial change is echoed by Anthony Carnevale (1980) who notes that the government's fundamental basis for economic policy is incorrect in that it has been directed toward the distribution of wealth, not the generation of wealth.

Given the assumption that a significant change in economic policy will occur in the 1980s, several trends appear to be relatively clear and of substantial importance for vocational education. First, the general trend of the public mood is toward fiscal conservatism, at least during the next several years. This suggests that although public support for vocational education increased during the 1970s, the same may not be true during the 1980s. Second, the 1980s will necessitate more emphasis on determining economic priorities, leading to a decade of economic winners and losers. Third, more discretion and flexibility will probably be extended to state and local governments in the utilization of federal monies and fourth, there will be strong competition for training dollars—private schools and the military will become increasingly strong competitors in the postsecondary training enterprise.

Information-Based Society

Shirley McCune in a presentation at the National Center for Research in Vocational Education emphasized that one of the major trends affecting vocational education in the 1980s will be the shift to an information-based labor market. In an article dealing with major trends in the United States during the 1980s. John Naisbitt (1980 p. 8) reinforced that position when he suggested that the impact of the shift to an information-based society "will be more profound than the nineteenth-century shift from an agricultural to an industrial society."

The impact of the shift to an information-based society and labor market has significant implications for the entire educational community, including vocational education. If the clients of vocational education are to function effectively at work or in their personal lives, they must possess the skills necessary to collect, synthesize and disseminate information. The flood of information and the rapidity to which knowledge becomes dated will create the need to focus on learning how to learn and on developing the ability to identify what is important to learn.

The advanced demands of an information-based society, plus the present public concern with basic skills, will pose a set of serious issues for vocational education during the 1980s.

A SCENARIO FOR 1990

It was noted that it will be important in the 1980s for vocational education to focus its energy on the issues and challenges derived from the needs of society at large. The previous section presented a set of trends that will probably be influential in driving those needs. In this section, a picture of vocational education in 1990 is painted. The picture is only a partial one; it futuristically portrays a selected set of changes that the vocational education enterprise instituted in the 1980s to be responsive to the noted trends of that period.

Economic Development

Vocational educators, particularly at the postsecondary level, played a major role in retraining the nation's work force during the 1980s. While some individuals in the early 1980s (Froomkin, 1980) questioned the extent of the demand for vocational education services in retraining and upgrading incumbent workers, those who envisioned a substantial role for vocational education (Bushnell, 1980) were proved correct. The difficulties experienced by the American automobile and steel industries were more than mere cyclical disruptions and led to the need to retrain a significant number of workers. Highly paid mechanically-oriented workers who tolerated past cyclical economic downturns and disdained retraining for lower paying high technology industries were forced to seek retraining as indefinite layoffs became permanent.

Manufacturing workers were not the only ones who saw the conditions of employment change. As the number of individuals in the 35-to-44 year-old range increased, a mid-level career crunch dashed the career aspirations of many workers. Fierce competition for supervisory and management positions frustrated many of those competing for such positions. Although some lost heart and shunned the competitive cycle, others sought training for more promising occupations or to upgrade and extend their occupational choices. Large numbers of women continued entering and reentering the labor force, increasing the demand for vocational education services.

Throughout the decade, vocational educators capitalized on the potential inherent in upgrading incumbent workers due to changes in technology. New computer applications, increased use of microprocessors and the revolution in word processing were but a few developments that made it necessary to upgrade the skills of workers. Bushnell's (1980) admonition that changes in technology would create opportunities for vocational education at all levels if vocational educators were sensitive to the impact and magnitude of the shifts in employment opportunities proved to be true. Although all institutional levels of vocational education engaged in training activities to upgrade incumbent workers, postsecondary vocational education played a particularly important role. The role played by community colleges in several states working with the industries during the 1970s had demonstrated the capability of postsecondary institutions for retraining workers.

In order to effectively deliver the training required for retraining and upgrading workers, vocational educators engaged in several strategies. First, they cultivated numerous arrangements with business and industry to conduct training on-site. This served the dual purpose of providing training on up-to-date equipment while reducing institutional capital outlays.

Second, since most employers wanted skill-specific training, specialized and intensive courses were designed to supplement the more traditional programs. Vocational education's role expanded further when the federal government provided adequate incentives to business and industry to undertake the training of disadvantaged and minority youth.

Third, vocational educators placed a greater emphasis upon establishing cooperative arrangements and new linkages with other training providers and new consumers. Specifically, vocational educators stressed the maintenance of close ties with the smaller high technology industrial firms that proliferated. Vocational educators changed their orientation and became more community-based in delivering training services. Individual students and institutions requiring training services were aggressively recruited. Implementing these strategies required vocational education leaders to develop new competencies.

An issue that was inextricably bound with changing technology and the need for upgrading workers was that of teacher training and retraining. The necessity of maintaining a teaching force that was responsive to existing training needs and clients, and one that was technically proficient posed a complex problem for the vocational education manager. Once again, cooperative arrangements with business, industry and labor were pursued in order to provide teacher upgrading. Programs in which teachers were sponsored in summertime employment by local businesses and industries served to upgrade teacher skills. While incentives to cooperate were not always adequate, labor shortages in certain areas of the country stimulated cooperative arrangements to upgrade teachers.

Basic Academic and Work Skills

Vocational educators had always addressed a spectrum of educational needs. At one end was the training necessary to fill existing occupations and to prepare workers for new or changing technologies. At the other end of the spectrum were the needs related to good work habits and basic academic skills. During the 1980s, secondary vocational educators devoted increasing attention to the latter end of the spectrum. Throughout the decade, secondary vocational education stressed developing basic academic and work skills and the importance of establishing a work record for students.

While cooperative education and other work experience type programs represented only a small percentage of the total secondary vocational education enterprise in 1980, that was not the case by the end of the decade. They had been so successful that the Carnegie Council for Policy Studies' (Grasso, 1979) recommendation that they be expanded so that all high school age students could develop both job knowledge and employability skills was adopted by many local districts. This development changed the focus of traditional secondary vocational education programs in many states. In order to implement this new focus and the emphasis on basic academic skills, secondary vocational educators increased their involvement with business and industry, as well as their coordination with other components of the secondary education enterprise.

Energy Awareness
The decade of the 1980s was characterized by an overriding concern with energy. Early in the decade the role of vocational education in addressing energy concerns had not been well defined. Perhaps this stemmed from confusion at the federal level as to how to best go about resolving the "energy problem." Until 1981 most of the talk surrounding vocational education's role had been in terms of training workers for the occupations that would grow out of the energy technologies—jobs like solar panel installer, geothermal technician and others. While at first glance this seemed plausible there were those who raised the question, "How is a solar panel installer substantively different from a carpenter or a plumber?" Would not existing construction trades programs, with minor modification, qualify graduates of those programs for the position of solar panel installer? Similar questions were raised regarding whether programs that prepared coal miners reflected new technology or new demand for an old technology.

The original question thus remained unanswered—what was to be the role of vocational education in resolving the nation's energy problem? A movement arose within vocational education to focus attention upon promoting energy awareness. Some felt that vocational education could have a major impact upon domestic energy consumption if it concentrated on preparing energy-conscious workers. By stressing conservation measures that might be applied in the work place, vocational educators could contribute to a reduction in industrial energy consumption. If that conservation ethic extended into the worker's home, private energy consumption could also be reduced.

Vocational educators did not miss this opportunity to assume an important function in the nation's effort to conserve energy. Just as soaring medical costs had driven employers and individuals to seek alternatives to the high cost of health care, so did high energy costs drive individuals and industries to maximize value received from energy consumed. Energy conservation was seen as analagous to preventive medicine, with the inculcation of energy conservation as a work ethic corresponding to establishing an awareness of the importance of proper nutrition for good health.

117

All vocational education curricula ultimately reflected energy awareness concepts. Programs emphasized using energy efficient practices on the job and in the home. Individuals were made aware of their roles as producers and consumers of energy. Vocational education institutions made their energy expertise available to businesses within the community and the community-at-large via training programs, community work programs, and energy "hot-lines." In short, vocational eduation established itself as a driving force behind the reshaping of America's thoughts and attitudes toward energy independence.

Concern for Equity

An area where vocational educators pursued a proactive stance was that of equity. Although the federal government retained an interest in equity issues relating to women and minorities, it had shifted the responsibility for ensuring equity to the state and local levels. While some individuals used this as an excuse to reduce their concern with equity issues, many vocational educators continued to strive for equal access to quality vocational programs for women, minorities, disadvantaged and handicapped persons. Few vocational educators wanted to revive the stereotype of vocational education being insensitive to the needs of cities, women and other special populations. Many programs needed an increase in level of activity as more support services had to be provided to allow students to cope with the problems associated with pursuing nontraditional employment. Minority and disadvantaged students also needed special assistance in developing the work habits and attitudes deemed appropriate by the business community. As more students received occupational training on-site in the work place, school personnel worked closely with employers to help reduce stereotyping at the worksite.

The large numbers of women seeking education and training to enable them to enter the labor force created great demand for career guidance, job placement and other support services. Vocational education's ability to supply them was stretched to capacity.

New Teaching and Training Techniques

The effect of new technologies upon the need for retraining and upgrading workers was apparent. Often overlooked, however, was the effect new technologies had on the way job training was conducted. While many educators had been disillusioned by televised instruction in the early 1960s, the state of the art had progressed so dramatically it could no longer be ignored. In addition, new computerized instructional programs permitted learners to interact with the program, allowing for individualized instruction and providing immediate feedback.

High initial cost and limited flexibility had hindered the adoption of new teaching technologies in the past. Due to sharp declines in price and the addition of more flexible options, these technologies were in widespread use by the late 1980s. As the use of electronic media for student instruction proliferated, the role of vocational teachers shifted more toward that of learning consultants.

An additional training development during the decade was that more vocational education came to be delivered by way of short-term, on-site courses. This was true not only of programs designed for upgrading incumbent workers, but also of those designed for preparing initial entry workers. For the latter group, basic academic and work skills were taught in an institutional setting with the student receiving actual working experience and specific skill training on-site. Such a model was especially appropriate for minority and nontraditional students who were ensured access to support services at the institutional level. Movement toward increased on-the-job training was not without problems. For example, there were questions related to determining the incentives required to encourage employers to participate. Postsecondary education, however, continued to enroll more part-time vocational students and to deliver more training at the worksite.

Epilogue

One definition of the word crisis is that it is a turning point—for better or for worse. The 1980s were a time of crisis for vocational education. One alternative was to maintain the status quo, to continue business as usual. The other alternative was to expand the purpose of vocational education to address the social and economic needs of the 1980s. By selecting the latter, vocational educators entered an era of renewed vigor and growth. By dedicating itself to helping people develop the capacities to learn new patterns of behavior and to adapt to a changing environment, vocational education assured its success.

SUMMARY

This chapter suggests that the 1980s will be a challenging and rewarding era for vocational education. It promises to be a period in which vocational education will be presented both the opportunity and the necessity to institute substantial changes. It was emphasized that vocational education must be responsive to the needs of society at large in developing and instituting the required changes. Four trends of the 1980s which will drive societial needs and hence be influential forces for vocational education were outlined.

In addition, a scenario for vocational education in 1990 was presented. Whether this scenario proves to be an accurate representation of our field in 1990 is not as important as the need for the vocational community to continue to think about and talk about the future. To achieve responsiveness in 1990, vocational education must remember and use its great history and address the needs of the decade of the 1980s.

REFERENCES

Bushnell, D.S. *The Role of Vocational Education in Economic Development.* Washington, D.C.: U.S. Department of Education, December, 1980.

Carnevale, A. "The Reindustrialization of America." A paper presented before the Interstate Conference of Employment Security Agencies, September, 1980.

Dede, C.J. "The Next Ten Years in Education." In K.M. Redd and A.M. Harkins (eds.), *Education: A Time For Decisions.* Washington, D.C.: World Future Society, 1980.

Dunham, D.B. "Vocational Education: Policies, Issues, and Politics in the 1980s." *Occasional Paper No. 65.* Columbus, Ohio: National Center for Research in Vocational Education, 1980.

Etzioni, A. "Re-industrialize, Revitalize, or What?" *National Journal,* 1980, *43,* 1818-1820.

Froomkin, J. "The Future Role of Vocational Education." A paper prepared for the National Institute of Education, October, 1980.

Grasso. J.T. and Shea J.R. *Vocational Education and Training: Impact on Youth.* Berkeley, Ca: Carnegie Council on Policy Studies in Higher Education, 1979.

Hood, F. "Planning Changes in Education: Futuristic Trends and Images." In K.M. Redd and A.M. Harkins (eds.), *Education: A Time for Decisions.* Washington, D.C.: World Futures Society, 1980.

Lewis, M and Russell, J. *Trends, Events and Issues Likely to Influence Vocational Education in the 1980s.* Columbus, Ohio: The National Center for Research in Vocational Education, 1980.

Naisbitt, J. "U.S. Trends for the 1980s." *Business Tomorrow,* 1980, *3* (1), 8-12.

Norman, C. "The New Industrial Revolution." *The Futurist,* February 1980, pp. 30-40.

Taylor, D.B. "Revitalizing The American Economy: A Research and Development Focus for the 80s." *Occasional Paper No. 64.* Columbus, Ohio: National Center for Research in Vocational Education, 1980.

Toffler, A. *The Third Wave.* New York: Bantam, 1981.

THE INFORMATION AGE: RATIONALIZED LIFE STYLES

David Pearce Snyder

The United States today is entering a new age—that of the "information society." Today fewer than one job in four is in manufacturing, while one job in three is in the services or professions. But most importantly, across all economic sectors, *better than one job in two is, in some fashion, related to the handling of information.* Further, according to research conducted by Marc Uri Porat (1976), 55 percent of this country's gross national product is related to the gathering, storing, transcribing, retrieving, analyzing, packaging and distribution of information.

This emerging preeminence of information work is, in part, what is implicit in the term "information society". But this transformation goes far beyond the nature of our work. It also goes to the source of our future economic wealth—knowledge, technology, problem-solving skills—and to the overarching need of our society to vastly improve the productivity with which it employs what has become our most valuable *and* costly economic asset—our human resources.

What does this mean? How can we begin to appreciate the potential for social and economic change that will arise as our markets, policies and applied technologies adjust to accommodate the primacy of information? It has been about 300 years since Western civilization has undergone so fundamental a transformation. The last occasion was, of course, the shift from an agrarian economy to an industrial economy.

Factory production technologies required large concentrations of workers and thus gave rise to cities and to salaried employment, which took economic production out of the home. To serve and sustain burgeoning urban populations, civil authorities copied the large-scale, high-production institutional model that had worked so well for the industrial sector. Growing public bureaucracies were thus created to provide welfare, education and medical services, further extending the institutional sector of our society while simultaneously reducing the role of the household.

In sum, over the past 250 to 300 years, the adoption of industrial technologies and institutional forms has substantially altered both

123

our economic geography and demography, concentrating most of our population in and around large cities, and concentrating most commerce and productive activity under the management of large institutions. Today, every American should clearly understand that the emergence of information work as our principal economic activity plus the simultaneous emergence of cheap, powerful information and communication *(infocom)* technologies pose the same potential for social and economic transformation as did the rise of industrialism.

It is equally important to understand that the very nature of industrial technology *necessarily* led to a physical concentration of social and economic activity, and to the expansion of institutional power. In contrast, the rise of infocom technologies will permit *either* a further concentration of power and meaningful activity in our system *or* a redistribution and decentralization of social responsibility and economic enterprise. And, while both outcomes remain possible today, the underlying social and economic factors summarized in the following pages appear to favor decentralization.

THE DEMAND FOR INFORMATION

Walk into a magazine stand and look at the astonishing variety of information, knowledge, expertise, reportage, opinion, insight and inspiration being offered there, including hundreds of new, nationally distributed magazines established during the past decade in an attempt to respond to and capitalize upon the ever-growing demand for more and more specialized information.

Consider, for a moment, the implications of the continuation of these trends. Given current growth rates, de Solla Price (1967) estimates that by the year 2000 there will be over one million different scientific, technical and scholarly periodicals being published throughout the world, a substantial portion of them in the U.S.

Newspapers on Computer

What will a magazine store be like then? Macy's? The continued growth and dispersion of knowledge requires, and is already forcing a change in our fundamental information medium—from paper to electronics. Through this change, by the year 1990 most U.S. households will possess their own, in-home magazine stores. Stored and delivered electronically, knowledge and information can be marketed more on a selective, individual demand basis (that is, economic pull), rather than a bulk output basis (economic push), as currently represented by newspapers, magazines, television programs, reference books, etc. A consumer-pull information economy will make possible much greater public access to much larger volumes and varieties of information and at a much lower cost than such resources cost today.

Not only will the mass production and consumption of information comprise an increasing portion of our economic activity, but the growing flow of performance-monitoring feedback should substantially enhance the quality of our goods and services and do much to restore consumer confidence in the products of our technology and our industry.

For example, electronic diagnostic equipment will provide the automotive and appliance industries with an automated performance feedback system. Armed with accurate, detailed and up-to-date performance data on their products, manufacturers can continuously re-design products for optimal performance, rather than concentrating on market-provoking style changes. So detailed will this flow become that such feedback will trace performance failures back to individual subassemblers, suppliers and specific workers on the production line. This ultimate extension of accountability is an achievable potential that could take the anonymity out of assembly line work and make such employment richer and more meaningful. It will also spark pressures for altered pay and performance criteria.

The easy access to information on an as-needed basis will have equally profound impacts on consumer behavior and on the functions of advertising. Consumers will be able to evaluate competing services (such as moving companies and exterminators) and alternative products (such as automobiles and appliances) simply by consulting up-to-date records of product performance and customer complaints collected by government licensing agencies and consumer interest groups. In such an environment, consumer behavior will become more rationalized because it will be based more on hard data and less on advertising ballyhoo.

Of course, any significant move by government to improve its information-handing efficiency through computerization and data-sharing will rekindle the public debate over privacy protection. But the national imperatives for intelligent public policy-making and improved economic productivity will become so clearly linked with the need for free information flow that sometime during the mid 1980s, the courts will substantially redefine and significantly narrow the legal concept of privacy.

In particular, the courts can be expected to rule that all information regarding sales and purchases of all kinds are in the "stream of commerce," and are thus not entitled to personal privacy protection.

In addition, data pertaining to specific individuals will be legally classified as personal property and subject to the same basic protections as money held in a bank or securities held in trust. This resolution of the privacy issue, based upon the Swedish model now being studied by other European countries, will remove the last major barrier to the emergence of a "wired society," where electronic mail, two-way television, wrist telephones and information utilities will become commonplace.

Management of Complexity

The major growth of the information economy will not, however, come from improving the performance of our industrial technologies, nor from meeting the "retail" consumer demands for knowledge. Rather, it will arise from the imperatives posed by what British cyberneticist Stafford Beer (1970) calls "the management of modern complexity."

Each year, we develop or discover 10,000 new chemical compounds; each year our local, state and federal legislators enact more than 50,000 new laws; every year our society produces 75 billion new documents. Electronic information and communication technology will make it possible for us to manage 10,000 new chemical compounds, to enforce and evaluate 50,000 new laws and to meaningfully utilize the contents of 75 billion documents, by providing us with the electronic equivalent of millions of typists, file clerks, librarians, research assistants, poll takers and computer operators.

Electronic technologies are already reshaping our institutions. Library card files have been replaced by computer printouts, which are now beginning to be replaced by video terminals. Telephones are increasingly being answered by electronic devices. Today, it is cheaper to create, distribute and store information via electronic media than in any other form. And the outlook for the immediate future is for massive, implemented change. The electronic office does not merely mean memory typewriters. It means electronic mail, interoffice communication and filing. Within the next several years, we will begin to see massive reductions of new hires of semiskilled clerical personnel as electronic information technologies become more widely adopted, due to their patent productivity and to the rising cost of labor.

Infocom Technology and Productivity

The compelling productivity of infocom technology is already being reflected in information-based businesses. For example, as newspapers convert to electronic composition, they are finding that where they once spent $2.00 to produce the news that they spent $1.00 to gather, this ratio is now reversed, and they can spend two-thirds of their operating budgets on the gathering and analysis of content. This basic change in employment patterns will affect not only the nation's 40,000 newspaper and periodical publishers and their one million employees, but book publishers as well. While the number of books in print rose 25 percent between 1973 and 1978 and the number of book publishers grew from 3,500 to 6,000, the publishing industry's share of the total consumer dollar remained relatively constant, at one percent of consumer expenditures (Applebaum, 1978). This rapid growth of output and product differentiation at a fixed cost attests to the sharply increased productivity of electronic composition.

In fact, our new understanding of information economics goes right to the heart of our current national concern for increasing the general productivity of our economy. Clearly, if information is the principal product of our national enterprise and information work is our principal employer, then our major efforts at productivity enhancement should be directed to these sectors of our economy. In this respect, the emerging electronic information and communication technologies could scarcely have become available at a better time.

Today in the U.S., only about $2,500 is spent on productivity-enhancing equipment for each white-collar worker, while nearly $26,000 is spent on productivity-enhancing equipment for each blue-collar worker and over $52,000 is invested in support of each American farmer. In a nation where white collar — that is, information — work is the largest and most rapidly growing segment of the economy and where such work is the source of over one-half the GNP, the compelling need to reverse recent downward trends in overall economic productivity, combined with the need to reduce the hyper-inflating energy and transport costs of all organizations, will collectively produce hundreds of billions of dollars in capital investments to automate communications and information work during the 1980s.

Our Most Important Product

In terms of economic value then, basic or applied knowledge and information will be our most important product in the coming decades. The U.S. is the best educated mass society in the world today. Our research capacity, public and private, is greater than any other nation's, as is our pool of technical personnel. Further, the U.S. has an acknowledged lead in the principal growth technologies of the 1980s and 1990s, including information and communication, aerospace and agriculture. With these basic components, while the nations of the Third World industrialize, the developed nations, led by the U.S., will be "rationalizing," as a logical progression in the sequence of cultural evolution.

The Western nations, as a whole, represent only 15 percent of the world's population, yet they currently control the bulk of the globe's productive capacity and technological knowledge and consume the majority of the world's output. But the West controls less and less of the world's raw materials.

As the Third World countries develop—industrialize, urbanize and "consumerize"—they will form growing markets for U.S. knowledge and technology in such forms as patents, licensing agreements, management, technical and systems consulting, training, turnkey operations, engineering design, service, testing and exploration, as well as high technology such as communications, electronic monitoring, sensing and control devices, manufacturing processes and equipment, software, prime moving equipment, etc. Global markets, developed as well as developing, will also generate much of the demand for our aerospace services, which U.S. space authorities currently estimate will be $20 billion per annum by the 1990s.

This space boom, too, will largely be driven by the growing demand for information and for communications, weather forecasts, navigational assistance, and geological and agricultural survey data that only satellites can provide.

Our Most Valuable Resource

During the past generation, our multi-trillion dollar private and public investments in education and health care have far outstripped our investments in productive plant, equipment and infrastructure. Today, America's human assets—her trained, productive workers— are her most valuable *and* costly resource. Our rising investments in education have been particularly appropriate, for they have been made just as white-collar work has supplanted blue-collar work as the nation's principal productive activity.

In 1945, only 25 percent of U.S. adults had completed high school; in 1980, 75 percent of adults had received a high school diploma. In 1945, 5 percent of all Americans had completed college; in 1980, 18 percent had finished at least four years of college and nearly 14 percent more had received a two-year associate degree. This means that more Americans today have a postsecondary degree than had finished high school in 1945.

As birthrates have declined, future increases in national education levels will be slower than those of the recent past, particularly in view of the rising costs of higher education. Currently, however, more than 50 percent of all 20 to 29 year-olds have completed at least one year of college, indicating a continuing popular commitment to learning.

A CONTENTIOUS WORK PLACE

As we contemplate the prospect of working in what promises to be a decade of dynamic innovation and opportunity, we must also understand that other powerful social and economic forces will be at play during the next five to 10 years, challenging and confounding both personal and professional development.

Mid-Career Compaction Increases Competition

Not only is the 1980s work force considerably more educated than previous U.S. labor pools, it is now getting older, after decreasing in average age for most of the past 30 years. The "baby boom" age cohort has now moved into full adulthood, and by 1990, 30 to 45 year-olds will constitute over 50 percent of the work force (up from 39 percent in 1970). As this group matures, the number of applicants for mid-career promotions may be expected to double, from 10 candidates per vacancy in 1975 to nearly 20 candidates per vacancy in 1985. Further, fully one-third of such promotions will be influenced by affirmative action requirements. All of these circumstances are expected to foster frustration and contentiousness among white-collar workers.

Productivity and Job Satisfaction Decline

In fact, mid-career compaction and affirmative action are only two of many powerful change agents that will bring turmoil to the work place during the 1980s. Other change agents will include the automation of white-collar work and the robotization of blue-collar work, both of which will eliminate millions of routine jobs while creating millions of new, more highly skilled openings. There are also volatile forces for change latent in the attitude surveys that show growing worker dissatisfaction among all levels and types of salaried employees. Closely linked with this decline in worker satisfaction is recent research evidence which suggests that *none* of the widely acknowledged techniques for improving worker productivity on repetitive assembly-line jobs or on menial or rote work have a *permanent* effect on employee performance. The studies indicate that the improvements produced by such innovations as "participative management," "team work," "job rotation" and "job enrichment" are almost entirely transitory.

A Society at Odds with Its Institutions

The declining productivity of America's workers is widely associated with the declining expressions of job satisfaction throughout the U.S. work place. During the 1970s, surveys of American workers reflected sharp drops in average job satisfaction levels of *all salaried* workers of *all* ages—blue collar and white collar—from rank-and-file employees to top management, including all salaried technical and professional personnel. And, while farmers and the self-employed have continued to report relatively high average levels of job satisfaction, fewer than 10 percent of America's workers fall into these categories. Over 90 percent of us are salaried employees, and over two-thirds of us work for large organizations (i.e., with over 100 employees). But public opinion polls also indicate that the vast majority of Americans have lost confidence in all of our major private and public sector institutions, and further, that the public regards all large organizations with a substantial degree of distrust.

Thus, in the work place of the 1980s, we will see a phenomenon that is reflected in the general opinion polls as well as in the worker attitude surveys: Americans are not happy with the institutions upon which most of us must depend for governance, for goods and services and for employment. We are presently a society at odds with its institutions, and in few places will the realities and consequences of this adversary relationship be as clearly demonstrated as it will in the dynamics of the American work place during the next five to 10 years.

Labor Movement Seeks White-Collar Recruits

Since the mid 1960s, most U.S. labor unions have experienced no growth or have actually lost membership. This has generally been due to the extremely slow growth of the blue-collar work force, the traditional base of the American trade-union movement. Labor's initial attempts to organize U.S. white-collar workers during the 1950s were largely rebuffed by employee populations who saw themselves as professional or quasi-professional. (Note: In an economy generally perceived as being based upon the physical substance of its agricultural and industrial output, there had also been a long-term tendency for white-collar workers to be seen as "administrative overhead"—excess baggage who could be dismissed without significant impact on the employer's central operations. Thus, a combination of gentility and insecurity made white-collar workers poor union recuits in the 1950s.)

Today, of course, white-collar and service work employs nearly 70 percent of our labor force, and this new worker majority understands that they are a crucial component to all productive enterprise. Further, many white-collar employees and salaried professionals perceive that they are less well paid for their time than many trade workers, often in spite of the white-collar workers' substantially greater investments in career preparation.

Organized labor's announced intention to actively recruit white collar employees, plus the worker attitude survey results cited previously, must be considered in the light of other basic background factors, such as the compaction of mid-career employees, the short-fall in the number of entry-level workers, the compelling need to automate millions of white-collar jobs and the intervention of affirmative action in the employee promotion process.

These sorts of dynamics, combined with the likely continuation of high inflation rates during the early 1980s, will serve to encourage the success of white-collar unionization. One labor leader was recently quoted in a national news magazine as suggesting that "the 1980s will be for the white-collar worker what the 1930s and 1940s were for the blue-collar worker."

A Troubled Public Sector

The foregoing dynamics will be working in public and private sector alike. But the public sector will also be confronted with ongoing political pressures to reduce government expenditures through such measures as hiring freezes, service cutbacks, and budgetary requirements to do more work for less pay at all levels of government. This will make public sector employees particularly susceptible to union recruitment during this time frame. Job actions—such as strikes, slow-downs and "work-to-rules" movements—throughout the public sector may be expected to seriously disrupt all forms of social and economic activity from time-to-time, at least during the first half of the 1980s.

Having already experienced numerous early manifestations of these looming circumstances, both managers and executives throughout the public sector are currently forming "professional associations," in order to represent their interests in a turbulent economic and political environment, which they see likely to provide them with fewer and fewer personal rewards for fulfilling more and more complex and demanding civil responsibilities with increasingly constrained resources. The emergence of these new power centers in the governmental labor-management relationship may serve to either moderate or exacerbate what promises to be the most troubled sector of a generally contentious work place during the next five to 10 years.

A Growing Service Sector

The combined increase in single-person households, single-parent families and dual-career marriages has stimulated a long-term growth in the demand for a wide variety of personal services. In 1950, about one-third of the average household's budget was spent for services, including shelter, medical care, transportation, communications, education and personal care. That portion had grown to 45 percent by 1978 (Linden) and the service sector continues to be the fastest growing major component of the U.S. economy. This reflects both increased disposable household income *and* a more rationalized attitude toward the economic value of time on the part of the general citizenry.

As long as women's labor in the household was regarded as a cost-free good, housewives performed a variety of personal services for their mates as a part of their culturally defined role. But as more and more women contribute increasing amounts of money to their household budgets, and as their income-earning potential rises, the economic value of women's time will continue to increase, and it will become increasingly compelling (rational) to pay for services previously performed at no cost by women in the home. Growth service fields are likely to include child care, health and dental care, yard and home maintenance, restaurant eating, prepared foods, travel, tourism and recreation.

It should be noted that a growing number of economists now believe that the rise of single life styles and the growing commercialization of personal services once performed in the domestic sector are among the principal sources of stagflation. If this perception gains general currency in U.S. economic thinking as we seek to manage our ailing economy back to health, it may lead to social and economic policies—such as social security/pension reforms and tax incentives—designed to encourage household formation and extended family collaboration. Such measures could be expected to curb or reverse long-term growth trends in some service fields, including child care, nursing and convalescent homes, residential maintenance, auto repair and private schooling.

An Evolving Industrial Sector

While the service sector will be growing and the public sector will be experiencing disruptive tensions and conflicts, the U.S. industrial sector will continue its long-term evolutionary adaptation to the growing value and cost of human resources. Since the Second World War, as America's investments in human capital have raised the value of the average U.S. worker, lower-cost foreign labor—especially in the "take-off" economies of the Third World—has permitted overseas producers to make substantial in-roads into U.S. domestic and international markets. Today, the U.S. is exporting an estimated 20,000 blue-collar jobs each month to competitor nations with skilled, low-cost industrial labor pools.

The make-up of the U.S. blue-collar labor market has also been undergoing changes in response to the rising value of the American worker. Once, mass production of manufactured goods and their components employed over two-thirds of our industrial workers. But today, due both to automation and our increased import of foreign products, only one-half of our factory workers are employed in mass production—that is, turning out automobiles, appliances, cans of food, boxes of soap, can openers or ball-point pens. About one-half of our industrial GNP comes from this type of production. The other half of our industrial work force—the growing half—is engaged in producing products in lots of 100 units or less, such as aircraft, computer main frames, materials handling equipment, communications satellites and the rockets to launch them into space, etc. America's blue-collar workers are migrating to the high-growth, high-tech industries, including energy and communications, which demand workers of a higher skill and knowledge level than was required of the rank and file industrial workers a generation ago. The Chrysler Corporation, for example, is reported to have lost over 6,000 skilled, mid-career employees to other industrial sectors during the 1970s.

RATIONALIZED LIFE STYLES AND A KNOWLEDGE-BASED ECONOMY

How will America's evolving values and life styles interact with these economic and taechnological developments? Are the two compatible or will we find Americans fundamentally at odds with what promises to be a high-growth global economy extensively dependent upon America's export of her technology and America's growing consumption of foreign products and raw materials?

Today Americans are increasingly pursuing "rationalized" life styles; that is, in our critical life decisions—our choices of careers, habitats, avocations and mates—and in our daily activities, we are increasingly being guided by pragmatic considerations, factual input and reality, and less guided by normative values and traditionally prescribed behaviors and expectations. In fact, Americans are demonstrating an adaptability and ingenuity that is entirely appropriate to a time of great change.

A Logical Progression

This is the combined logical outcome of such diverse long-term factors as soaring levels of public education and sophistication (brought about both by public schooling and the media) and distrust of the prior generation's institutions, technology and values (brought about by the events and perceptions of the 1960s and 1970s) plus long-term prosperity (brought about by the prior generation's institutions and technologies) and a massive benign welfare system (brought about by the prior generation's values).

This rationalization of life styles is manifested in a myriad of ways. But before proceeding, an important, fundamental point should be made about this American rationalism. And that point is, that rationalization of life styles is a natural, long-term phenomenon reflected in all modernizing societies.

Average family size, for example, has been diminishing throughout the developed world since the advent of industrialization; family size has begun to diminish in the developing nations in consonance with increasing levels of education, industrialization and urbanization. Reduced family size is a natural result of any society's conversion from agrarian to industrial society. It is also the natural result of the rising role of public institutions as providers of education and social welfare. *There is simply a diminished economic utility for large, cohesive families in a cosmopolitan, industrial society.*

This does not mean that the family does not serve critical social and economic functions in modern society or that the family is destined for oblivion. What it *does* mean is that the diminished size and apparent diminished importance of the family in our society, at least up to this point, is a natural phenomenon, concurrent with the changes in the household's social, technological and economic environment.

Thus, the waning of the family is not some uniquely American phenomenon. The recently declining birthrates in the Third World are a manifestation of this reality. At the other end of the spectrum, Europe is conceded to have moved further toward many more key elements of social, political and economic rationalization than has

134

the U.S. As a result, birthrates there are so low that Germany actually lost population in 1980, and all European nations except Ireland are expected to decline in population by the end of this decade. In Germany and Sweden, single persons make up 35 to 40 percent of all households, nearly twice the proportion as in the U.S.

THE NEW DEMOGRAPHICS

Until recent months, birthrates in the U.S. had been falling steadily since the late 1950s and they have been below replacement levels for nearly a decade. One powerful economic consequence of this long-term trend in social behavior will be reflected in the sharply reduced growth of the labor force during the 1980s. During the past decade, swelled by the maturing "boom babies," the U.S. work force grew by more than 17.5 million persons; but in the 1980s, the worker population is expected to increase by only eight to 10 million, with the increased competition for young workers resulting in inflationary pressures on entry-level wages and accelerated robotization of routine, semi-skilled work.

Clearly, a continuation of the past two decades' dwindling birthrates would ultimately find the U.S. confronted with the same shrinking labor pools and domestic consumer markets that are presently troubling the Europeans. But historical data make it clear that the household unit is a flexible, highly adaptive social form, which adjusts to the circumstances of its social, economic and technological environment. Various combinations of change in the family environment during the 1980s could reverse the long-term shrinkage of the household and even result in the emergence of new household forms.

For example, under conditions of increasing per capita income (along with other demographic and economic influences) the percentage of the U.S. population which lives alone has grown from 10 percent to 25 percent just during the past 25 years (1955-80). During the Great Depression, the percentage of live-alones went from approximately 15 percent in 1929 to nearly 40 percent in 1939, because economic conditions so discouraged the formation of new households. (It is important to note that the vast majority of one-person households during the Depression years lived in group quarters—boarding and rooming houses—while the majority of today's live-alones occupy solitary residences, with all of the appliances, overhead space, equipment and operating costs typical of an independent household. Thus, similar demographic phenomena may have differing socioeconomic manifestations.)

During the past two to three years, short-term trends have begun to suggest some potential directions for adaptive household behavior during the 1980s. The rapid appearance of a growing number of "group houses" in most larger American cities suggests the emergence of a new form of collective housing for singles anticipating less prosperous times. In a related development, the Sindlinger Organization has noted there was a sudden, precipitous drop in the number of households in the U.S. during the last nine months of 1980. Over 700,000 households "collapsed" into one another, with children moving back in with parents and parents moving back in with their children. Sindlinger's surveyors reported that the principal reason given for these household reintegrations was economic, specifically the high cost of living—especially housing—or loss of a job.

If this recent short-term reduction in households were to continue for 10 years—admittedly not a likely event unless we were to go through a 1930s-style depression—average household size, given nominal population growth, would rise from 2.6 persons in 1980 to 3.7 persons in 1990, roughly equivalent to average household size in 1940. If this decline were to last only five years, that would still leave us with an average household size of 3.3, about where it was at the peak of the baby boom.

There is also historical demographic data to suggest that the coming shortfall in entry-level workers—and the resulting increase in their wages—should foster earlier marriages and higher fertility rates among young adults, since a single entry-level income once again will be sufficient to support a household. And, as the members of the baby boom generation move toward the second half of the normal child-bearing years (27 to 43 years of age in the U.S.), most demographers expect the fertility rate for this group will also increase throughout the 1980s. Indeed, during the 18-month period from the middle of 1979 through the end of 1980, there was a 25 percent increase in those giving birth among the 25-to-34 year-old age group, and an increase in the marriage rates for all Americans aged 17 to 45 years.

Overall, then, there is clear historical evidence that demographic and economic factors can interact to sharply alter residential patterns in the U.S. over a relatively short time span (five to 10 years), and further, that potential factors will exist during the 1980s and 1990s to promote such social dynamics.

Alternate Population Projections
Because marriage and fertility rates are so responsive to changing components of the social environment, and because of the dispropor-

tionately large number of Americans currently at the child-bearing age, the growth of the population and of the number of households represent two of the most volatile base variables for the next two decades. For this reason, the U.S. Census Bureau makes several alternative population and household projections, using different assumptions.

The U.S. population is expected to increase within a range of 13 to 31 million persons, with growth rates ranging from about one-half percent per year to a little over one percent per year. Households are expected to increase within a total range of 10 to 19 million units at growth rates ranging from one percent to two percent per year. By comparison, the number of persons in the U.S. increased by 21 million (about one percent per year), while the number of households grew by 17 million during the 1970s, a rate of about 2.7 percent per year.

Based on current Census Bureau forecasts, the number of households in the 1980s will increase by no more than the same amount per year as they did in the 1970s, with alternate growth projections ranging downward to increase by about one-half the amount they did in the 1970s. In fact, most demographers anticipate that fundamental sociological and economic realities of the 1980s will produce higher birthrates and lower household formation rates than did the 1970s.

More Women Participate

The shift from blue-collar to white-collar work has facilitated the expanded participation of women in the work force. Women made up only 30 percent of the paid labor force in 1950, rising to 44 percent by 1980. Historical changes in labor force makeup indicate that female participation in the labor market is sensitive to several economic and demographic factors and thus, like the future marriage and fertility rates of the baby boom generation, it is not possible to forecast future increases in women workers with certainty. However, if the U.S. economy during the 1980s merely maintains the modest 2.9 percent average annual increase in GNP that it experienced in the 1970s, certain basic influences—such as the shrinking entry-level labor pool—will coerce some increases in female employment, to at least 45 percent of the workers by 1990.

The "Boom Babies" Grow Up

Finally, in seeking to identify the most likely scenario for the U.S. during the next decade, special notice must be made of the movement of the baby boom generation into middle age. Throughout the remainder of this chapter, detailed reference is made to the specific, predictable consequences of the maturation of this age group. Because of the unusually large number of Americans born during the 20 years following the Second World War, the members of this age cohort have been destined to be a powerful force for social and economic change throughout their lives.

In their infancy, the boom babies fueled the development of our modern medical establishment and triggered a housing explosion that temporarily made home-building America's third largest industry and permanently encircled all of our cities with suburban sprawl. When the baby boom reached school age, society provided them with over 2 trillion dollars in education and they responded by providing the nation with a decade-and-a-half of social unrest and political upheaval.

Today, both educators and home-builders are carefully watching the slowly rising birthrates of the post-war generation to determine if the current, short-term "baby bubble" will become a new baby boom. And Madison Avenue is speculating on the emergence of an affluent, highly educated, middle-aged consumer market during the 1980s and 1990s. Overall, it is not yet clear just what social, political and economic impacts the baby boom generation will ultimately have on America during the next 10 to 20 years, but given the track record of the last three decades, we can be certain the results will be remarkable.

An Economically Powerful Domestic Sector

Around 1910, the annual rate of investment by households in themselves—in the form of purchases of real property and hard goods—exceeded for the first time the rate at which the business sector was investing in plant and equipment. By the mid 1950s, the total assets of the domestic sector had surpassed the total assets of all business. Today, individuals and families own approximately 38 percent of America's total assets, while business owns 31 percent, governments own 22 percent and agriculture (which also includes extensive family holdings) controls 9 percent. The domestic sector's principal asset is the nation's housing stock, which is worth an estimated 33 percent of all U.S. wealth, greater than all business assets.

This long-term, underlying trend may fairly and simply be regarded as reflecting the massive realization of the "American Dream"—owning your own home, two cars in every garage, a kitchen full of labor-saving devices and ample leisure time for avocational and recreational activities involving further capital investments in boats, second homes, mobile homes, ski-mobiles, etc. No other economy has ever been so successful in providing its participants with so many affordable personal investments. In no other nation do home ownership, auto ownership, television ownership, etc., exist on so large a scale as they do in the U.S. The low rate of personal savings in the U.S.—often lamented by U.S. business leaders and economists—largely may be explained by the affordability of our goods and services in general and of our hard goods in particular.

In those economies where hard consumer goods are more costly, they often are saved for over a long time, generating a high rate of personal savings and concentrating capital goods consumption in the older members of society. The higher general level of private saving ultimately puts more venture capital in the hands of institutional decision-makers and planners—banks, corporations, bond-issuing public agencies, etc.—than does the current U.S. economy, where the domestic sector has been accumulating its own economic "reserves." Society's future use of this reserve, the political efforts to enhance or protect it through tax policy, government transfer programs, local development and zoning restrictions, referenda, etc.—plus future patterns of domestic sector consumption and investment in the face of persistent inflation—will all be significant variable factors in the unfolding of the next five to 10 years in America.

It should be noted that the long-term trend toward increased domestic sector capital investment has been augmented by the nation's sharply increased expenditures for education and health-care over the past generation. Since individuals may be said to "own" themselves, it is reasonable to assert that the productive use of America's huge "human capital" asset—roughly equal to the value of our total national productive plant, equipment and infrastructure—is under the direct control of society itself, rather than under the guidance or management of any institution. This remarkable distribution of economic power—unique among modern nations—makes social behavior an extremely potent determinant of economic performance and evolution in America.

The growing value of human resources will, among other things, increase the leverage of employee organizations in their job actions and wage/benefit negotiations. But more important by far, the long-term accretion of economic power by the domestic sector means that the most important economic decisions in the U.S. during the next 10 years will be the collective choices—made by millions of individuals and households—regarding how they will invest their resources and their lives. It is of particular importance, then, to take note of the current literature in anthropology and social history, which strongly suggests that, given the opportunity, societies are highly adaptive to changes in their economic, political and technological environments. This further suggests that society itself—through its individual and small group investments of time and money—is considerably quicker to undertake adaptive innovations than are its institutions.

In view of the socioeconomic dynamics described above, this would appear to be an extremely opportune moment in our nation's history for our resources to be so broadly distributed throughout our society, particularly when the literature in the management science fields makes it so clear that large institutions are ill-suited to initiate significant changes except under crisis conditions. But, given the rich mix of factors that will shape our social environment during the coming decade, can we possibly make any coherent assessment of what living in the 1980s will be like? The answer is "Yes." Emerging trends in U.S. values and life styles give us some very solid indications of the kinds of adaptive behavior that will characterize life in post-industrial America.

RATIONALIZING SOCIAL VALUES

We have reviewed the demographic, economic and technological changes that will shape the social environment of the 1980s and have further suggested that people will rationally adapt to these changes. But what ends will society be seeking to achieve? What practical goals will motivate society's investments and commitments during the next five to 10 years?

What Do Americans Want Out of Life?

A review of the desires most commonly expressed in public attitude surveys over the past 10 years provides us with a sense of the motivating life goals held by the vast majority of all Americans today:

- People want more control over their own lives and the destinies of their families.
- People want opportunities to learn and develop throughout their whole lives.
- People want meaningful work or significant roles that give them a sense of accomplishment and contribution to the larger community.
- People want to participate in and actively experience life rather than to watch or experience others performing.
- People want challenges to their creative and problem-solving abilities.

- People want to live and work among open, happy, trusting people.
- People *do not* want to be unwittingly or unwillingly jeopardized.

The strong commitment of most Americans to the foregoing values can be expected to powerfully influence the manner in which people arrange their lives and spend their time and money. Products, services and public policy measures that permit people to satisfy these goals are likely to win popular support in the marketplace and the voting booth during the next five to 10 years.

CHANGING HEALTH STYLES

The current nationwide movement toward rational health styles began in the 1960s with the emergence of the health food craze and the public debates over the deleterious effects of chemical substances in the environment, including foods. Extensive research, much of it made economically possible only by the existence of the computer, began to reveal statistical correlations between some consumables and some diseases. Recent sharp reductions in death from some forms of heart disease, hypertension, cerebro-vascular disease, diabetes and arteriosclerosis are directly laid by medical experts to improved diet and exercise, voluntarily adopted by large numbers of Americans.

Basically, the rational behavior of the society in response to factual information—feedback—completes a "cybernetic" loop which is characteristic of rationalized life styles. A word to the wise, they say, is sufficient.

Preventive Medicine: HMOs

An even more important trend, already prevalent today, is the promotion of health maintenance organizations (HMOs), which have the purpose of prescribing, monitoring and particularizing programs of behavior designed to prevent illness in individuals. The promotion of HMOs is "rational," because the per patient costs of a *preventive* health care program are lower than those of traditional medical insurance coverage for *curative* costs, particularly when incorporating the benefits of a healthier work force. Further, growing union promotion of the use of HMOs reflects the perception that such applications of medical technology are both beneficial and antiinflationary.

Private HMOs are emerging, run by single doctors or nurses or as private clinics, suggesting a competitive edge for the preventive approach. These enterprises hope to take advantage not only of the rationality of HMOs but also their cost-effectiveness. They are entering an excellent market, since Americans spend more money on medical care than on any other personal service except shelter.

A final element of the rationality represented by HMOs is found in their employment of human resources. Because they deal in preventive medicine, the bulk of their work can be done by nurses and medical technicians—freeing highly trained, costly doctors for more productive work and reducing the overall labor costs for care provided.

A Growth Industry

Rationalized health styles promise to grow during the eighties. Home health care, bringing the return of the visiting nurse, has been supported in congressional hearings as a means of reducing hospital costs. Other examples include birthing rooms at hospitals, practicing the LeBoyer childbirth methods, and hospices, where terminal patients may go to die in pleasant surroundings, without heroic measures at life maintenance.

Other elements of rationalized health styles in the 1980s will include exploration of the noetic sciences, such as folk medicines, and acupuncture, both by researchers and by the general public. In the political arena, there will continue to be extensive attempts to legislate the quality of foods and drugs and to restrict the use of physically harmful substances.

In Sweden, a nation where rapid progress into a rationalized society has often lead to its being seen as a precursor to the U.S., food quality and labeling standards are extremely rigorous. For example, all perishable foods must bear a chemically treated sticker that changes color when its shelf life expires. Restaurant food is similarly controlled. For example, if food has been heated for a long time, its fibers and nutrients essentially vanish. Food that passes such time limits in Sweden must be thrown out.

CHOOSING NEW HABITATS

The 10 to 20 million increase in households during the decade of the eighties will place some severe burdens on the nation's housing markets, particularly in view of escalating costs for new residential construction. The average purchase price of a new housing unit has soared from $28,000 in 1971 to a little over $67,000 in January, 1981. Moreover, without some form of government subsidy, we will be producing not much more than 1.1 to 1.2 million single-family homes per year during the early 1980s, while the number of new households will increase an average of 1.5 million each year.

The shortage of moderately priced housing units is largely a function of increased costs of land and money. In 1947, labor and materials represented about 70 percent of the cost of a new home; today they make up only 45 percent. Land prices have risen with the spread of suburbia and the cost of money has escalated with inflation.

A Return to Center-City

One result of these high costs is growth along urban fringes is slowing, while there is a palpable return to the center-city and near center city by thousands of households in many urban areas throughout the nation. Singles and childless couples, particularly two-career couples, find center-city living extremely compatible with rationalized life styles. Of course, extensive public and private money has been spent during the past 15 years to enhance the quality of center-city living, but the actual adoption of urban life styles by increasing numbers of middle class households has occurred only with the emergence of rationalized living.

Center-city living dovetails with rationalized life styles in numerous ways. The location is particularly appealing, for it patently reduces transportation costs and dependence on the automobile. Since rationalized families are created late, often after one or both members have attained career maturity, city-dwelling rationalists count on being able to send their offspring to private schools if the public system is not acceptable. As children of suburbia, many also have the expectation that when the time comes they will be able to improve the quality of the city schools through political action. There are others who see city living as a transitional step before mature adulthood, when they may move to the suburbs.

Alternate Possibilities

City dwelling generally encourages bicycling, walking and public transit, all three fashionably rational modes of travel for the 1980s. Center-city space also offers greater variations in configuration to allow for alternative household arrangements. For example, large old houses, characteristic of near-center urban areas, offer opportunities for two or three couples or several individuals to pool their resources to acquire unique and attractive living space. Restoration of old center-city residences not only permits the owners to build equity in their appreciating property, but it also permits the residents

143

to engage in meaningful, tangible work that will be beneficial to both themselves and the community at large.

If they continue, inflation and dwindling housing starts may force even further housing consolidations. Intergenerational housing is on the increase, and attitudes toward the acceptability of sharing one's dwelling with one's parents or relatives, as reported by government surveys, show that more than 50 percent of the general public would find such an arrangement acceptable (Department of Commerce, 1977).

The pressure for an expanded, quality housing market is particularly great at this time, as the market for owned residences grew rapidly in the 1970s (from 61 to 67 percent of the market) with the growing perception of residential housing as a sound investment and hedge against inflation. The increased demand for purchasable housing also reflects greater average household prosperity, and an increased desire for the independence and personal control provided, in the public's mind, by home ownership.

CHANGING WORK STYLES

Another fundamental manifestation of rationalizing value systems is reflected in changing attitudes toward work. Opinion surveys today show that the majority of American workers want their work to be *meaningful.* This characteristic is repeatedly reported as the single most important job characteristic cited by workers in most developed nations, easily topping salary, job security and working conditions. Some social psychologists suggest such attitudes merely reflect the fact that most U.S. workers already have good salaries, sound working conditions and fair amounts of security, but that they *do not* have meaningful work.

Commitment to Self-fulfillment

Whatever the reasons, the desire for meaningful employment is significantly affecting the behavior of the labor force, particularly the lower age groups. Individual motivation for improved job performance, greater productivity and professional development is relatively low among today's younger workers. Turnover is high, as a general commitment to self-fulfillment consistently takes precedence over employer loyalty. This tendency was amplified in the late 1970s by the fact roughly 26 percent of the labor force was in the 16-to-24-year-old age group—double the proportion of 1950.

But this fact is already changing. In the 1980s, the proportion of young workers will diminish rapidly. And due to the reduced number in the youngest segments of the labor market, performance demands on the now-maturing workers of the World War II baby boom will increase. A large portion of the young people who entered the labor force during the 1970s did not follow expected career patterns. For example, while college enrollments from among upper and lower income portions of the population remained fairly stable—for differing reasons—enrollments from among the middle class tended to fall off. In opinion polls, these "drop-offs" expressed a belief that college did not appear necessary to get a good paying job (Fields, 1978). But as automation and foreign competition continue to reduce the labor market for semi-skilled literates in America, these people will have to look to other fields for advancement, and these fields will demand special skills and knowledge. The "retreading" of these workers will represent a major element in the 2 to 2.5 percent growth per annum in the demand for adult education in the 1980s.

Sequential Careers

The emergence of sequential careers has been noted with increasing frequency during the past decade, but many of the factors cited in the preceding pages will combine to make multi-stage, evolutionary careers the normative work style of postindustrial America. Automation, robotization and foreign competition will force millions of people to find new jobs during the 1980s. Mid-career compaction will lead millions of others to seek new fields or employers out of frustration. The enactment of five-year pension vesting and full pension portability will clearly encourage sequential careers. And, while hundreds of thousands of American women will continue to enter the commercial labor market after having completed an initial career in child-rearing, demographic projections indicate that an even larger number of women can be expected to leave their commercial careers—at least temporarily—to begin parenting.

Underlying all of these changes will be the basic, motivating social values of the 1980s and the pursuit of both economic security and personal self-fulfillment in a work place where meaningful roles will continue to demand increasing amounts and varieties of both experience and knowledge. In such an environment, the average 55-year U.S. adult life span, plus the substantial accumulated resources of our domestic sector, will provide the majority of Americans with the time and money to pursue life strategies designed to acquire the most personally appropriate mix of experience and education.

The heuristic, step-by-step life-long learning process is exactly

145

suited to the present period of rapid economic and technological transition, since it enables individuals to acquire a broad variety of skills and knowledges, thereby promoting the individual's capacity to adapt productively to an uncertain and changing career environment. In fact, throughout the 1980s, we can expect to see blue-collar work of all kinds to become increasingly "classless," as a stint of industrial and/or service work will become a normal career stage through which most young people of both sexes will pass. Thus, by the end of the decade, the blue-collar labor pool will largely be made up of the 16-to-30-year-old age cohort.

GROWTH IN ENTREPRENEURSHIP

As mentioned earlier, while America's salaried employees have been reporting increased levels of dissatisfaction with their work, the self-employed in our economy continue to report themselves to be happy. These assessments are all the more significant because social and economic indicators show that, on the average, the self-employed person works longer hours for less pay, has higher personal debt and less financial security than does the average salaried worker. This suggests that the self-employed are not only the happiest members of our work force, but that they are also the most productive. Because of this, we should take note that after nearly 50 years of declining self-employment, individual entrepreneurship is again on the rise in the U.S.

During the mid 1930s nearly 20 percent of the U.S. work force was self-employed. This proportion declined slowly through 1950, when the percentage of self-employed workers stood at 17 percent. During the next 25 years there was a sharp decline in self-employment, and in 1975 only 7.5 percent of U.S. workers were self-employed. In 1976, however, this trend reversed, and while the number of self-employed in the agricultural sector has remained unchanged, the number of self-employed in the non-agricultural sector has been growing better than twice the rate as the number of salaried workers since 1977.

The reversal of this long-term trend is the result of a combination of diverse factors. In the first place, with the rise of information work, a growing amount of gainful employment can be accomplished with no more overhead than an education or specialized experience. Thus, the amount of front-end capital needed for individual entrepreneurship is declining. In addition, relatively low-cost small computers, plus word processors and photocopiers can substantially amplify the productive capacity of an individual information entrepreneur.

146

Beyond this, declining job satisfaction on the part of salaried employees and high job satisfaction among the self-employed may also be contributing to the shift toward entrepreneurship. At the same time, government regulations and social pressures have stimulated requirements by most large institutions for expert knowledge that lies outside of the organizations' specialized areas of activity. The easiest, quickest and cheapest way to acquire such expert knowledge is to "buy it," in the form of contract consultants. As a consequence, consulting is one of the fastest growing components of the private sector. Gross receipts to individual and corporate consultants were estimated at $30 billion in 1978.

EDUCATION'S ESSENTIAL ROLE

The adoption of a life-long learning policy by the U.S. Department of Education is a clear manifestation of the acknowledgement of education's growing and changing role in our society. Education is already the single most commonplace adult discretionary time activity outside of the home. As a pursuit, education clearly appeals to the rational life style emphasis on self-fulfillment and meaningfulness and is seen by many as a means of achieving greater independence.

At the same time, as the public policy issues and decisions faced by the U.S. become increasingly complex, a well-educated electorate will be essential to the continued effectiveness of the democratic process. If the majority of the citizenry cannot comprehend the factors at stake in such policy issues as energy, genetic engineering, ecology, public health and the uses of technology, decisions on such matters increasingly will be determined by an educated elite. In such a case, the potential for bad decisions and for conflicts between the public and its political leaders would rise, with obvious serious risks for the well-being of our society and the world.

The Problem of Adult Competency

It is essential to recognize that there are members of our society who are ill-equipped to benefit from the coming of the information age—indeed, who are ill-equipped to survive day-to-day life today. For example, according to Barron and Kelso (1975), 15 to 25 percent of Americans over 18 are unable to do an effective job of managing their own lives because they cannot comprehend the intellectual tasks required of day-to-day living. Further, their studies suggest that perhaps an additional third of our population are only marginally competent in these skills.

These figures pose both a challenge and a threat for the nation. We can either address the problem of adult competency, with all of the power that infocom technology and the social and didactic sciences can bring to bear or we can choose to ignore the situation, and watch an ever-increasing proportion of our population lose the ability to manage their own lives. Unless we intervene, the "information poor" will increasingly join the "resource poor" in the backwaters of society, becoming more and more dependent upon the largesse of the state bureaucracy and alienated from a socioeconomic system they cannot comprehend.

Yet at the same time that the education industry is facing burgeoning responsibilities, it is being confronted with reduced public sector support, both at federal and local levels. How can these two apparently disparate vectors be wed?

From "Push" to "Pull" Functions

In the first place, education must shift economically from a "push" function to a "pull" function. Educational establishments must increasingly be geared to deliver custom-tailored products on demand, both to institutions—business, government, professional and trade associations, etc.—and to individuals. Education must come to regard itself more and more as competing for the consumer dollar in the market place, rather than as a timeless, sinecured component of our institutional infrastructure with functions that may be satisfied merely by furnishing a standardized product line.

The rationalization of life styles and values is not selective; education must be rationalized too. It must be accountable. It must be utilitarian. It must monitor feedback and revise its output to meet the needs of consumers. In such a context, constrained public sector funding will increasingly be augmented by consumer payments for education purchased in a competitive marketplace, a marketplace made lively by the demands of a rationalizing society and an information economy.

A Life-Span Learning System

Second, in order to accommodate increasingly individualized life-long learning and sequential careers, educational systems must integrate their products and their operations with all of the productive roles and learning experiences that the life-long student may be expected to pursue. An individual's record of educational achievement will have to be expanded to cover not only performance in the graded schools and institutions of higher learning, but also technical and on-the-job training, as well as actual performance and advancement in the work place. The acceptance of "practicum" as an essential for degree certification—as has long been practiced by such cooperative work-study institutions as Antioch College—will have to become a routine arrangement. The educational establishment should already be working with employers to develop universally-accepted work-performance rating standards to facilitate the integration of work and learning.

Employers, on the other hand, may be expected to capitalize on the growing popular demand for practical experience by designing particular career programs—both short and long term—to provide documented educational credits, thereby offering potential employees a highly competitive and motivational fringe benefit at relatively little cost. Ultimately, by acknowledging and stressing the educational/developmental nature of all work experience, the basic employer-employee relationship may be significantly changed. A more creative, collaborative work place could emerge, serving to enrich the jobs of millions of salaried employees and to reverse the long-term decline in job satisfaction in the U.S.

Electronic Education

Third, education must move as rapidly as possible to exploit the productive efficiency and powerful capacity of the infocom technologies. The predicted 30 million home computers to be sold by 1990 implies 30 million potential "school-households," capable of offering their members an almost limitless variety of packaged self-instruction programs. If 40 million homes are going to be linked to at least one cable telecommunications network within 10 years, then there will be a potential market of over 100 million citizens to be provided with interactive, televised classes, such as those now being offered over the QUBE network in Columbus, Ohio (Jordon, 1978).

Electronic courses could also be taught over computerized conferencing networks, such as the Electronic Information Exchange System (EIES), operated by the New Jersey Institute of Technology in Newark. Some of the elementary schools now being closed around the country could be turned into operations centers for such electronic education systems. Modularized, heuristically structured curricula are already being developed that can be employed by a broad range of students, each at his or her own individual pace. All of these technologies and many more must be utilized to enhance the effectiveness and productivity of American education.

And finally, the educational establishment is going to have to develop and promote a new image—a new perception of education's role in the overall scheme of things, both as an essential life-long service and as a vital public utility that stands ready to provide one or 100 million individuals with the proper course content to meet their needs for self-fulfillment and meaningful participation in the common national enterprise.

REFERENCES

Applebaum, Judith, Ed. "The Question of Size in the Book Industry Today." *Publishers Weekly,* July 31, 1978.

Barron, W. E., and Kelso, Charles R. *Adult Functional Competency,* Report submitted to the Adult Education Division, U.S. Office of Education, March, 1975.

Beer, Stafford. "Managing Modern Complexity," in *The Management of Information and Knowledge,* papers for the 11th Meetings of the Panel on Science and Technology, Committee on Science and Astronautics, U.S. House of Representatives. Washington, D.C.: GPO, 1970.

de Solla Price, Derek J. *Science Since Babylon.* New Haven, Conn.: Yale University Press, 1967.

Fields, Gregg. "Middle Class Youths Increasingly Choose Work and Not College." *Wall Street Journal,* July 20, 1978.

Jordon, Gerry D. "Education on QUBE—An Approach to Life-Long Learning." *Educational and Institutional Television,* May, 1978.

Linden, Fabian. "Services, Please!" *Across the Board,* August, 1978.

Porat, Marc Uri. *The Information Economy, Vol. 1.* The Institute for Communication Research. Stanford, Calif.: Stanford University, 1976.

U.S. Department of Commerce. *Social Indicators, 1976.* Washington, D.C.: Author, 1977 (Lib. Cong. No. 77-608307).

U.S. Department of Commerce, Bureau of the Census. *STATUS.* Washington, D.C.: Author, 1976 (Lib. Cong. No. 76-600037).

AN INVENTORY OF RESOURCES

Roy Amara

The usual futurist presentations fall into one of two categories: either the U.S. and the world are headed for a major crisis, or a series of crises, which can be avoided, if at all, only by mending our ways or sharply curtailing our lifestyles, or, we are on the threshold of a fantastic "gee whiz" world of high technology, affluence or abundance where worldwide per capita incomes of $20,000 to $30,000 (in 1978 dollars) are just around the corner if we only play our cards right.

I will attempt to paint what I hope is a somewhat more realistic picture in which, on the one hand, all is not lost and, on the other, we probably will not play all our cards right either. It will be the big picture, warts and all so to speak, reflecting my own personal interpretations but also reflecting a distillation of considerable information and perceptions of many individuals from both inside and outside the Institute for the Future (in Menlo Park, California).

My approach is to view prospects for the U.S. in the next decade and beyond by taking stock or inventory of our resources—human as well as natural, and including, if I can stretch the notion a bit—technological, economic and political resources as well. Primary emphasis will be placed on human resources and, in particular, those related to labor force characteristics.

NATURAL RESOURCES

The quadrupling of oil prices in the early 1970s was, in many ways, a blessing in disguise—some of you would say that if this is so, it was very effectively disguised. The basic reason: it has provided the stimulus and time to rethink our whole energy supply problem, which we would have had to do any way since the transition out of oil has to be made in the next 20 to 40 years.

The events of the early 1970s—and the steady rise in energy prices—have given and will continue to give a spur to develop new sources of energy, to use fossil fuels more efficiently through conservation and redesign and to make a smoother transition out of oil. During the decade of the 1980s, we will move toward diminishing dependence on oil and natural gas and increasing dependence on coal and uranium; other sources can play only a small role in that period.

No major long-term problems exist in the supply of nonfuel resources —in other words, minerals and the materials derived from them. This is so even though we import heavily—aluminum, tin, chromium, asbestos—a total of up to 23 minerals or materials, being dependent on others for more than half of our supply of these, even though third world countries are increasingly nationalizing their mining activities and even though rising costs of energy make the mining of leaner ores very expensive. In time, new sources of supply can be developed or alternative materials adapted that serve the same function. In addition, stockpiling and recycling are two other alternatives that can act as very successful deterrents to cut-offs or large price increases. Included in such deterring practices might be the opening up of federally owned land for extracting minerals from indigenous materials.

It is interesting to note that with fairly reasonable energy prices the long-term prospects for materials can be considered inexhaustible based on the following eight basic materials: iron, aluminum, magnesium, titanium, wood, glass, cement and plastic.

Generally, air quality from polluting sources is not becoming worse and, in some instances, is improving considerably, thus halting the long-term degradation that had been going on for decades.

Water supplies can be a major problem in certain western and southern states. But even here, if we learn to manage this valuable resource by conservation, sound pricing policies and limitations on the discharge of toxic substances (pesticides, dyestuffs, inorganic compounds), it should not be a long-term problem.

Agricultural land is clearly one of our most valuable assets. It is the best in the world in terms of size, geographic location and fertility. In the next decade and beyond, we are not likely to have any major climatic changes, and even the less likely scenarios (large warming or large cooling) would have almost negligible effect on the enormous food-producing capacity of the United States.

TECHNOLOGICAL RESOURCES

We must recognize that—properly used—technology is a friend and an ally and not an outcast to be shunned. To be sure, we have gone through what I call the end of a period of infatuation with technology, preparing now to settle down to a much more mature relationship. The ways we deal with technology may be among the most important choices we make.

An overselling of technology, a proper concern for health and safety, a rapidly changing regulatory environment and even a "loss of nerve" have put us on a curve of technological descendency. We are now in an excellent position to get on the long road to recovery.

We need to stimulate investment in research and development (R&D) to overcome higher risks, costs and uncertainties. Among the most important incentives would be tax credits for R&D, joint industry-university arrangements and, most of all, a stable, understandable regulatory environment.

There are many promising areas for new R&D opportunities. These include:

1. *energy*—solar (photovoltaic, thermal, biomass, space collection) coal in situ to gas, tar sands, shale, fission and fusion;
2. *materials*—mining of indigenous materials, recycling, substitutability, new uses for wood as renewable resource (e.g., into liquid fuel by hydrogenation);
3. *bioscience*—chemicals from living cells in fermentation-type reactors; antiviral and bacterial agents by genetic modification; methanes, alcohols and sugar from biomass by microbes; and proteins from food plants by nitrogen fixation; and
4. *information sciences*—terminal devices, memories, microprocessor/minicomputers; office (automation); and home (videotex) systems.

ECONOMIC RESOURCES

If technology is to be one of our best allies, then its closest twin is increased investment in U.S. industry. We need to raise the level from 10 percent of the Gross National Product closer to 12 to 14 percent by investing in new energy-generating and energy conservation systems; processes for recycling import-dependent materials; the transportation sector (renewal of our automobile, railroad and ship-building industries); soil-water management projects; modernization of industries threatened by foreign competition and, as previously noted, by investing in R&D, one of our last truly great frontiers.

The incentives required for this include tax credits for capital spending, lower corporate income taxes and elimination of double taxation of corporate dividends. As a result, we can, with an investment-led boom, grow at a real rate of 3 percent per year; inflation and unemployment can also be reduced to below 5 percent levels, with discretionary income growing at a grand total of 13 percent per year.

Internationally, we can lead from strength even though we will be faced with a much slower growth of world trade, incipient protectionism and a host of new competitors. To do this, we have got to lead from our most important strengths: agriculture, chemicals, computer/communication systems, aircraft, control systems, measuring instruments, optical/dental/medical equipment, oil field/construction machinery.

POLITICAL RESOURCES

The best news of all is that government expenditures at all levels as a fraction of GNP have decreased and will level off after 1981. If that is not something to cheer about, we can also expect less government regulation in energy, communication, transportation and financial sectors.

The political arena will become one of the most volatile and active because of the influence and independence of large numbers of eligible adult (not young) voters. The dominant theme, one we are already experiencing, is likely to be a new conservatism, accompanied by more participation and activism by citizens at all levels in first by-passing, then modifying and changing institutions.

Our biggest threats during this period will *not* be from foreign sources (although the threat of a nuclear exchange by accident, escalation or sabotage will certainly be there), *not* national economic planning, *nor* nationalization of industries (except for railroads). Rather, the largest threat is internal and would come from divisiveness and lack of consensus. This may be described as a failure to form and exercise national will and represents the darker side of the coin, the bright side of which reads individuality, pluralism, diversity. This is a point I will come back to later.

HUMAN RESOURCES

Birthrates are at their lowest levels ever—essentially at replacement levels after the largest baby boom in history—providing us with a time to "pause and refresh." By far the largest growth in the next decade or two will be in the working-age population 18-64, reflecting the passage of the end of the "bulge" into the labor force. The resulting dependency ratio (the number not in labor force divided by the number in the labor force) will be the smallest ever. And since at the same time we can let up on the allocation of resources for schools, playgrounds and roads, we have an enormous opportunity to invest for future growth and quality-of-life improvements.

The demand for housing will continue at a very high level, reflecting peak levels of household formation into the 1980s.

The South and the West will continue to enjoy a disproportionate share of national growth.

Some—not all—urban communities may start a turn-around by the end of the 1980s, partly because the suburbs will become somewhat less attractive and crime and unemployment rates are likely to decrease appreciably in the cities and elsewhere.

Although no dramatic changes are expected in longevity, we are likely to experience a tapering off of the large annual (8 to 10 percent per year) increases in medical care costs, as we shift our attention more effectively to preventive and self-help measures rather than almost total dependence on after-the-fact medicine.

Values and attitudes best describing the 1980s are those of individuality and independence of thought, acting to control decisions affecting our life; pluralism, with an affirmation of differences (ethnicity, lifestyles); fiscal conservatism, brought about by inflation and disenchantment with government generally; quality consciousness, made possible by increasing affluence and higher levels of education and conservation-mindedness, reflecting concerns about the environment, energy and natural resources.

THE LABOR FORCE

In the past decade, the U.S. economy has successfully expanded the number of jobs to meet the needs of an abundant labor supply—particularly of youth and female workers. Many of these people found work in clerical, service, sales and state and local government occupations. But as the baby-boom generation is absorbed into the labor market, comparatively low numbers of new entrants will follow. The overall composition of the labor force is changing, and the interests and skills of available workers may not match up with available jobs.

Size and Composition

From average annual increases in the civilian labor force of well above 2 percent per year in the late 1960s and throughout the 1970s, the average rate of increase will drop to under 1 percent beyond 1985. One major factor contributing to this change is the decline in birthrates since 1958. (In 1975 there were 66.7 births per 1,000 women as compared with 118.5 per 1,000 in 1955.) Between 1976 and 1990, the total number of labor force entrants in the 16-to-24-year old age group will fall by 14 percent. By 1990 there will be about a half million fewer labor force entrants from this age group annually.

155

A second contributing factor is the gradual slowdown in rates of female participation in the work force. In recent years, more and more women have taken jobs to maintain family living standards under inflationary pressure or to support themselves, and frequently children, independent of a male breadwinner. Although women's participation rates will continue to increase, they will rise more slowly than before and begin to level off at slightly over 50 percent. Since women in their early twenties traditionally have had the highest labor participation rates among women, the decreasing portion of young women in the labor force will significantly influence female participation rates. Also, some revival of traditional childrearing is likely.

Considering the relative reduction of young entrants and female entrants of all ages, on the average there will be three-quarters of a million fewer persons added to the labor force each year during the 1980s. Viewed another way, employment growth will be half of what it has been in the previous two decades.

These demographic trends will push unemployment down to the low levels of the 1960s and will act as a brake on the economy after 1985. Beyond 1985 unemployment rates in the U.S. are likely to remain at about 5 percent.

Perhaps the most important trend in the composition of the labor force is the large increase expected between now and 1985 in the proportion of minorities comprising new labor force entrants. Minorities currently account for about 17 percent of such entrants. Because of higher immigration rates, the increasing number of illegal alien workers entering the labor force, and the generally higher birth rates of minorities, it is estimated that by 1985 minorities will account for well over 25 percent of new labor force entrants.

Wage Rates

The tightening of the labor market will cause not.only a general escalation of wages, but a shift in the wage structure. With fewer new entrants available, many of the lower-skill positions—clerks handling banking/credit card forms, typists, health aides, mail-handlers, textile workers, stenographers, assemblers, drivers and laborers—will be harder to fill with people who have good basic skills and experience. Labor-saving technological innovations will become increasingly attractive to business as wage rates of lower-skill positions escalate.

While virtually all occupational categories will experience real wage gains, some occupations will do better than others. In comparison to the average worker, professional and technical workers will gain about 10 percent in wages, and clerical, sales, and service workers will improve their wages by about 5 percent. Wage rates of blue-collar workers will remain stable, and managerial and administrative wages will fall by 10 percent relative to the average. It is expected that fringe benefits now enjoyed by most professional, technical, managerial and unionized workers will be more widely extended to other occupational categories.

While new entrants will be much scarcer in the 1980s, there will be a relative abundance of older, more experienced workers vying for middle-level positions in business organizations. As the first of the baby-boom group reaches middle age around 1990, competition for middle-level, nontechnical positions will rise dramatically. For example, in the 1960s approximately 10 workers vied for each middle-management supervisory position. By the end of the 1980s, this ratio will increase to about 20 to one. Many workers in this middle age group will be forced to accept jobs with status and pay scales below their expectations. Discontent among these older, experienced workers is likely to increase as they observe rising wages for lower-skill workers.

Generally escalating wages will add to inflationary pressures on the economy. Signs of this inflationary impact can already be seen in the consensus of economists concerning the inflationary "trigger point" of the unemployment rate. During the 1960s, government spokespersons set the frictional unemployment rate (workers moving from one job to another) at 4 percent. Most economists outside government agree the inflationary trigger point now is between 5 and 6 percent. As the labor market tightens through the 1980s, the risks of wage-induced inflation will be even higher than they are now.

Impact of Technology

Technological change will be both a cause of and a response to trends in the labor force. Rapid changes in technology will continue to escalate the demand for skilled workers in certain professional and technological occupations — design, marketing and services centered in advanced technology industries, including data/word processing, communications, pharmaceuticals, instruments and transportation equipment.

In the computer software field, the proliferation of small computers will cause a great expansion in the demand for software packages that are usable by general office personnel without extensive retraining. The need to write simple, widely usable software packages will exacerbate the shortage of skilled programmers. Currently, computer companies are hiring as many hardware and software "superstars" as they can find to design systems that are simple to use. This should help ease the need for highly skilled programmers at the user level and promote general societal acceptance of computer-based innovations.

In electronic assembly, technological innovation will not affect employment levels as much as it will radically change the functions of jobs. Incorporating all digital electronic functions on a single programmable microprocessor chip will greatly reduce the need for workers to interconnect and test circuitry, while increasing the demand for workers in final product assembly.

Another aspect of technological change concerns its effect on the shortage of entry-level workers. As wage rates escalate, the incentive for technological substitution will increase. Labor-saving innovations could eliminate many of the positions created by the information and paper-processing explosion of the past two decades. The substitution of capital equipment for labor is likely to have the greatest impact on employees in commerce, banking, public administration and office work.

In the office, for example, innovations could greatly increase the productivity of the support staff and eliminate some positions. Word processing machines that allow all corrections to be made in the machine without additional retyping and that store documents electronically speed up production and often yield a better quality product. Electronic filing systems cut down on storage costs, as well as personnel.

In the service sector, demand will continue to rise as increases in discretionary income allow for more travel, meals away from home, entertainment, health care and personal service expenditures. For example, the number of workers in the allied health sciences has greatly increased with growing demands for improved health care. Although this trend will continue, the escalation of labor costs will bring about the widespread use of devices such as electronic diagnostic machines operated by a lower-paid technician (or the patient himself) rather than by a physician. Electronic devices will be more commonly used in educational services, but this trend will be gradual, and it is doubtful that any substantive displacement of education personnel before 1990 will be due to technological advances.

Education and Job Skills

Surveys show that students in high school and college today are becoming more pragmatic about career goals. They are paying more attention to stories of unemployed teachers and liberal arts Ph.D.s (a recent study for the Mellon Foundation predicts a national surplus of 60,000 humanities Ph.D.s by 1990 if current trends persist). Clearly, *more* education is no guarantee of a job. Yet it is hard to know what skills will be needed within the next decade—especially since many future jobs do not yet exist.

It is paradoxical that with educational levels currently the highest in U.S. history, many employers are finding it increasingly difficult to hire workers with appropriate skills. Part of the problem stems from a general decline over the past decade in the level of basic skills, as measured by standardized tests. The entry-level worker often has inadequate reading, writing and mathematical skills. Yet even individuals who have a firm knowledge of the basics may be hard pressed to keep up with the rapid pace of change. From the perspective of the labor force, what is needed is a better meshing of educational focus and industrial needs.

Elementary and secondary schools are already responding to pressures for a return to basics. There is a widespread movement afoot at the state level to set minimum standards of achievement and adopt competency tests that go beyond writing and mathematical skills. Such tests measure life or survival skills; for example, they test students' competence as consumers and job seekers.

The increasing disparity between job demands and educational backgrounds, combined with the continuing high demand for technical skills, will accentuate current trends toward learning more marketable professional, business, analytic, technical and engineering skills in college. Two and four-year colleges are likely to shift gradually toward curricula to accommodate tomorrow's more pragmatic student, who will be concerned about his or her place in the tight labor market.

A growing number of adults are returning to school on a part or full-time basis to update their skills or train for a new career. These mature learners often have work and family responsibilities that make attendance at traditional classes difficult, if not impossible. Postsecondary education programs that use electronic media and external degree programs that serve geographically separated learners are providing alternatives to meet students' changing needs.

Corporate training programs will undoubtedly experience a substantial upswing. In the face of the increasing skills shortage, business will concentrate on upgrading the skills of the employees it has. Expanding the capabilities of workers already familiar with company practices may be more advantageous for the corporation that searching for such skills in the increasingly expensive labor market and will provide employees with opportunities for advancement and greater job satisfaction.

Currently, about four-fifths of industry training funds are spent on in-house training facilities. Because of the increasing complexity and rapid changes of many skilled positions in offices and factories, businesses will find it difficult to provide adequate in-house skills training.

Larger corporations will likely respond to these training needs by establishing central training facilities that serve multiple company locations or by expanding the size and the curricula of the facilities they already have. They will also make increasing use of local public and private educational facilities. In the past two decades, the percentage of major companies that provide tuition assistance to employees attending outside educational institutions has risen from 53 to 90 percent. Not only have more companies provided assistance, but the number of workers and size of tuition-aid program budgets have risen. While on average the percentage of the eligible work force using tuition-aid currently is less than 5 percent, such programs could be expanded in the future to meet corporate needs by changing program provisions and incentives.

SUMMARY

How would I sum up our prospects? Generally, I remain a cautious optimist.

We still have a lot going for us, much more than perhaps any other country: natural resources second to none; unquestioned leadership in some sectors of high technology that are key to long-term productivity gains; an economic system that is still the envy of many, with political stability unobtainable anywhere else. And all of this backed up by one of the largest, best-educated, most stable and productive labor forces anywhere. Where then is the problem?

The problem is "keeping it all together." Our biggest threat stems from *divisiveness*—the inability to reach any kind of consensus on major issues facing us. Joseph Kraft has called it "the crumbling of consent" while to others it suggests the "balkanization of America." What we need above all is to learn how to participate in decisions affecting us without "hanging up" the whole process.

What can vocational educators do? A great deal. They can help by preparing individuals to contribute to society through their work—at peak levels of individual capabilities—while at the same time providing each individual the breadth of understanding and knowledge that will make him or her a responsible U.S. and world citizen. A large order indeed. But few activities are more central to an individual's life and outlook. I believe the authors of that old standby *Work in America* said it very well:

> [We are dealing with the] functions of work: its centrality in the lives of most adults, its contribution to identity and self-esteem, and its utility in bringing order and meaning to life. Work offers economic self-sufficiency, status, family stability, and an opportunity to interact with others in one of the most basic activities of society. Consequently, if the opportunity to work is absent or if the nature of work is dissatisfying (or worse), severe repercussions are likely to be experienced in other parts of the social system.

There is no greater challenge.

LIVING WITH SCARCITY

Warren Johnson

There is a lot of gloom and doom about the economy these days. Each time the price of foreign oil rises, more billions of American dollars leave the country, the economy shudders a bit, the price of everything else heads upward and more workers lose their jobs. Even the government and the captains of industry have very few good things to say. The question in many minds is "How will we get by?"

COPING WITH THE CRUNCH

We'll get by. We'll have to, there's no other choice. The halcyon days are over—the days of resource abundance, cheap gasoline, cheap food and rising productivity. We are now past the high point of abundance and are peering down the other side for the first time.

But getting by with less is not the worst of the problem. Whoever produces the things people cut back on will find their jobs disappearing. Doing with less is one thing; losing a job is quite another, especially if the lost jobs are part of a long-term trend rather than the cyclical ups and downs we have known in the past. We already know about the first of it—layoffs in the auto industry, the airlines and a drop-off in tourism. But with each drop in energy supplies more steam will go out of the economy. And our confidence is not helped by the fact that unemployment funds in many states are already exhausted.

The Opportunity

But behind each problem is an opportunity; they are the two sides of the same coin. We are seeing the new opportunities already. The high price of heating oil has created a boom in wood stoves and firewood and the insulation industry is strong. The high cost of gasoline and small cars has made it worthwhile to recycle fuel-efficient cars out of junk yards. The high price of new housing has made it possible to fix up old houses and sell them for good prices. Hand-made houses using indigenous materials are being built in many areas. And more opportunities will appear as energy prices continue upward.

163

The first thing is to understand why scarcity will drive prices up and our purchasing power down and then to try to figure out ways to take advantage of this tangled situation. What follows are some ways to think about the crunch, though individuals will have to figure out their own ways of approaching it.

The Shrinking Coin

New opportunities will appear, but they are not likely to be as lucrative as the jobs that will be lost. A few will be and there will be new millionaires, but on the whole, the size of the coin of the economy will slowly but steadily decrease in the coming years.

Why? Basically because we have consumed many of the high quality resources this land provided us. For many years we have been cranking them through the machinery of the affluent society as fast as we could. The best resources went first, such as the oil in the fields of Texas and Louisiana, and now we have to go to Alaska and to off-shore sites. All of that expensive new hardware would not have been necessary if we could just keep the old pumps going in their convenient locations, using the same pipelines and the same refineries. The best hydroelectric dam sites were occupied years ago and to build dams on the remaining sites would mean flooding farmland or other valuable resources. The old-growth timber is gone in most places, the trees that were frequently 10 feet in diameter and all clear heartwood. Now we're using primarily second-growth timber, where a two-foot tree is considered a good one. Most copper ores being mined now contain less than one percent copper, and new agricultural lands are a far cry from the deep, black soils the first settlers worked in Illinois and Iowa.

But in today's world, energy is the critical resource. With abundant energy we could do practically anything. Big machines could mine and process ores with only one pound of copper in a ton of rock. We could produce man-made substitutes for wood such as plastics. We could make desert soils bloom by transporting water to them and make poor soils productive by applying fertilizers. Without low-cost energy, very little of this can be done. So far, oil drilling off the East coast has turned up no commercially feasible oil or gas. Nuclear energy is turning out to be more dangerous than expected and uranium is scarce and already expensive. Coal is available and we are beginning to appreciate it more all the time, but is mean stuff to mine, handle and burn, and turning it into synthetic oil and gas is also expensive.

In the meantime, petroleum prices rise regularly. Each dollar of increase in the price of a barrel of imported oil aggregates to a total of three billion dollars. These are dollars leaving the country, coming out of the pocketbooks of American consumers, dollars that once had other uses. If this keeps up, the United States could be progressively impoverished by the dollars lost in sustaining its energy habit. The country has become an energy junkie, willing to do almost anything to keep shooting energy into the economic system to keep it on its "high."

In practical terms, high energy prices result in higher prices for everything. Only increased productivity could salvage some of the purchasing power being lost, but productivity is also stagnating.

For some time now we have tried to deny this. It was so much easier to blame the government or the oil companies than it was to face the implications of scarcity for our way of life. Trying to keep the price of oil and gas down, it turns out, was the big mistake. Artificially low prices for energy kept the wrong jobs booming and made it impossible for the right jobs—the ones that produce energy or save it—from getting started. Solar energy limped along even with substantial tax advantages because fossil fuels were too cheap a competition for solar. At the same time, Americans kept on buying big cars for the same reason—gasoline was cheap—and Detroit was happy enough to keep on producing them since building big cars is what they did well. Detroit lost money on small cars because most people looking for small cars would buy foreign autos anyway, the products of countries where the price of gasoline was often three or four times as high as it was here. Then all of a sudden the dam broke, gasoline prices skyrocketed, and the car makers began losing billions of dollars as they frantically tried to do what they should have done years ago—make fuel efficient cars.

The "Detroit Syndrome"

Surprisingly, the same problem that Detroit faces is the one that will make the task of coping with the crunch difficult; it is hard to know when the crunch will hit. Like Detroit, it is so tempting to hang onto a current job, and to hope something will come along to remove the dark clouds hanging over the job. But it is just as likely that these dark clouds could open up and pour out, washing everything away. It is hard to give up a job before this happens, but afterwards may be too late.

It would be nice to make the right change before the deluge comes, and get in on the ground floor of the emerging opportunities, but as with the solar industry, it can be risky to get there prematurely and starve for years. Timing is all important, but it is also the hardest thing to predict. With hindsight, it is easy to say that we should have done what the Europeans and Japanese have done and placed high taxes on energy to encourage the evolution of an energy-efficient way of life. But that was not politically popular and the country did just the opposite: kept energy prices down and sustained an energy-inefficient way of life. We are now in a corner, so much so that we are having a hard time competing with European nations and Japan, countries with far fewer natural resources.

It is important to realize how dangerous the "Detroit Syndrome" is, of holding onto a job in a declining industry. Detroit provides the best example, but it is not the only one.

A decline in auto sales will mean a decline in the steel industry, in rubber, glass, plastic and all the products that go into the making of cars. The entire industrial establishment around Detroit will be hit, so it will not be possible for laid-off workers to shift to other industries. Wages are likely to fall, too, as unemployed workers compete for what work is available. The unions will have very little clout. It will be hard to sell a house because who would be looking for a house with the job situation so bleak? And why buy a house in a declining market? Potential buyers would be inclined to rent and to wait for a bargain, like a distress sale of an unemployed auto worker who can no longer make regular payments. In other words, after the crunch hits, it is hard to get out without major losses.

What is the other side of the coin of a sinking auto industry, the brighter side? The way to look for the emerging opportunities is to first ask the question, "For what purposes have people been using their cars?" The second part is to find ways to provide those same services without requiring the use of an automobile. For example, people use cars to go shopping. While a neighborhood store might have to charge higher prices than a big chain in the shopping center, savings from not having to drive would offset the higher price. Similarly, how about providing nearby recreation opportunities as it becomes more expensive to drive to Miami Beach, the Rockies or Disneyland? How about organizing bus tours to resort areas? Hotels are happy to give huge group discounts with so many of their rooms empty. And neighborhood entertainment and theaters will have a better chance competing with the flashy places along the freeway that are big enough to advertise heavily and bring in the big attractions, but where the prices are high and the line are long.

As people come out of suburbia to be closer to their jobs and shopping places, there could well be an urban renaissance in response to the energy crunch, bringing life back to the sidewalks, the corner coffee shops and the parks. The key to good life in the cities is the people one is acquainted with on the sidewalks. People out walking not only make cities sociable and keep the shops open, but they also discourage the criminal who thrives on the lone individual on a dark, empty sidewalk. Perhaps that is one profession that will decline along with the auto industry.

The Fear: Inflation and Bust

How soon these opportunities materialize depends on whether or not we can cut imports and reduce energy consumption. We could well do what we have been doing for several years, continuing down the inflation path as far as we can, pushing up wages with the cost of living and ignoring the fact that energy is taking more of our economic resources while productivity is stagnating. We may well be able to maintain a make-believe world of abundance for some time, starving out those who are "on the ground floor" and then watch the whole thing fall apart in a real depression. Then all the money needed to make the change would have been washed away by a sea of red ink; the Chrysler solution is not possible on a national scale. The future is going to be tough enough as it is—learning how to live with less—but there is no point in making it any worse than it has to be by going through the last of the "easy" energy as if scarcity did not exist.

The Energy Industry

Because energy is the limiting factor in the economy, it will be a strong industry whatever way the economy goes. Other than oil and gas, the domestic energy industry has almost been stalled in its tracks; even imported oil has been cheaper than many of our domestic alternatives. But with each increase in imported oil prices and the gradual removal of price controls on domestic oil and gas, the domestic energy industry will begin to take off.

Surprisingly, it has been firewood that first became competitive with fossil fuels, and in only a few years it has come to surpass the energy produced by nuclear sources. In the many parts of this country having an abundance of wood, people are making their living cutting firewood, enjoying an independent livelihood out in the fresh air, working with their hands. A big advantage of firewood is the short start-up time and minimal expense—whatever it takes to buy a chain saw and a truck—compared to 10 to 15 years for a nuclear power

167

plant and a billion dollars. And the potential has hardly been touched. There are huge acreages with what the lumber industry calls "trash" trees growing on them, hardwood trees that compete with the more valuable softwoods being grown for lumber. The foresters are happy to have these hardwoods removed, often without charge. Hardwoods have roughly half the energy content of coal, so they can be transported a fair distance profitably.

The burning of coal is already following firewood. Coal-burning stoves and furnaces are available, and though handling coal has none of the pleasures of wood, it burns longer than wood and is much cheaper than oil; use of coal is a way to cut heating bills almost anywhere in this country. Coal merchants may well be the next millionaires we hear about.

The authentic boom towns today are in the coal-mining areas, mainly those in the upper Great Plains states. Rock Springs, Wyoming seems to be the classic one, with problems of crime and corruption, with poor housing and services, but offering the chance to make some money fast. For a young person it might be an experience for a year or two, working in the huge strip mines of the wild west to earn a stake to get started somewhere else. It is one way to get off the ground, although not without some risk.

If in fact this country is able to reduce its oil imports without knocking the economy too far off keel, it will be through the development of the huge coal resources. We have used only one-twentieth of our coal, while the comparable figures for oil and gas are now well over half; oil is a declining industry. There will be huge industrial developments to mine coal, transport it, process it into oil and gas, to burn it directly and to clean up the mess it makes all along the line. There will be many well-paying jobs, primarily in science and engineering, but also in construction, picking up some of the slack in the construction industry elsewhere in the country.

There is also likely to be a great deal of effort to develop renewable energy resources, but they may not turn out to be the growth industries some predict. Solar's best prospects are in the passive form, the careful placement of windows, the provision of heat storage walls and other design features that are a part of the building process. The active systems, the ones that go on rooftops with circulating pumps, storage tanks and controls, are still quite expensive. The large-scale schemes to provide electricity for cities and industries are clearly uneconomical now and promise to remain so for the foreseeable future. Making alcohol from grains is seen by many as a gimmick promoted by farmers to increase demand for the food they produce;

there is very little net energy produced after one subtracts the energy used to raise the crops and convert them to alcohol.

Nuclear energy appears to be the big loser. Jobs are more likely to dry up rather than to be created. With a huge federal bureaucracy and several of America's biggest corporations involved, nuclear energy was oversold; we were told it would be "too cheap to meter." Now it looks as if we cannot afford it, at least not safely.

There are many other possibilities—energy is everywhere, as the optimists keep telling us. The person who finds a way to get a hold of it at a price competitive with coal will not only become a millionaire, but probably a billionaire. But a lot of sharp people have been working on it for years, and one of the surprising things of recent decades is that none of their ideas have panned out. We are back with coal as the best alternative to keep the industrial machine going.

Conservation with a Kick

The way things stand now, a forced reduction in consumption during the 1980s is likely; the energy simply will not be there to do otherwise. A good part of the savings can be achieved through a reduction in waste, which is the most efficient way to save energy. It should be kept in mind, however, that cutting out wasteful products will also cut out products made by people—throwaway bottles and cans, recreational vehicles, air conditioners, electric toothbrushes, etc.—and in that process some people will lose jobs. We are back then to the basic problem: unemployment. What, then, are the industries to avoid and where will the opportunities lie?

Transportation uses 40 percent of the energy consumed in this country, 25 percent in fuel tanks and the rest in the provision and maintenance of the transportation systems. That figure almost has to fall, and it will take with it more than just the private car; all transportation will suffer. But in one case at least—the movement of goods and materials—a huge opportunity will be created. Small local and regional producers will be able to avoid many shipping costs that are already beginning to be a significant cost item to the national firms.

The big manufacturers became so dominant because they held all the right economic cards in the era of cheap energy. Their automated plants used little labor but considerable energy and resources to turn out a mountain of goods very cheaply. Coupled with cheap transportation, they could undersell smaller producers everywhere. Yet that scheme is going to go sour in the future as the cost of labor becomes a relatively better value than energy and raw materials. The large corporations are going to find it harder and harder to sell all the goods they can produce.

A Renaissance for Small Manufacturers?

If all goes as this author hopes, and this may involve some wishful thinking here, small producers will thrive and encourage others. Consider the advantages. By avoiding transportation costs, other costs are also avoided—overhead, middlemen and distribution, costs the large corporations cannot avoid. To the degree old plants and equipment can be used, start-up costs will be reduced. Being small also enables a quick response to a changing economic scene. Sears and U.S. Steel did not produce the woodstoves that have sold by the millions; they came out of small foundries all across the country. Nor do small outfits attract the attention of unions, government inspectors or consumer groups as much as large ones do.

The best opportunities to win at this game are with bulky or heavy items that are expensive to transport. Building materials provide a good example. We already see adobe, rammed earth, stone and poles used in house construction, and small mobile lumber mills are available that can be moved onto a piece of property to mill the lumber needed for a house from the trees on the property. Using materials available on or near a site means that many material costs can be reduced in addition to transportation costs. This takes more labor, but those are the rules of the new game we are playing; it is the way to avoid paying eighty to a hundred thousand dollars to have a house built, plus ending up with a custom-built house as well.

One small industry that is certain to grow is the repair business. The throwaway society was inevitable with manufactured goods being so cheap relative to the price of labor. As this reverses, people will take care of what they have, and repairing something will be the economical thing to do.

The general handyman is almost certain to be one of the winners in the future, the person who can fix anything, who can get a machine going and keep it going, and who can improvise and make do with what he has. He will be the valuable person, an authentic craftsman in an era that is certain to honor craftsmanship more highly than today.

Hand-made goods are likely to continue to expand as they have for some years now. While they take more time to make than machine-made goods, they are, in general, of better quality and they give more pleasure, both to the maker for the skill and creativity involved, and to the purchaser because they can be made to the buyer's specifications and because they have a human touch. In cold economic terms, the only advantage of this admittedly inefficient form of production is the enjoyment and independence it provides, for which the craftsmen have been willing to forego a higher income. But the prospects of human labor will improve as machine labor grows more expensive.

One general principle holds: to be highly specialized will be a dangerous thing in the future. Today it is the way to go but already, for example, the highly specialized craft unions are feeling the squeeze and are less willing to shut down a steel mill, an auto plant or the trucking system as they were a few years ago. If people are specialized and the need for their particular skill dries up, they could find themselves competing with unskilled laborers for other kinds of work. Our economy doesn't hesitate to jetson workers as it has no need for them, as happened to millions of small farmers and businessmen in the past. The key is to diversify if possible.

The Urban-Rural Shift

A major opportunity in the future should be associated with the population shift toward rural areas that has already begun. In the past, when the population movement was in the other direction, businesses in small towns slowly dried up while the enterprising individuals who moved to the city at the right time did well. Now just the opposite is beginning to happen. Small towns and rural areas have been growing faster than metropolitan areas since the 1975 mid-decade census, and this is creating a whole range of opportunities to serve this growing population, from building to retailing to government services. And most of the opportunities are ones that are virtually impossible for big business to take advantage of; rural populations are too thin to be served other than by small operations, usually individuals.

This decentralization trend must be considered a desirable one since surveys regularly indicate that most people do not care for big cities, just as they do not care for big corporations and big government. But each person that leaves the city makes it a little bit easier for those who do enjoy the cities and wish to stay there.

Why are people heading for small towns and rural areas? There are many reasons, but one is cost; they are cheaper than big cities. Cities take more energy for their metabolism than rural areas. It takes energy to ship in food, water and materials, to move people around within the cities and to process its wastes. All this is reflected in high costs for food, shelter and transportation. And the declining economic prospects of the large cities adds to the economic squeeze. In smaller towns or rural areas, by contrast, people are closer to the renewable resources of land, water, woods and sunlight, and therefore food, fuel and water are easier to obtain. Wastes are easier disposed of and indigenous building materials are available. Many of the jobs appearing in small towns and rural areas will not pay much, but with lower living costs this will not be such a disadvantage. And since it is the renewable resources that have the best long-term prospects, rural areas have the advantage of being close to them and therefore less dependent on the workings of a complex, vulnerable and increasingly expensive industrial system to obtain the basic necessities of life.

Geography

What parts of the country have the best prospects, assuming that no fast easy solution to the energy problem appears? Just look at which parts of the country have the best renewable resources plus coal, the one non-renewable resource that is likely to be important for a long time yet. On this basis, it seems fairly clear that the midwest has excellent prospects. It has plentiful coal, excellent soils and plenty of summer rains so irrigation isn't necessary. It has rivers and lakes for waterborne transportation, the most energy-efficient kind and relatively dense rail networks. Many of its cities are older, with relatively high densities and more of an urban character than the sprawling cities of newer areas that were built largely for the private car.

The Pacific northwest is probably second, with its mild climate, diverse soils and timber, plus abundant hydroelectric power. The south has a number of advantages, but heavy rainfall and poor agricultural practices in the past have depleted the soils in many places. The northern tier of states in the eastern half of the country have vast amounts of woods and much good soil, but the winters are hard. Since many people today are heading for the sun belt, this north country is where the best buys in land can be had. Because of this, the back-to-the-land movement is strongest there; if a person is interested in that, it is nice to have others of the same disposition for neighbors.

The best coal deposits are in some of the most God-forsaken parts of the west, and a major unanswered question is whether industries will go there or whether the coal will be shipped to existing industrial areas elsewhere; the latter seems more likely.

The southwest has perhaps the worst overall prospects. Almost everything is transported in except sunshine, which is not too useful by itself.

Farming

The abundant land and good soils of this country are, when you get right down to it, far more valuable than all of OPEC's oil, which will be gone a few decades after our oil is gone. As an industry, however, agriculture may start to weaken when Europe and Japan decide they can get by with less meat and dairy products easier than they can get by with less oil and correspondingly reduce their imports of American feed grains. California and Florida farmers are already faced with higher prices to process their fruits and vegetables and to transport them to distant markets. The only prospect for farming that looks at all decent is truck farming, using the organic wastes cities produce in abundance for fertilizer and producing fruits and vegetables that can be sold locally without processing. Such agriculture would be analogous to local manufacturing for local consumption.

Inflation or Deflation?

Periods of rapid inflation do not go on forever. At some point the bubble bursts; the faster the run-up in prices, the bigger the bang. In the 1920s it was the stock market. Today it seems like it is almost everything else: gold, real estate, art, coins, stamps, farms, old cars, on and on.

Still, it is hard to say just what will derail the inflationary trend that is so strong today. My guess is it will stem from the staggering private and public debt we have all been running up for years. It is fairly easy to imagine inflated house prices breaking in a number of urban areas, speculators frantically trying to unload their properties all at once and billions of dollars of paper profits vanishing. I can imagine a number of weak industries going bankrupt when sales fall off. Many farmers are only in business today because the increasing value of their land has enabled them to borrow against it; if this value slipped they would be out of business. And if even a part of these things happened, it would put tremendous pressure on the federal government, increasing welfare costs at the same time that tax revenues were down. Even serving the national debt could become a difficult trick. The federal government is almost certain to favor inflation, just like any other debtor, because inflation reduces the burden of the national debt and keeps the government in business.

For the individual, however, trying to decide whether it will be continued inflation or a bust in the coming years, a hard dilemma is created. The standard advice is to get your money out of the bank and invest it as fast as possible to capitalize on inflation. This has certainly been the way to make money in the past, but given all the deflationary forces now, of higher energy prices, the huge public and private debt and unemployment, it is getting to be an increasingly dangerous strategy. Prices could fall, and fall quite a ways, even for the safest hedges against inflation such as real estate. If one knew that was going to happen, of course, the thing to do would be to cash out now and purchase outright whatever would be the best thing to own in an energy short future, or to hold onto your money and buy at depressed prices after the fall. But if you did this and inflation continued, you would be doing all the wrong things. The best advice is to do both, to be covered whichever way it goes, inflation or recession, but that requires quite a bit of capital.

That is one advantage of not having money; the poor do not have to lay awake nights worrying about whether they have done the right things to safeguard their hard-earned assets. A survey in California showed that renters were much more optimistic about the future than homeowners, a rather surprising finding when you consider how renters have taken a beating compared to buyers in recent years.

Renting or Buying Today?

With house prices as high as they are now, however, buying is becoming riskier. One of the saddest things to imagine is a young couple working for years to get together the monsterous downpayments needed today—often as much as an entire house cost 10 years ago—and both having to keep on working to make the high payments associated with today's high interest rates, and then in the end see it all disappear in a bust. Renting is cheaper in many parts of the country today and it is only the expected appreciation that causes people to go the more expensive route of buying, an expectation that is becoming less justified. If a person bought a house 10 years ago and has a substantial equity built up, then it is a different story. Even if prices fell back he or she would still be well ahead.

It is possible that real estate prices might continue upward for some time; the markets do some pretty irrational things at times, such as the run-up in the price of gold in 1979. Yet to work hard to buy a house today is to give up a lot of one's life to buy an over-priced commodity and a risky one at that. It doesn't seem to be worth it. Spend money instead for something that is a better value, perhaps land to build a house on or use extra money for starting some kind of part-time business that might grow into a full-time one.

The Pleasures to Enjoy

The important thing in these unstable times is for people to keep their eyes and ears open and to think about what they are doing; the world is changing and to live in the past is likely to be a big mistake. Yet at the same time, there is no point in planning too seriously for a future we cannot know very well. The only thing we know for sure about the future is that life will be poorer materially than it is now; that seems absolutely inevitable given the energy situation. With all the unknowns, however, we might as well enjoy the authentic pleasures that life provides, most of which are not expensive. It is the status symbols that cost so much, the newest styles (that often look foolish anyway), the fast cars (that go twice the speed limit), the recreational vehicles (that make a vacation pretty much like everyday life), the second homes (as if trying to take care of one wasn't enough) or the slick vacation (complete with hassles at the airport and surly hotel people). Compare these strenuous, expensive activities with an evening with good friends, a night out dancing, a delicious meal, possibly one prepared at home, a winter evening with a good book, a walk through the park, being in good physical condition or the luxury of a Sunday afternoon nap.

The affluent society is very competitive and can take a lot out of a person, not only to earn a high income but to spend it as well. There is much to be said for living simply, for giving up the quest to make it to the top and for enjoying the simple pleasures that are available if we open our eyes to them, to do what we want to do, rather than what the advertisers tell us we should do. Such a strategy is certain to make life with scarcity much more comfortable.

One of the most stressful things to do is to live beyond our means, to have to worry about paying bills and making ends meet. That way can only get harder as prices go up faster than incomes. One key advantage of living simply is that we might end up by saving some money, money that could enable us to make changes if we want, such as getting away from dead-end jobs or places where we live but do not enjoy, and getting started in something else more to our liking or better suited to an energy-short future. Money is freedom in our society and if we are up to our necks in debt we are pretty well trapped where we are.

To cope with the crunch should not require grand plans or hair-raising risks. More than anything else, it means that we moderate our material needs, that we keep our minds open to what is happening and that we be willing to change and to adapt as necessary. There are opportunities; things are starting to happen and the exploding energy prices of the last few years could well turn out to be a watershed point.

It is certain to be a challenging time. If we are creative and adept, we could well build a way of life much better than the present times when so little satisfaction seems to come from all our affluence. Although sparcer materially, the future may well be richer personally and culturally. Whatever it is, it will be what we make of it.

SECTION V

THE CLIENT SYSTEM

The array of client groups served in programs of vocational education during recent years can be traced to two major developments, both of which emphasized the importance of client groupings. One was the growth of an employment or placement orientation for vocational education, particularly within the rather immediate and proximate employment market. The other was the growth of the civil rights movement from a crusade for social and political rights in the South to a quest for educational and economic equality on a nationwide scale.

Within the context of these developments, two categories of group characteristics began to appear. One possesses characteristics which are involuntarily acquired such as race, age, sex, ethnic background. The other possesses characteristics acquired to some degree by choice or by preferred circumstance and are identifiable in such groups as immigrants, migrants, drop-outs, offenders and those who choose to identify with a certain industry or community.

The expansion of enrollment in vocational education and the heightening of its operational complexity is a direct consequence of these two major developments, along with the emergence of an increasing number of both categories seeking avenues for opportunity. The responsiveness of vocational education institutions has exceeded the response capability of the occupational structure of the employment market.

What will be the nature of the future client system? Lawrence Davenport and Joel Galloway describe it as becoming even more differentiated and complex. George Copa identifies youth unemployment as a special problem and a special set of circumstances. This section explores the range of these views.

177

THE CHANGING CLIENTELE
FOR VOCATIONAL EDUCATION

Lawrence F. Davenport

Vocational education is a major supplier of the nation's manpower resources. Therefore, the needs of industry as well as the economic and political climates of the future play an important role in determining future vocational education populations.

In the 1960s changes in the client population were characterized by larger numbers of ethnic minorities, resulting from the awakening social consciousness of those groups and an increase in civil rights activities. The general client population also increased. At the same time, national attention was focused on vocational education. The intensifying competition with the U.S.S.R. in space technology, as well as the women's movement of the 1970s, brought increasing numbers of women into the client population. Women began to seek skills in areas formerly considered to be male domains.

During the decade of the 1980s, increasing inflation rates, decreasing natural resources, economic recession and soaring energy costs will continue to be of worldwide concern. Productivity is viewed by industry as the key to remaining competitive and the chief means of increasing productivity is technological advancement. All of these factors foretell changes in the vocational education client population.

THE NEW STUDENT PROFILE

Although the client population is made up of individuals and groups whose needs, orientation and expectations vary, there are certain general attributes that will characterize vocational education clients of the next 10 to 20 years. The Carnegie Council on Policy Studies in Higher Education (1980) has identified certain characteristics of the new higher education student population in general that can be related to changes expected in vocational education clientele: (1) lower levels of developed aptitudes; (2) more concentration on professional and vocational subjects; (3) less political activism; (4) less interest in academic reforms with efforts for campus change directed at tuition charges, better counseling and so forth; (5) less respect for rules and regulations, with more cheating, vandalism and defaulting on student loans; (6) less hope about the world and (7) on the other hand, more confidence in their own individual futures.

According to census statistics, the nation is growing older. The median age of Americans has risen to 30 for the only time in history, with the exception of the 1950 census. This is attributed largely to longer life expectancies and smaller families.

At the same time, people are changing careers more often to keep pace with changes in technology and economic conditions. In one five-year period in the 1970s, one-third of the labor force changed not just jobs, but careers.

Reflecting these conditions, vocational education clientele will vary greatly in age. Increased numbers of older people may be expected. Variations in age will lead to increased numbers of part-time students. Older clients tend to be employed and seek programs that allow them to gain skills while they continue to meet the financial obligations of families and mature life styles.

Future clients will be drawn toward variable entry programs. They will desire easy access to programs, the capability to gain quickly the skills they need and to leave the program upon mastering skills necessary for employment. In general, the client population will be older; there will be greater ethnic and cultural diversity and more women. Clients will have attained higher levels of education and will be seeking training in a wide variety of fields.

Women: The New Opportunity for Vocational Education

Although recession is expected to slow the rise of inflation, continued high rates of inflation are predicted. Currently, 51 percent of American women are in the labor force. As inflation erodes individual spending power, and as the number of single-person households and households headed by women rise, the number of women in the labor force can also be expected to rise. Department of Labor figures indicate that most women work for economic reasons and that two-thirds of those working outside the home in 1979 were single, widowed, divorced or separated, or had husbands earning less than $10,000 per year (DOL, 1980).

For women who desire good jobs with substantial salaries, vocational education will be more important than for their male counterparts who can get good jobs with less training. Women now graduate from high school at a rate of 3.3 percent above that of men yet on the average make only 59 cents to each dollar earned by men (U.S. Department of Commerce, 1977). Women of varying ages, interests and needs will be turning to vocational education for training and career guidance to upgrade skills and to gain the new skills necessary to change career directions.

Ethnic Minorities in The Work Force

As a nation, we point to great strides in providing employment opportunities for Americans in the 1960s and 1970s. Statistics indicate these strides did not include blacks and other ethnic minorities.

Although the number of families making more than $25,000 grew twice as fast among blacks as among whites between 1970 and 1978, only 13.4 percent of all black families fall within this category, compared with 29.5 percent for whites. Moreover, black family income fell from 60 percent of the white level in 1969 to 57 percent in 1979. The unemployment rate among blacks with college educations is 27.2 percent, compared with 22.3 percent for white youths who are high school dropouts (*Time*, 1980, p. 20).

The situation for Mexican-Americans as compared to whites is similar to that of blacks. While median family income in the United States in 1977 was $16,000, the average for Mexican-American families was $11,740 or about 75 percent of that for all U.S. families. The dropout rate for Mexican-American students is estimated at about 50 percent. In 1978, only 45 percent of employed Mexican-American women were in white collar jobs as compared to 64 percent of all employed women in the U.S. *(Time)*.

Blacks and Mexican-Americans are the largest ethnic minorities in the U.S. It may be reasoned that their situation is in many respects similar to that of other ethnic minorities that are subject to discrimination on the basis of color and/or cultural differences.

Ethnic minorities are not new clients of vocational education. However, emphasis on programs to provide skills training to minorities may be expected. New approaches may be required to reach the hard-core unemployed and to upgrade skills of the employed in order to improve work and economic mobility.

In addition to skills training, there is a need for basic work orientation that covers such areas as employer expectations, the nature of career ladders and where and how to attain advanced skills.

Just as individuals are different and have varying needs, so also do individual groups. It may be necessary to approach the problems of ethnic minorities differently than one approaches those of the majority group. More comprehensive programs that continue to serve clients after they attain a specified level of skills training may be necessary. Programs that include follow-up after employment, in the form of continued counseling and training for advancement may be required.

New Arrivals in Search of the American Dream

Economic and social pressures are driving the world's poor and oppressed to the U.S. in numbers that exceed the great wave of immigration that brought more than eight million immigrants into the country from 1900 to 1909. Experts calculate that as many as 800,000 immigrants will enter legally . . . hundreds of thousands more will enter illegally, mostly from Mexico, Central America, and the Caribbean ("The Economic Consequences of a New Wave," 1980, p. 80).

The majority of immigrants in this new wave are poor and unskilled. They are arriving at a time when the U.S. unemployment rate is 7.5 percent and is predicted to rise as high as 12 percent. Most of the immigrants will compete for employment in industries that are the first to experience business decline and, therefore, can be expected to contribute heavily to sharp rises in the unemployment rate.

Business Week has calculated that if U.S. citizens held the jobs now estimated to be held by four million illegal aliens, a drop of almost four percentage points would be seen in the unemployment rate ("The Economic Consequences"). As recession deepens, the competition for available jobs will increase, leading to historical intensification of social tensions.

The U.S. is just beginning to address the shifts in immigration trends and the rising population of illegal aliens. Current policies, or lack of them, have resulted in a large pool of immigrants and undocumented persons vying with large numbers of ethnic and economically disadvantaged citizens for low-paying, entry-level jobs.

As the trend toward increasing numbers of unskilled immigrants continues, we may anticipate growing emphasis on programs that provide skills training and develop career ladder opportunities for immigrants. Current thinking on the problem of undocumented persons tends toward recognition of their existence. Attention is being paid to improving their lot in this country, rather than to identification and deportation. It is foreseeable that this group may become new clients of vocational education.

U.S.-sponsored vocational education programs in foreign countries may become a means of dealing with the large influx of immigrants. This would provide career opportunities in the native country and lessen the need to emmigrate to improve standards of living.

Employers as Clients

As industry, the military and public service agencies attempt to increase productivity and decrease costs, we may expect an increasing demand for in-plant programs—courses for employees provided at the work site. A number of businesses and agencies currently conduct their own programs and employ their own training staffs.

Increasingly, industry, the military and public agencies are finding that instructional programs can more effectively be contracted to educational institutions. Military personnel formerly assigned to teaching and curriculum development are freed for more relevant military duties. Applying the same principle to industry and other major employers, the client population may be expanded to include employees seeking specific skills required by their employers.

Liberal Arts Graduates in the Work Force

People with liberal arts degrees will be turning more to vocational education. They find frequently they lack the skills necessary to compete in the job market. Many of these people are disillusioned, primarily as a result of long and fruitless searches for employment in their field. Those fortunate enough to find employment are discovering that because of low salaries and intense competition, the dream of living the "good life" that sustained them through long years of higher education is often impossible to fulfill.

This group tends to hold strong antibusiness attitudes. They frequently view themselves as humanists while seeing the business world as harsh, brutal and corrupt. Their manner of dress and general appearance is sometimes unsuited to the business world. Although highly educated, they are disillusioned with their chosen fields but lack the understanding and skills required for work in other areas. Programs for these students must address not only skills, but attitudes toward business and self as well, if this group is to survive in new careers.

Public demands for accountability have resulted in more regulation of some professions. For example, such fields as real estate, nursing and certified public accounting all require continuing education units for retention of certification. Professionals seeking to keep up-to-date in their fields may account for certain percentages of the client population in vocational education.

Individuals with higher levels of education are more likely to continue taking courses on a part-time basis throughout their lives. Therefore, this group most likely will return to vocational education programs to upgrade their skills, seek assistance in changing careers and/or to remain current with advancements. They may, in fact, form the core of continuing consumers of vocational education.

Senior Citizens — America's Untapped Resource

People are living longer and enjoying better health. Legislation now permits people who formerly would have retired at age 65 to continue to work. Others who take advantage of early retirement programs sometimes find they are not ready for a life of only leisure. Most significantly, retirees are finding inflation has eroded their fixed incomes to such an extent that a return to work is essential.

Thus, increasing numbers of older people who normally would have left the labor force are either remaining or re-entering. Military personnel with salable skills may decide to try new fields after 20 to 30 years of service. Others with skills not in demand in the civilian world may seek retraining in skills that have current marketability.

It is expected that many individuals seeking new careers will be turning to vocational education. In addition, accelerated change in our society has led economists and sociologists to predict that the average American worker will change careers at least three times in his or her lifetime. Many of these people will turn to vocational education for assistance in making career choices, as well as for training.

Unemployment: The Challenge for Vocational Education

In times of high unemployment, enrollments in vocational education programs increase. The unskilled unemployed person seeks skills as a means of insuring future job security, as the skilled unemployed person seeks to upgrade current skills or to gain new skills in areas where the employment outlook is brighter.

The current unemployment situation has a troublesome aspect that differs from previous periods of high unemployment. In the past, those laid off during economic downturns could expect to be rehired when the economy was in full swing once again. Today, even many of the larger companies may not be able to re-employ everyone laid off during periods of recession. Increasing foreign competition, energy costs, automation and decreasing world markets may lead to permanent reductions in operating levels and manpower requirements. For example, the late changeover to emphasis on smaller, energy-efficient automobiles in the American automobile industry has resulted in steadily decreasing market shares worldwide. Although American companies have introduced small cars that have gained in popularity, foreign companies are strongly entrenched in this market, and market shares formerly held by American companies continue to be eroded.

Ever-increasing concern for productivity has led to a new emphasis on the use of robots. *Business Week* ("Robots Join the Labor Force,"

1980, p. 62) reports that "New technology is making it possible to replace increasingly skilled workers. . . . A new generation of robots that 'see' and 'feel' and even 'think' . . . provide improved productivity, faultless performance, and lower labor costs." General Electric has launched a program that is expected in the foreseeable future to replace nearly half of its 37,000 assembly workers with robots.

Proponents of robotics hold that the use of robots ultimately will not reduce manpower, but merely shift its emphasis. Instead of large numbers of people working on assembly lines, workers will be required to program and repair robots. However, no plans have yet been made for retraining large numbers of displaced assembly line workers, and the skills needed by these two groups of workers are obviously very different.

The widespread introduction of computer-based technology—microelectronics—while increasing productivity is resulting in a net loss of jobs. *World of Work Report* ("Microelectronics Revolution," 1981, p. 2) notes that when National Cash Register began converting from the manufacture of mechanical or electro-mechanical cash registers to electronic cash registers, it was able to produce the electronic cash register with a 25 percent decrease in labor. Between 1970 and 1975 it was thus able to reduce its work force in the United States from 37,000 to 18,000.

Clearly, the challenge for vocational education will be to plan and provide retraining for the "new" unemployed. We can expect in the future large numbers of unskilled workers seeking technical skills, as well as skilled workers seeking retraining. We may also expect an increased enrollment in computer technology and robotics programs.

CONCLUSION

As the profession gears up to meet the needs of more and diverse clientele, we must realize we cannot do it alone. To a large extent, success will depend upon the willingness of state and local governments to commit resources to meet the manpower needs of the U.S.

The clientele is there and will increasingly seek out our services. It is our responsibility to advise government what it will cost to meet those needs and to guard cautiously against making promises that we do not have sufficient resources to keep.

REFERENCES

Carnegie Council on Policy Studies in Higher Education. *Three Thousand Futures: The Next Twenty Years for Higher Education.* San Francisco: Jossey-Bass, Inc., 1980.

"The Economic Consequences of a New Wave." *Business Week,* June 23, 1980.

"Microelectronics Revolution Will Result in Worldwide Job Loss, Predicts Report." *World of Work Report,* January, 1981.

"Robots Join the Labor Force." *Business Week,* June 9, 1980.

Time, June 16, 1980.

U.S. Department of Labor (DOL), Office of the Secretary, Women's Bureau. *20 Facts on Women Workers.* (three-page flyer) Washington, D.C.: DOL, December, 1980.

NEW APPROACHES FOR A NONTRADITIONAL CLIENTELE

Joel D. Galloway

In the upcoming years, this nation faces a need for increased programs of vocational education and of a wider variety than were previously necessary. There is no question that in a reindustrializing America there will be more demand for skilled technical labor and less demand for highly professional people. The plight of the unskilled and poorly educated will continue to worsen as the country comes to grips with its number one economic problem: declining productivity, which lies behind inflation and the adaptation to the energy problem ("A Conversation with Amital Etzioni," 1980, p. 54).

The type of product and expectations of vocational education by business and industry has to be one of quality as the nation faces labor shortages in a period of high unemployment. A careful examination of the pool of unemployed people in this country clearly indicates that the majority still have limited, if any, marketable skills for today's job market. That the unemployed in America are mainly unemployable still remains the basic problem for public and private vocational education.

INTRODUCTION

The implications of trends in the nation's job market, along with the educational needs of growing numbers of minorities, handicapped and women in vocational education programs give some indication of the clients to be served in the 1980s.

Of all the factors influencing client composition, few will have a bigger impact than the shifts ahead in the American population. The big increase, four-fifths of the population growth, will be in persons in their thirties and forties, with most of the remaining increase in the 60 and older bracket.

The number of Americans under age 20 will fall below 30 percent of the population for the first time in history. Societal values for youth and the opportunities for these young people will increase considerably. Qualified students and workers will be sought after by all segments of our society with vocational education offering upward

socioeconomic opportunities never before realized by previous generations of minorities and disadvantaged young people (Boaz, 1980, pp.
45-47).

A large component of the nation's population shift will be racial.
Blacks will increase both in number and as a proportion of the total
population during the next decade, giving them increasing political
and economic influence. It is estimated they will number 30 million,
12.2 percent of the nation's population by the end of the 1980s. Asian,
Hispanic, and other racial minorities are expected to increase even
faster, but from a smaller base—up from 1.3 percent in 1970 to 2.7
percent by 1990 ("Challenges of the '80s," 1979, p. 49).

Many of the above trends are already obvious. Postsecondary
vocational education programs are enrolling fewer veterans, as the
various federal assistance programs for them wind down. The changing
student population includes an increase in average age, a shift from
full-time to more part-time students, and an increase in both the
number and proportion of older female students and racial/ethnic
minorities (Holt, 1979, p. 22). Preparing quality education for
tomorrow's student offers a challenge and an opportunity unequalled
in the history of American vocational education.

THE CHANGING SCENE

The federal government, in its involvement with vocational education,
appears to wish to limit future funding to special needs programs for
the disadvantaged, handicapped and minorities. There are several
reasons for this position, primarily the shrinking population of young
people. This change will provide more opportunities for this particular
age group; therefore, an emphasis will be placed upon helping those
who need special assistance.

Since the passage of the Vocational Education Act of 1963, the
sensitivity of vocational educators to the needs of disadvantaged or
minority individuals has been heightened (Evans & Herr, 1978, p.
305). Community colleges and technical colleges can take considerable credit for expanding the base for education beyond high school
for minorities through flexible admissions policies, low cost and a
broad mix of educational programs (Gilbert, 1979, p. 5).

Minority student enrollment was 26.7 percent of the full-time
enrollment at two-year colleges, and 19.8 percent of part-time enrollment, according to the new *Minorities and Community Colleges,*
an American Association of Community and Junior Colleges (AACJC)
publication. These figures reflect 38.8 percent of the nation's minority
students. From 1970 to 1978 there was a 52 percent increase in

minority enrollment. Black enrollment increased 65 percent (Gilbert, p. 13). Although the statistics in some ways are encouraging, the total outreach program to assist these clients in the future will have to be modified and expanded considerably.

The Nontraditional Become Traditional

Since 1970 the characteristics of students in two-year colleges changed more than those of students in four-year colleges. More learners in two-year colleges were older, married, attending part-time, from less affluent homes and with parents who have less education than students in four-year colleges and universities. Women, minorities and persons over 24 have now become the "traditional" rather than the "nontraditional" students. Within this group of two-year college students, there has been a definite shift for both men and women away from arts and sciences and general programs, to occupational curriculums (HEW, pp. 19-26).

It is estimated that 40 million adults in America will be making a career change in the next 10 years. Twenty-four million will be turning to institutions like community colleges for training and/or retraining. These adults will enroll as part-time, employed students seeking specific courses and skills (Guzzardi, 1979, p. 103).

Studies of part-time and full-time mid-life adults show that most are attending community colleges for job or career-related reasons. Current employment was high among part-time students, with about 93 percent employed and working an average of 41.5 hours per week. About 52 percent of the full-time students were also employed and worked an average of 33 hours per week; thus, the current population of vocational education students are already operating in the primary sector of the economy and are very work-oriented. Counting the part-time credit students and all the non-credit students as adult learners, a new report from the National Center for Education Statistics (NCES) reports the "average" adult learner is 36 years old, has a family income of $20,300, two years of college and is seeking career and/or personal enhancement (Boaz, pp. 4, 127).

The higher the level of education already achieved, the more likely the person is to be enrolled in an adult education activity. This also correlated with personal income. The report just being completed by NCES shows that over 18 percent of those with incomes of $25,000 or more, 15.1 percent of those with incomes between $10,000 and $14,999, 9.7 percent of those with incomes between $7,500 and $9,999, 6.3 percent of those with income between $5,000 and $7,499 and 4.9 percent of those with income under $5,000 comprised the adult education enrollment in 1978. This study has major implications for those agencies administering adult education programs (Boaz, p. 4).

The significance of this relationship between education, personal income and participation in adult education, appears to be that the longer a student stays in school the more apt the student is to continue to use the educational service available. Very few adults having a low socioeconomic and educational background participate in present adult educational programs. Apparently the best chance to get involvement in adult education programs for these clients is to catch them as soon after leaving the secondary school system as possible. Retention within the educational system will continue to be a primary mission of secondary vocational education. Relevant occupational training for a large segment of low socioeconomic young people will be crucial to their mobility within society.

CLIENTELE IN THE 1980s

The United States is witnessing a changing labor force in terms of individual values and aspirations. Today's diverse groups of workers are more affluent, enjoying more fringe benefits, better educated, more likely to work in offices than factories, enjoying more leisure time and are more mobile than any previous generation. With all of these improvements, many workers remain dissatisfied. A 1979 study published by the University of Michigan's Survey Research Center shows worker dissatisfaction is at the highest point in the last decade ("New Breed of Workers," 1979, pp. 35, 38).

Worker Alienation

This trend is most noticeable in the declining participation of males, from 90 to almost 70 percent, in the nation's labor force over the last 40 years. This decline in men's participation has come mostly among the less educated. The sharpest withdrawal has been by black men, many of whom did not complete high school. The younger generation of black high school and college graduates, reversing the pattern of older blacks, is not withdrawing from the work force. Black women continue to maintain a higher participation rate than white women (Guzzardi, pp. 92, 106).

Vocational education, through adult education programming, has yet to reach this segment of our society. Something needs to be provided for people who quit work because they are unhappy with work. This activity will have to address such factors as personal aspirations and self-esteem. Although a portion of this group drops out because

190

they feel underpaid, most alienation and work studies report the feeling of unused skills and over-qualification for the job as part of the rationale for quitting. These factors should be taken into account in developing innovative outreach programs to encourage people over 40 years of age to enroll in vocational education programs.

The other segment of this group of alienated workers is the employee who continues to be dissatisfied with present employment, but is unable to change jobs due to lack of knowledge of and access to educational and job placement services. Their present environment and perceptions of such services hold few options other than their present situations or dropping out of the work force. It is to this group that vocational education must deliver new and different services in the 1980s.

Although the Comprehensive Employment and Training Act (CETA) has historically addressed itself to working with this unemployed population, its mission is limited by the very nature of the legislation. CETA dollars within the framework of disadvantaged and minorities are still funding clients on the basis of those most apt to succeed in the training process. Neither vocational education nor CETA appear to be reaching those who may benefit considerably from such occupational training, even though pretraining testing and evaluations indicate marginal chances for success. Service to many within this population will call for a different criteria for what constitutes progress, along with acceptance on the part of the funding agency of flexibility and a high risk factor.

Specialized Occupation Training
Another expanding area for vocational education will result from state and local training initiatives in specialized occupations. These efforts will be based upon particular industrial manpower needs and directed toward local economic development programs. Such activities will abandon federal guidelines for both vocational education and apprenticeship training. The clients to be served in this situation will clearly be the talented and those having the potential to succeed. Many states and communities will attempt to utilize vocational training to attract industry into their localities.

Some institutions in higher education, suffering from decreasing enrollment yet viewing the success of technical institutions, will attempt to provide program offerings in various fields of technology. This effort will be to attract the already college-bound student and to create new employment opportunities for the present clientele. Although this should provide educational opportunities for part-time

191

students in the urban setting, the students recruited will be limited to those having the necessary academic skills to succeed. Concern on the part of state technical institutions is that the end result of such activity will not result in an increased production of qualified technical people, but only a dilution of already limited state resources for occupational training.

The technical institutes and community colleges will become more interested in providing occupational training for the talented student having special aptitudes in the various fields of vocational education. The need for this type of education will increase as the reindustrializing of American industries create even greater opportunities for a highly skilled work force.

Importance of Instructional Delivery

In preparing for its new clientele, vocational educators need to realize that the most critical area demanding a new look is instructional delivery. Instructional approaches have remained traditional despite the fact that most students are nontraditional and fall far short of many "standard" academic prerequisites. The following example given by Hattie R. Jackson in the AACJC *Minorities and Community Colleges* report (Gilbert, 1979) is just too typical: two-year college faculty members will agree that most of their first-term students display problems expressing written ideas. These problems are manifest in such areas as spelling, organization, idea development and in students' inabilities to construct clear and complete sentences. Despite this knowledge, too many instructors continue to use the straight lecture method and to require difficult written assignments during the first transitional term. This impedes the mission of the institution by imposing pedagogically unsound instructional modes on a different population and it is an important factor in explaining the high attrition rates among blacks and other minority students.

A very positive role vocational education will continue to play at the postsecondary level is to "demystify" education for minorities and disadvantaged students. Too often education and the process of going on for further schooling has been viewed by these groups as a frightening, anxiety-producing and unconquerable endeavor. Counteracting hopelessness and providing a second chance for self-discovery and growth are key accomplishments of vocational education (Gilbert, p. 26).

Serving the educational needs of students in the 1980s will be more than meeting society's needs for workers. It will include providing relevance of education to many through application of "traditional"

192

general education topics. Instilling the purpose and motivation to utilize computational and verbal ability skills through the application of social and scientific information is fundamental to vocational education activities. For many of these clients, this role for vocational education will be the turning point in their education and will significantly affect the options available to them in the future.

REFERENCES

Boaz, Ruth L., ed. *Participation in Adult Education 1978.* Unpublished advance report. Washington, D.C.: U.S. Department of Education, National Center for Education Statistics (NCES), 1980.

"Challenges of the '80s." *U.S. News & World Report,* October 15, 1979.

"A Conversation with Amital Etzioni." *U.S. News & World Report,* April 14, 1980.

Evans, Rupert N., and Herr, Edwin L. *Foundations of Vocational Education 2nd Edition.* Columbus, Ohio: Charles E. Merrill, 1978.

Gilbert, Fontelle, ed., *Minorities and Community Colleges.* Washington, D.C.: American Association of Community & Jr. Colleges (AACJC), 1979.

Guzzardi, Walter Jr. "Demography's Good News for the Eighties." *Fortune,* November 5, 1979.

Holt, Dione. "Planning for Tomorrow's Students." *Community College Review,* 1979, 7(2).

"New Breed of Workers." *U.S. News & World Report,* September 3, 1979.

U.S. Department of Health, Education, and Welfare (HEW), National Center for Education Statistics (NCES). *Transfer Students in Institutions of Higher Education,* National Longitudinal Study. Washington, D.C.: HEW, 1980.

UNEMPLOYED YOUTH: RENEWED EFFORT AT SERVING A CLIENT GROUP

George H. Copa

Youth unemployment is a problem of tremendous proportion in this country today. Because of its cyclical nature, it likely will be a problem of the future as well, presenting one of the more challenging client groups to vocational educators.

In the past, the nation often had a "holding tank" for its youth—the Civilian Conservation Corps in the 1930s, World War II in the 1940s, the G.I. Bill of Rights in the early 1950s and the Korean and Vietnam wars of the 1950s and 1960s—all which served to occupy youth who might otherwise have been unemployed.

While it certainly is a relief not to see youth going off to war, the most common of the holding tank devices, nevertheless since the 1970s the number of unemployed youth has steadily risen. Hubert H. Humphrey, during Congressional hearings, called it a "national disgrace," saying:

> ...I believe that it is incredible that a government will sit around paralyzed in its own indifference with a national unemployment rate...of 3.5 million young workers of the age 25 or under. Here are young people in the full vitality of life....for our nation's economy this is a terrible waste of millions of young people who have unlimited amounts of energy and desire and talent, and who want to become productive and useful members of our society. (U.S. 94th Congress, 1976, p. 2.).

It is difficult to know if unemployment comes first and then profound and implacable cynicism or vice versa. However, they do seem to occur together and perpetuate themselves in a spiraling sort of way. To suggest that one has *the* answer that promises to break the downward spiral is a risky endeavor.

Is the promise of entry to work, even to those youth with an adequate education, a sufficient "carrot"? Will it match and surpass the competing alternative ways of making a living? One must enter the business of reducing youth unemployment with eyes open to the realities of the individuals and environments involved and the strength

195

of the services being advocated.

Complicating matters is the issue of who is to blame, individual or society, for the existence of youth unemployment. The corresponding question is how much each should be expected to contribute to a solution. Human resources are special in that they cannot be stored like other raw materials for later use. It also appears that youth unemployment is not distributed randomly in the population with a different group affected over time. Rather, it is concentrated in certain areas and there are "hang-over" effects so that once affected, the same individuals are likely to be affected by it again. The result is certain individuals bear a relatively larger share of the burden and are likely to bear it for long periods of their lives.

Education generally has its effect on the supply side of the labor market—the individual—with little direct control over occupational demand. Jobs cannot be promised to those contemplating education; only a competitive advantage should be expected. If a competitive advantage is offered by education and if resources are not available to give it to all, then who should have easiest access to it—adults or youth, rural or urban, black or white, male or female, employed or unemployed? Is some level of unemployment desirable to keep a cap on inflation? Does education serve only as one of many mechanisms to redistribute the "pie," with little control of the size of the pie itself and the decision as to what is a sufficient piece?

The focus of this chapter is on identifying and describing what vocational education *could* do in reducing youth unemployment. This is a responsible endeavor because claims to do more may be damaging to the individuals being served and to those offering other services that could be more viable. It seems untenable to hold the position that there is one simple answer.

DEFINITIONS TO CONSIDER

The complexity of interpretations and perspectives of the youth unemployment problem makes a clear definition of terms a mandatory first step to profitable discussion. Who is covered by the youth unemployment rate often quoted as evidence of crisis?

Unemployed

According to the U.S. Department of Labor (1978, p. A-4) the definition of unemployed is:

> All those (age 16 and older and non-institutionalized) who did not work during the survey week, made specific efforts to find a job within the preceding 4 weeks, and were available for work or would have been available during the

survey week except for temporary illness. Also included as unemployed are those who did not work at all, were available for work and:
a) were waiting to be called back to a job from which they had been laid off, or
b) were waiting to report to a new wage or salary job within 30 days.

Some of the limitations of this definition are that it does not take into consideration the amount of time worked during the survey week which could have been only one hour, the number of weeks worked per year or the amount of wages or salary earned by working. Nor does it include the person who has become discouraged in job seeking and is no longer actively looking for work. Of particular concern is that the definition does not include the person who is underemployed (working at a job which does not make full use of capabilities) or is working in the secondary labor market (working at a dead-end job, with little opportunity for vertical advancement.)

The unemployed also can be subdivided into several groups depending on the reason for being unemployed. Some of the more common terms used to identify reasons are: cyclical, frictional and structural (Bloom & Northrup, 1965: Bowen & Finegan, 1969). Cyclical unemployment is associated with the rise and fall in business activity over time, between years or within a year. Frictional unemployment results from persons who are in between jobs, that is the time required to move from one job to the next. A minimum frictional unemployment is estimated to be 2 to 3 percent. Structural unemployment results from loss of job due to technological change, such as replacing labor with machines or creating new qualifications for a job.

These definitions are important to note because the solution to each type of unemployment is held to be different. Cyclical unemployment usually is treated by tailored services to particular groups, involving retraining, area economic redevelopment and geographic relocation. Frictional unemployment requires better services in the job transition process, that is, quicker matching. Structural unemployment is usually treated by tailored services to particular groups involved, such as retraining, area economic redevelopment, geographic relocation.

Youth

As used in the *Employment and Training Report of the President* (1978), the term *youth* or *young worker* refers to the age group 16 to 24 years old. For descriptive and analytical purposes, youth often are subdivided into two groups: teenagers (age 16 to 19) and young adults (age 20 to 24). These definitions will be used in this chapter.

POSSIBLE CAUSES OF YOUTH UNEMPLOYMENT

Causation is an illusive concept. To prove that any one variable causes youth unemployment would be next to impossible. Rather, one is forced to talk in terms of *possible* causes, based on observation of certain phenomena or characteristics that regularly appear together or at least in some relationship in terms of time and location. It is one thing to say that two occurrences happen together and quite another to show they are connected, for the connection really can never be observed, only hypothesized.

Scriven (1973) describes four types of situations encountered in searching for causation:

1. Experimental cause—wherever and however the causal variable occurs, the effect occurs.
2. Observational cause—the causal variable accompanies the effect and the effect doesn't occur on other occasions.
3. Compound causes—more than one causal variable is needed before the effect occurs; one of the causal variables alone is not sufficient.
4. Multiple causes—any one of several causal variables accompanies the effect; each is sufficient by itself.

Experimental causation is very difficult to show with any social phenomenon, especially if the phenomenon is complex. It usually is demonstrated only in physical sciences. With youth unemployment, the evidence at this point as to possible causes is only observational. It is highly likely that the situation with youth unemployment as an effect has multiple or compound causes.

What follows is a listing of hypothesized possible causes of youth unemployment, obtained by reviewing syntheses of research and evaluation and expert testimony on youth unemployment (Barton & Fraser, 1978; U.S. Congress, 1976; U.S. 94th Congress, 1976; U.S. 95th Congress, 1977; Vice President's Task Force on Youth Employment, 1980).

The resources consulted, while not exhaustive, represent some of the best current thought. Certainly the possible causes could be subdivided and aggregated in various ways for different purposes. No attempt is made here to provide the evidence as to why the listed factor is suspected to be a cause of youth unemployment; rather the factor itself is described briefly. For organizational purposes, the list of possible causes has been subdivided into three categories: (1) characteristics of individuals, (2) characteristics of the environment and (3) characteristics of institutions.

Characteristics of Individuals

The possible causes of youth unemployment included in this category are inherent in the affected persons themselves. Treatment would mean focusing on changing individuals.

Lack of Education. The education of an individual as it relates to employment can be subdivided into *general* and *specific-to-work.* General refers to basic cognitive skills in areas such as reading, speaking, mathematics and social studies, as well as physical (psychomotor) and interpersonal (affective) skills. These are general skills important to all of the roles played by a person in society. The specific-to-work education refers to cognitive, psychomotor and affective skills, useful primarily in the work role. This latter category can again be subdivided into *seeking/coping, general-work* and *specific-work* skills.

Seeking/coping skills are those useful in obtaining, holding and advancing in a work role of any kind. They include using labor market information, assessing one's capabilities and interests, career decision-making and relating to supervisors and co-workers. General-work skills refer to skills useful in the performance of several occupations, that is, the more basic of the specific-to-work skills. Specific-work skills are those useful in a single occupation. (Work skills which are even more specific apply only to a particular work site but these usually are taught on the job).

Lack of Work Experience. Experience refers to time spent working at paid or unpaid employment. Perhaps its importance comes as an indication of a person's likely performance in the real world of work. Work experience is seen to provide some additional education beyond that obtained inside the classroom or laboratory of the school.

Lack of Resources. Resources here refer to financial resources to purchase items such as transportation, food and clothing while seeking and becoming established at work.

Lack of Support System. Support system refers to the personal support of family or friends to make it through the ups and downs of getting established in a work role. This entails providing the needed encouragement to "stay at it," serving as a sounding board to solve problems, functioning as a source of security necessary to independent action and serving as a role model for normal behavior relating to working.

Lack of Information. The information is about self, the work environment and the means for making a successful transition to work.

It could involve knowing such diverse information as one's vocational interests and aptitudes, the jobs presently vacant in a given community or the education most suitable for entry to a particular occupation.

Wrong Geographic Location and Unwillingness to Relocate. The person is living in a geographic location where jobs are not available at all or where jobs are not available for which the person is qualified. The person is unwilling to move to secure a better possibility of employment. There may be several legitimate reasons for not moving, such as a family not willing to move, school demands and so forth.

Poor Attitude Toward Self and/or Work. The person has low self-esteem; that is, he or she does not feel capable of securing a job and then advancing in it. Or the person does not see working as an important part of living, perceiving that the work available is "not worth the effort."

Competing Roles. The person has other roles that constrain the type of work that can be accepted. These other roles may involve school, family or leisure activities in the person's life. It may be that the person is not interested in working but it may also be the person has other interests of stronger intensity.

Lack of Consequences to Not Working. The person may want to work and actually be searching but may not be under hardship while in the process. The person may be living at home with a substantial allowance or be receiving welfare payments so there is no incentive to work at a low-paying job.

Characteristics of Environment

The possible causes listed in this category are inherent in the environment and external to the young person seeking work. Treatment would mean focusing on changes in the environment of the youth and work.

Inadequate Labor Demand. Job vacancies of the type for which young persons are prepared are not available in sufficient number or are not in the same geographic location as unemployed youth. Youth looking for work simply outnumber job vacancies.

Successful Competition from Other Groups. Older workers, migrants or those previously unavailable, such as women re-entering the work force, those retired from the military or those discharged from institutions, compete with unemployed youth and are more successful in entering work. The size of the "otherwise unavailable" category has been increasing substantially in recent years.

Discrimination: Discrimination in hiring based on age works to the disadvantage of all youth; that based on sex or race affects particular subgroups of youth.

Unrealistic Job Requirements. Job requirements are used for screening and selecting job applicants that are above those actually necessary for successful performance of a job. Requirements may be stated in such forms as education, experience, licenses and union membership.

Restrictive Laws and Regulations. Laws and regulations related to hiring, such as minimum wage legislation and insurance requirements regarding the age of workers, can force employers to pay unrealistic wages for youth based on their productivity. These regulations may restrict employers from hiring youth for certain jobs and make employers wary of the legal risks of hiring youth.

Negative Peer Pressures. A young person's friends can exert pressures as to the types of work that will be acceptable. Peers form an important social reference group for youth.

Characteristics of Institutions

The third category of possible causes of youth unemployment are inherent in the institutions and organizations, which through their services to youth, assist in the process of transition from school to work.

Lack of Service. The exact type of service needed may not be in existence anywhere. Perhaps it has not been developed or tested to the point of being operational, or maybe no one has identified the particular service as being needed. Types of non-existent service may include preparation for work, career guidance, job placement and employer education.

Insufficient Quantity of Service. The service is available but not in enough quantity to serve all youth needing assistance.

Inadequate Access to Service. The service is not available to those who need it because of factors such as geographic location, costs, admission requirements, scheduling or physical access.

Ineffective Service. Services are in existence and accessible but are not effective. They do not diminish the problem they are designed, operated and funded to affect.

Uncoordinated Services. Service institution and organizations do not avoid unnecessary duplication and gaps in service. Individuals are not able to move from service to service in a smooth flow; multiple needs are not taken care of with appropriate schedules and overall concern for individuals.

Sorting Out Possible Causes

Multiple or compound possible causes have been posited for youth unemployment. The delimitation of all the sufficient sets of causal factors has not been accomplished by research and experience. Several of the possible factors can vary from "cause" to "not a cause" depending on circumstances or the intensity of manifestation. For example, when is a service such as career guidance, job training or equity in hiring procedures ineffective enough to become a real cause of youth unemployment? Or, how intense does negative peer pressure have to become before it affects a young person's decision to take a particular job?

The task of sorting out possible causes is even more difficult when causes are separated from the effect by time and space. For example, it may be four or more years from the time a ninth grader gets career guidance in selecting a set of high school courses to the time the student searches for work. A student obtaining job training in one community may end up searching for work several hundred miles away.

Possible causes also can be organized in terms of primary, secondary, tertiary and so forth. That is, the unemployment of a particular homogeneous group of youth may have as a primary cause "lack of education." Lack of education may in turn be caused by several possible factors, such as poor instruction, wrong curriculum content or poor student attendance (termed secondary possible causes). Poor student attendance may in turn be caused by poor health, lack of transportation or family obligations (tertiary possible causes).

It is important to document the conditions under which each possible cause is likely to be a real "contender" for causing youth unemployment. The task of identifying the actual cause(s) of unemployment for a particular youth becomes one of considering all possible causes, determining if the possible cause was present for the youth in question and then determining if the cause was actually operating as would be expected.

ALTERNATIVE TREATMENTS FOR YOUTH UNEMPLOYMENT

Potential treatments for reducing youth unemployment are not always alternatives in the sense of being substitutes for one another; they may work on different possible causes of youth unemployment. Again, the treatments are drawn from a review of synthesized research and evaluation, expert testimony and the author's experience. Concern is with both the "flow" to and "pool" of unemployed youth—with those who are predicted to become unemployed youth sometime in the future, as well as those already unemployed. In this section, youth will refer to both groups of individuals.

Outreach

Outreach involves making all members of a community, particularly the youth already or potentially unemployed, aware of the services available to alter their condition. Outreach not only provides information but sees that it is received and understood. It could occur in many places, such as the home, school and church, at many times and through a variety of media, such as print, radio, television and personal communication.

Recruitment

Recruitment goes beyond outreach. The intent is to attract those in need of service to actually procure the service. For example, if occupational training is needed by particular individuals, several active means might be used to enlist them in a service such as vocational education. The intent is not simply to wait passively for youth in need to enroll on their own.

Assessment

Assessment pertains to assisting youth to see their own needs, abilities and interests. It involves development of valid and fair procedures for testing and communicating results of assessment to youth and others who may need to know.

Guidance

Guidance refers to services that help youth make better decisions regarding preparation for and actual transition from school to stable careers. It includes offering direction relating to secondary and post-secondary education, jobs, personal matters and family, as they affect transition and maintenance of a work role. Ideally it should lead to an individualized plan for development of employability.

General Education

General education refers to improving the more general skills useful in several different life roles, all of which may affect success in a work role. Areas of improvement include focus on the basics (e.g., mathematics, reading, speaking), nature of industry, culture, leadership and human relations. Some of the effort here may be characterized as remedial for skills which should have been, but were not, learned in other educational experiences.

Job Readiness Training

Job readiness training involves teaching the skills necessary to seek employment and to cope in the labor market. Techniques of career decision-making, interviewing, using sources of job vacancies, relating to employers and co-workers and advancing in the same job or to another job are examples of such preparatory training.

Skill Training

Skill training emphasizes cognitive, psychomotor and interpersonal skills directly related to and most useful in work roles. Training could take place in institutions (public and private, residential and non-residential), on the job or in some combination of the two (cooperative experience, apprenticeship).

Education Information

Information about educational processes includes types of occupations for which training is offered; cost, length and likelihood of completers getting the jobs for which they are trained; location and qualifications of staff. The information should serve to make youth aware of their educational options and the consequences of selecting an option. It should make other deliveries of educational service aware of duplication and gaps (areas for decline, expansion or coordination) and let employers know what to expect from someone who has received educational services of a particular kind.

Labor Market Information

Labor market information refers primarily to services directed toward communicating characteristics of the labor market to youth and institutions serving youth.

Current job vacancies, future estimates of vacancies, location of jobs, wages, working conditions, job entry requirements and advancement possibilities represent labor market characteristics of use in providing effective guidance, instruction and placement.

Secondarily, this service could entail actually gathering or stimulating others to gather and communicate needed information not currently available.

Age Integration

Age integration involves providing opportunities for youth to come in close contact with persons of all age groups. It allows youth to observe, question and develop perspectives of the various stages in the career development process all the way to retirement. Age integration helps youth develop an understanding of how various forces interact and why things happen as they do and thereby provides a sense of control over or security in the work environment.

Role Model Development

Focus in role model development creates and communicates "success images" to youth. It involves providing youth the opportunity to come in contact with and be influenced by individuals who can serve as concrete examples of desired performance in a work role, from both the individual and more general societal perspective. Success images can be especially useful as mentors for youth, regarding how to act, operate and get ahead in a work role.

Occupational Experience

Occupational experience means providing youth with work experience that will be useful in the transition to a suitable career. Experience can be paid or unpaid; it can come before, during or after participation in school. Experience can be obtained through activities such as shadowing (spending some time observing and talking with those working at particular jobs or group of jobs), supervised occupational experience programs (this usually happens while the youth is going to school, with supervision by a professional to see that it is an effective educational experience), internships (usually full-time work experience before, during or after classroom instruction with less supervision by professionals) and transitional employment (usually some kind of meaningful work while moving from school to stable, desired work role).

Testing and Licensing

Testing and licensing refer to the special requirements to obtain certification for certain occupations. This often is based in part on education, such as a license for a practical nurse, acceptance in a carpenters' union or a diploma for high school graduation. Service to youth to meet these requirements can include checking the validity and fairness of the testing and licensing procedure, recommending changes if necessary, and assisting youth to be able to meet the criteria.

Job Placement

Job placement involves directly helping young people who want to work find suitable jobs. The notion of matching is involved, but in the dynamic sense that both individual and job are likely to be constantly changing with regard to the characteristics of each. Placement, therefore, is a continuous rather than a one-time service.

Placement services include developing a bank of information about present and future job vacancies, employment trends, and data on youth in the locality, particularly those unemployed or likely to become unemployed. Providing placement involves being accessible at times, places and at no or low cost to the youth being served. Placement is the physical linking of an individual and suitable work.

Job Development

Job development means stimulating new labor force demand, and may be accomplished by manipulating the economy or by directly creating jobs. Jobs could be created either by the public or private sector; particular geographic areas and industrial sectors may be targeted for economic stimulation. A shift from less to more labor-intensive methods of production is a possible option. Schools could be involved in job creation by actually operating small businesses.

Another aspect of job development is job redesign, that is, the changing of job descriptions to make the jobs more satisfying work roles and/or subdividing jobs to make, for example, two part-time jobs out of one full-time job.

Support Services

Support services are those supplementary services needed to prepare for and make the school-to-work transition. Assistance in having room and board, clothing, medical, dental and legal help, as well as follow-up monitoring after the transition to work has been made, all fall within this category. Support also could take on the social and psychological reinforcement necessary for job searching and job maintenance.

Community Involvement

Community involvement means making members of a community — including organizations serving youth, taxpayers, and employers — aware of how they can facilitate the youth transition-to-work process and benefit from it.

Laws and Regulations

Laws and regulations refer to those that affect work and include ones on discrimination, minimum wage and occupational safety requirements. Service in this area means informing youth and employers of rights and responsibilities, becoming active in changing undesirable laws and regulations and influencing those institutions—be they schools, unions, employers or whatever—that are not implementing the laws and rules effectively and fairly.

Geographic Relocation
Relocation refers to assisting youth move from areas of relative job deficiency to areas of job surplus.

Alternatives to Paid Work
Stress on developing alternative, personally and socially rewarding roles other than paid work serves to reduce the number of youth who want salaried jobs. Alternative roles include family, volunteer and leisure.

Coordination of Services
Coordination of services involves linking all the institutions and agencies assisting youth in the transition to stable employment. Major institutions and agencies involved include the total high school program (including vocational education), the employment service and business and industry. The linking could be formalized by having one particular agency or a joint group designated to monitor coordinated activities.

SELECTING APPROPRIATE SERVICES
The services described represent a set of options or alternatives that could be deployed singly or in combination to reduce youth unemployment. Several of the service alternatives focus on particular possible causes of unemployment.

In developing and selecting appropriate services, care must be taken to avoid creating a bigger problem than the one being solved. For example, setting lower minimum wages for youth may lead to high unemployment rates for adults, as youth are substituted for them. Or it may lead to large numbers of youth employed at work that does not pay just compensation. It is possible some causes of unemployment cannot be treated; treatments simply do not exist or are not feasible because of cost or side effects.

Each treatment alternative must be documented in terms of the conditions under which it will and will not work. Care in this process will lead to realistic expectations and relatively high success rates. An understanding that the labor market and transition from school to work are highly dynamic, interactive processes should cause speculation that treatments are likely to have multiple consequences. Little can be absolutely guaranteed. Guarantees for individuals are even more tenuous than guarantees for groups.

RECOMMENDED STRATEGY FOR POLICY

This section sets forth a series of recommended program thrusts or purposes for vocational education new or expanded programs focusing on reducing youth unemployment. The recommendations serve as suggested steps for action. Four program directions or thrusts are recommended, along with a brief description and rationale.

Thrust 1: Prevention of Youth Unemployment

Purpose: Increase the employability of youth as a means of *preventing* unemployment.

Description: Prevention would be accomplished by providing a comprehensive set of director services or linkages with other agencies providing such services to assure a smooth school-to-work transition. Services currently offered by vocational education would be used. The major new thrust would be to expand the quantity and quality of services and to extend the service beyond the school building and beyond students "while in school." Some of the services to be expanded are guidance, job readiness training, education information, labor market information, age integration, role model development, occupational experience, job placement, community involvement and coordination of services.

Rationale: The consequences of extended periods of unemployment early in work life can have major life-long hang-over effects. It is an experience that estranges youth from the opportunities, laws and institutions of our society. It is a waste of millions of young people who have unlimited amounts of energy, desire and talent. A program of prevention requires a comprehensive set of services focused on all possible causes of youth unemployment. The goal is to deal with the cause before it has the opportunity to have an effect.

Reliance may be placed largely on the conventional services known to be preventive and on combinations of services rather than on single remedies. In order for preventive services to be continuous and coordinated during the transition from school to work, they will have to be extended beyond the school building, into the community, employment site and home—the places where transition occurs. Further, allowance must be made to follow youth after leaving school, through gaps they may experience before finding meaningful and stable work.

Thrust 2: Remediation of Unemployed Youth

Purpose: Increase the employability of youth who already are unemployed.

Description: Increased employability would be developed through the planning and provision of selected services personalized to the needs of each unemployed young person. Current vocational education services would be used but major new efforts would be made in services such as outreach, recruitment, assessment, guidance, job readiness training, education and labor market information, age integration, role model development, job placement, support services, community involvement and coordination of services. Particular emphasis would be made on outreach, recruitment and assessment.

Outreach services would make students aware of services available while recruitment services would be used to get unemployed youth to participate. Assessment would be a major activity with each unemployed youth. Assessment should result in an *individualized employability plan* very much like the individualized education plan developed for handicapped and disadvantaged elementary and high school students. The employability plan would be an extension of the training agreement now used extensively in cooperative vocational education programs. Student, parents, employer (when appropriate) and school staff would all participate in formulating the plan.

Under this effort, a larger share of services are likely to be provided to out-of-school youth. In assisting unemployed youth, focus is on having a comprehensive set of services available but then selecting certain services for actual delivery that match the needs of particular youth. Linkages would be developed with other agencies to make available a comprehensive set of services that are accessible, effective and efficient.

Rationale: The longer youth are unemployed, the more manifest and paralyzing their symptoms become. This results in a higher probability of longer-term hang-over effects, such as chronic employment problems, and more difficulty in reaching and rehabilitating as quickly as possible those already unemployed. Targeted services should be aimed at the most serious cause of unemployment for each individual young person.

Vocational education has the capacity to provide efficiently a large share of the services required. Special efforts are necessary to make youth aware of these services and to secure their participation.

Through assessment, the most serious causes of unemployment can be diagnosed and an individualized prescription for services developed. Single services, such as job placement, guidance and labor market information may be used extensively to make an impact along with radical approaches to delivery. Services are likely to be individualized and may require rather direct intervention to achieve results quickly. In some cases, symptoms of unemployment, such as lack of food and clothing, may have to be treated while causes, such as lack of training, are being ameliorated. Linkages will be required with other agencies to provide a full range of services as efficiently as possible.

Thrust 3: Indirect Job Maintenance, Development and Creation

Purpose: Increase the opportunities for employment for youth.

Description: The present capabilities of vocational education would be expanded explicitly to recognize and plan for its effect on employment opportunities for youth. Major activities would involve working with employers, particularly small businesses, as a means to insure their stability and thereby insure they remain potential employers of young persons. Services to small business might occur through adult vocational education programs.

Job development would be accomplished by cooperating with employers using the job analysis procedures of curriculum planning to develop new jobs particularly appropriate for entry by youth. Further possibilities involve educating employers about the laws and regulations concerning the employment of young persons, thereby alleviating some misconceptions and "fear of the not-understood."

Job creation would be affected through teaching entrepreneurial skills to youth, by operating model small businesses as part of training programs that would also provide employment opportunities, and by initiating joint ventures with community agencies or groups to provide community services or community development projects employing young persons.

Rationale: The employment of young persons is predicated on the availability of job openings. It makes little long-term sense to improve the employability of young persons without considering opportunities to use that employability. Vocational education traditionally has had its major focus on the support side of the labor market—that is, on those wishing to enter or advance in the work environment. However, vocational education can have important indirect effects on employment opportunities if it decides to make this purpose explicit and plan accordingly.

Much of the technique already is available to mobilize this purpose for vocational education. What is needed is an incentive to use this technology on a much larger scale than at present. With this third thrust, employers and the larger community become an explicit client of vocational education, thereby providing additional opportunity for interaction and spin-off benefits to the direct services to youth, described in the first and second thrusts.

Thrust 4: Program Information and Improvement

Purpose: Conduct program improvement activities through research, development, demonstration, evaluation and training to increase the effectiveness and efficiency of vocational education's role in reducing youth unemployment.

Description: A planned strategy for program improvement of vocational education's services focused on reducing youth unemployment would be organized at the national, state and local education agency levels. Activities would involve assessment of existing weaknesses and gaps in programs, conducting research, development, demonstration and/or training as appropriate to reduce weaknesses and gaps and follow-up evaluation to determine the general applicability of improvement activities. Planning would be used to determine if improvement activities focused on a particular weakness or gap are most appropriate for national, state or local efforts.

Rationale: The causes for and ways of eliminating youth unemployment are not fully understood. The improvement in services in terms of effect and cost will be related to the increase in disciplined investigation of the problem and current solutions, as well as development and trial of new ideas and development of supportive people. Some problems and solutions related to youth unemployment and the role of vocational education are unique to local community and state situations; others are appropriate for federal level concern. Without this thrust, programs certainly will improve, but not at the increased rate needed to overcome youth unemployment, a problem considered by many to be a social time bomb.

REFERENCES

Barton, R.D. and Fraser, B.S. *Between Two Worlds: Youth Transition From School to Work.* Volume 1: A Synthesis of Knowledge, Volume 2: A Summary of Program Evaluation, Volume 3: A Research and Experimentation Strategy, Executive Summary: A Strategy for Research and Experimentation. Washington, D.C.: National Manpower Institute, August, 1978.

Bloom, G.F. and Northrup, H.R. *Economics of Labor Relations.* Homewood, Illinois: Richard D. Irvin, Inc., 1965.

Bowen, W.G. and Finegan, T.A. *The Economics of Labor Force Participation.* Princeton, New Jersey: Princeton University Press, 1969.

Scriven, M. "Causes, Connections, and Conditions in History" in Broudy, H.S., Ennis, R.H., and Krimerman, L.I. (eds.), *Philosophy of Educational Research.* New York: John Wiley & Sons, Inc., 1973.

U.S. Congress. *Policy Options for the Teenage Unemployment Problem.* Background Paper No. 13. Washington, D.C.: U.S. Government Printing Office, September 21, 1976.

U.S. 94th Congress. *Youth Unemployment.* Hearings before the Joint Economic Committee, Washington, D.C.: U.S. Government Printing Office, September 9, 1976.

U.S. 95th Congress. *Youth and Minority Unemployment.* A study prepared for the use of the Joint Economic Committee. Washington, D.C.: U.S. Government Printing Office, July 6, 1977.

U.S. Department of Labor. *Students, Graduates, and Dropouts in the Labor Market.* October, 1977. Special Labor Force Report 215. Washington, D.C.: U.S. Government Printing Office, June, 1978.

Vice President's Task Force on Youth Unemployment, Summary Report. Washington, D.C.: The White House, 1980.

SECTION VI

ORGANIZATIONAL AND ADMINISTRATIVE CHALLENGES

The domain of vocational education is immense, and it has many separate dimensions. It has a macrodimension requiring a response to such aggregated forces as unemployment, occupational outlooks and human resource policy. It has a microdimension requiring attention to training sites, job content and the work places. A third dimension is related to individual and group values expressed individually or through voluntary institutions such as the family.

The domain and the dimensions of vocational education are so extensive that the field appears to be operating without an organizable agenda. Yet individuals, communities, states and the federal government each have what appears to be a separable agenda for vocational education. The organizational and administrative considerations for the future of vocational education require attention to the multiple agendas.

Samuel Halperin views organizational and administrative questions from a federal perspective and he offers a plea for consistency, for a way in which subsidiary jurisdictions can have some assurance that their inheritance from the federal level is not merely indifference or worse, intransigence.

Robert Seckendorf highlights the difficulties of viewing vocational education as a system. He dispells the notion that even states have more similarities than differences. He describes the organizational and administrative problems as needing an evolving structure for definition and specification, not a system of regulatory action.

EDUCATION POLICY FOR THE FUTURE: WE CAN'T GET THERE FROM HERE...

Samuel Halperin

Social changes over the next few decades will place a burden on our educational system as great as any it has ever faced. Unfortunately, our present federal aid system is inadequate and has *not yet* obtained sufficient results to justify the substantial public investments in it. It is inconceivable that federal aid programs and federal education agencies, as structured today, can meet tomorrow's demands. In short, "We can't get there from here. . . ."

In taking a step backward from the futuristic theme of this book, to look at some realities of the present, one is reminded of Kenneth Boulding's sage observations about future studies:

> It's nice to be the drafter of a well-constructed
>   plan
> For spending lots of money for the betterment
>   of man.
> But audits are a threat, for it is neither games
>   nor fun
> To look at plans of yesteryear and ask, "What
>   have we done?"
> And learning is unpleasant when we have to do it fast,
> So it's pleasanter to contemplate the future
>   than the past.

In viewing the current federal aid system, three areas are of immediate concern: (1) fragmentary versus wholistic policy; (2) overload: too much complexity and too much change; and (3) policy as if people didn't matter. Unless there is substantial improvement in these areas, it seems very doubtful that federal agencies will be able to cope with a most uncertain future.

FRAGMENTARY VERSUS WHOLISTIC POLICY

The current fragmentation of our "non-system" of federal aid militates against a wholistic view of education and the maximum development of human potential. We give far too little time and attention to assessing the impact of a given act on education or learning as a whole. Rather, our vision and our inquiry seem limited too often to narrower questions of schooling or of specific concerns, such as Title X or Program Y. This year we legislate for higher education, last year for elementary and secondary, next year for vocational. There is scarcely ever time to consider the relationship of one educational program to another, of one level of education to another.

Virtually every congressional committee and over 70 executive branch departments and agencies take dozens of actions each year which affect the health of our educational enterprise. When, for example, the labor committees of the Congress helped to enact P.L. 95-256, "Age Discrimination in Employment Act Amendments of 1978," they played havoc with both educational practice and budgets by requiring some institutions to retain staff they might otherwise have replaced with younger, presumably less costly, instructors. Similarly, energy policy — or lack thereof — greatly affects the solvency of educational institutions. While manufacturers pass along higher fuel costs to consumers and when the president deregulates prices of oil or natural gas, to whom do the schools and colleges turn when their heating and lighting bills soar?

And how educationally rational is it for public policy to subsidize child care and day care through tax credits while denying similar financial support for the same age child whose parents would prefer educational benefits in the form of tuition, books and fees? Is there educational sense in policies which, through tax deductibility of educational expenses, encourage individuals to improve skills needed in their current employment but deny support for training that same individual for new employment, presumably of greater worth to both the individual and society? Currently, television, the most powerful educative medium of our time, lies beyond the jurisdiction of the education committees of the Congress. So do telecommunications and many of the new technologies of tomorrow.

The Proper Role of Oversight

These are only a few examples of the ad hoc, fractionated character of contemporary policies affecting education. Even limiting our inquiry to issues within the jurisdiction of one specific congressional committee, for example, the House Subcommittee on Elementary, Secondary and Vocational Education, it would be fair to say that — for all its many and real successes — the legislative process, as now constituted, gives inadequate attention to legislative oversight. Too often the predominant interest in inspecting federal aid programs is to find out what's failed and especially who's at fault. Too often the in-

216

quiry is conducted in the spirit of prosecuting attorney, rather than in the spirit of a partner who also loses when things go wrong and who, out of self-interest, tries to learn how to make things go right.

Most oversight gives too little attention to questions of what it would take to get the job done right. Are the burdens and responsibilities imposed upon the implementing bureaucracies—federal, state, local, institutional—administratively feasible? Do they have the necessary personnel to do the job? Are their staffs properly trained for these new roles? Are state legislatures and school boards likely to come up with the matching resources necessary to make the federal mandates more than paper promises?

When Congress authorizes specific studies, will the executive be given the personnel ("slots") and the dollars to carry them out, or will they remain hollow gestures? And, after a reasonable period of trial and error, and a truly collaborative and constructive attitude on the part of the Congress, will the Congress have the courage to consolidate, terminate or otherwise replace defective programs?

OVERLOAD: TOO MUCH COMPLEXITY, TOO MUCH CHANGE

I am an unreconstructed champion of federal aid to education generally, and of categorical aid in particular. But sometimes a good thing can be carried too far.

According to the National Center for Education Statistics, there are now almost 1,100 federal education and training programs. Depending on how one counts them, the U.S. Department of Education manages at least 150. This amount of programming is counterproductive, for it faces educators and implementing bureaucracies with a degree of complexity and cumbersomeness that must ultimately be self-defeating. True, these programs can be "managed"—in the sense that the agencies can pass out their appropriations, on time, with complete compliance to managerial rulebooks. But so many programs —spreading dollars, expectations and dreams a mile wide and an inch deep—can never measure up to their potential. The human mind cannot really comprehend that degree of complexity. Of necessity, it focuses on a few central tasks and, in fact, defaults on a host of others. Everything can't be a priority.

How Much Change Is Too Much?

As the president of California's State Board of Education, Michael W. Kirst, a former Congressional and Office of Management and Budget (OMB) staffer as well as U.S. Office of Education Title I

217

manager, has written: "The question becomes how much change can an organization take, and continue to deal effectively with its clients?" This is a particularly cogent question, since the way we Americans seem to cope with change is by loading a new reform or innovation on to the old system, scarcely ever reducing the original burdens. Shall we have Minimum Competency Examinations, School Site Management, Individual Educational Plans? Yes! Let's add them to Team Teaching, Early Childhood Programs, PPBS, ZBB, Flexible Scheduling, Open Classrooms, Educational Television, etc. And then we mandate or promote new curricula for every new problem or emphasis of society: Intergroup Relations, Driver Education, Sex Education, Drug and Alcohol Education, Consumer Education, Metric Education, Environmental Education, Education for Death and Dying, Career Education, Ethnic Heritage, etc.

Overall, federal aid objectives are far too ambitious in scope for the amount of actual assistance they render to educational institutions. In a country as large as ours, we simply cannot hope to achieve large goals—such as educating all handicapped, educationally disadvantaged and non-English speaking children—as long as our resources are as widely dispersed and our personnel as thinly stretched as they are today.

Reassessment Based on Goodwill

A major reassessment and reevaluation of categorical programs is long overdue. However, that process must be based on goodwill. It should start from the assumption that the goal is not to reduce the amount of federal assistance but, if at all possible, to increase it in the interest of more effective learning. Increase it to the point that the federal contribution is large enough that one can legitimately measure what difference it makes in the achievement of school districts—and maybe even individual schools and students. Not like the present mode in which we appropriate $5 to 10 million in Washington and then expect "results" in the academic lives of 50 million Americans! (With Charles Beard, we need to remind ourselves constantly that "The truth of an institution is to be found not at its center but at its circumference"—where it touches the lives around it.)

One of the most important ways the Congress could help American education to meet the changes and challenges of the future would be to develop a *few* clearly articulated themes or roles of federal aid and then to pursue them consistently and in a financially responsible fashion over a period of years, not subject to the ups and downs of educational whim and fancy.

The Temporary Nature of Federal Aid

This last point deserves underscoring. School systems throughout the country still regard federal aid programs as "temporary." From Washington, they have come to expect only the unexpected: Perhaps a new administration will wish to de-fund an "old" program? Perhaps a new Congress will change its tastes in federal aid fashions? Even with forward funding, what assurance is there that the executive won't try to impound or rescind an appropriation? Since the Congress reauthorizes programs virtually every two or three years—and department guidelines and regulations lag one to three years behind the new law—educators and administrators scarcely know whom to believe. Their educational associations in Washington that faithfully report what the Congress has authorized and promised for the future? Or the executive rulemakers who, sometime in the future, will have much to say about the substance of those plans and promises?

It would be highly desirable for the Congress to consider a moratorium on reauthorization of major educational programs. We need to get away from the syndrome identified by a former U.S. Commissioner of Education in which the Congress routinely pulls programs up by the roots in order to see how they are growing. The Congress and federal agencies need to send clear signals to the people in the field, assuring them—as much as humanly possible—that at least certain central federal aid programs are here to stay. State and local educational leaders need to be encouraged to integrate federal aid into their own long-range planning and into their own comprehensive school finance programs.

In addition to reducing the rate of change and level of uncertainty, there are several other "surgeries" Congress could consider. For instance, the House Committee on Education and Labor has three or four different subcommittees, each dealing with some part of education or youth programs. It may be that by having these separate subcommittees, the expectation is created that each is supposed to produce more and more legislation, more and more change, and consequently, more and more uncertainty for those who have to live with the consequences of the subcommittees' actions. It seems fair to ask whether a single subcommittee might not help to give education legislation a more wholistic, comprehensive and constructive view than is now the case.

Too Many Policy Centers

Similarly, it is essential that the Congress reduce the number of policy-making centers that affect education. As of now, important policy changes affecting education emanate from eight or 10 "policy shops" and planning and budget offices in the Departments of Education, Health and Human Services, and Labor, not to mention OMB and the White House. Policy is too often made in the whirlpool of tradeoffs among these competing and overlapping centers. As far as I can detect, there is no evidence that this excessive number of policy advisors — incidentally, usually men and women of high competence and personal integrity — has in any way contributed to the making of *better* policy than was the case when there were fewer and, hence, more accountable policymakers and policy advisers. Indeed, I think George F. Will was at his insightful best when he observed of this general phenomenon:

> Washington has many "bright young men" who are not so young any more. They came hoping to be consequential, and just became irritable. Theirs is a distinctive Washington irritability that afflicts ambitious people when they face this fact: as the state expands, it employs more people, but fewer of them are consequential.

When the new Department of Education was proposed, OMB was predicting that the new department would reduce the number of staff officers dealing with education (legislation, management and budget, planning and evaluation, executive secretariat and public affairs) from 22 to four. The problem is, it just didn't happen. An incredible array of staff offices produced new veto powers in many different places instead of clearly enunciated "policy" in one.

Continuity in Leadership

In a closely related matter, the Congress should consider what can be done to provide greater continuity to the managerial leadership of federal education programs. U.S. commissioners and deputy commissioners of education, responsible for billions of the public's tax dollars and for our most ardent hopes for educational improvement, have passed through the U.S. Office of Education — and now the Department of Education — at a rate exceeding that of Latin American and African military coups. In the 20 years since John F. Kennedy was inaugurated President in 1961, we have seen 15 commissioners of education (including long-term acting commissioners) come and go and we now have our second secretary. This "revolving door" sort of leadership does not seem a proper way to administer the federal education enterprise.

POLICY AS IF PEOPLE DIDN'T MATTER

Former Representative William L. Hungate spoke eloquently of the national mood about government when he retired from the Congress in 1975:

> Politics has gone from the age of "Camelot" when all things were possible to the age of "Watergate" when all things are suspect.

Watergate has passed but, regrettably, our national mind-set continues to denigrate the public sector in general and education in particular.

The Congress, itself sorely criticized, exhibits too little respect—and extends too little support—to the men and women who manage educational programs. "Bureaucrats" at all levels of government and education are subjected to blanket condemnation as a class in what John Kenneth Galbraith has aptly remarked is "the only form of racism that is still respectable in the United States."

The Scorned Bureaucracy

Much of the appointed leadership of the federal education bureaucracy—itself of often undistinguished character and even lesser duration—is openly scornful of the bureaucracy, scarcely masking its suspicion and even its contempt. The civil servant's role in making federal aid effective is belittled and overlooked. Frequent and precipitous reorganization further unsettle personnel and their programs. Bureaucrats are severely chastised for mistakes, told that they are lazy, incompetent and unimaginative.

So, in many ways, subtle and overt, they are dissuaded from taking reasonable risks of professional judgment. Little discretion is allowed. All is increasingly reduced to elaborate routine designed to diffuse and share responsibility. Civil servants learn to spend their time securing multiple sign-offs to every conceivable memorandum—what are referred to, in their lingo, as C.Y.A.s, which means to cover your posterior.

All in all, with morale near rock bottom, the bureaucracy is reduced to a preoccupation with techniques of survival, rather than with the *purposes or effectiveness* of federal aid: "What the heck. Let's do it by their rulebook and who cares if the program works?" To Congress' fondly legislated hopes, the bureaucracy responds by administering despair.

221

A Lack of Professional Training

One point deserves elaboration: Few training opportunities are provided at any level of our educational system for staff to become truly competent in their tasks. Congress and the executive have jointly done away with most of the personnel training programs which offer the only hope that the people who manage our educational system can rise to meet their many complex challenges.

Overlooking the stark fact that most of the school principals, administrators and others now working in the system will be there for decades to come, we have defaulted on the opportunity to help those individuals become truly potent and effective in the conduct of their tasks. Ignoring an increasing body of research evidence linking the performance of school principals to the success of the instrumental process, we fail to help them gain competence. Similarly, state education agency personnel, student financial aid officers, school administrators, state and city school board members and a host of other critical educational personnel whose work deeply affects the learning process are all left to fend for themselves.

Despite declining school enrollments, the case for training educational personnel and leadership has never been more compelling. With fewer and fewer opportunities for change in career, and less and less room for advancement within education, morale will remain "in the pits"—unless educators feel themselves enabled "to make a difference" in their work, to gain the professional satisfactions that attracted them to education in the first place.

There are no easy solutions to the problems enumerated here. Leaders have to respect and care about the people they lead. Leaders have to recognize that no program—no matter how well designed—is self-executing. People make the difference. Therefore, investment in personnel training is at least as critical as support for the program itself. Congress should take the lead in assuring that implementing bureaucracies at every level of government and in every program are assisted to reach the highest possible standards of professional performance. Only in that way can the dreams of the past and the challenges of the future be merged into a credible present for all who care about the federal aid system in education.

Alfred North Whitehead said, "It is the business of the future to be dangerous." Present-day conditions are no less dangerous to the cause of federal aid and to the health of American education generally. They need to be addressed *now*.

Education Policy for the Future

This article originally appeared, in slightly different form, as the prepared statement of Samuel Halperin for the Foresight Hearings on Future Trends in Elementary and Secondary Education before the Subcommittee on Elementary, Secondary and Vocational Education of the Committee on Education and Labor, 96th Congress, First Session, held in Washington, D.C. on April 25 and 26, 1979. See pages 145 to 155 of the published hearings, which are available from the subcommittee.

EXTERNAL INFLUENCES ON INTERNAL ORGANIZATION

Robert S. Seckendorf

Many forces and factors will emerge in the coming years that will influence the nature of vocational education. The diversity of systems in the nation will require states to examine individually their program goals and organization. Such factors as changing population, makeup of the labor force, occupational structure, financial conditions, economic development and technology can be examined in relation to each state's program. These factors may affect where and why vocational education will exist or whether vocational education will exist at all in the future.

Concern over the very existence of vocational education has been debated for as long as it has been a part of the public education systems of the nation. Its role has been considered endlessly by educators, industry, organized labor, economists, elected officials and taxpayers since it was first included in the general school structure. The arguments, challenges, support and denigration of vocational education have been documented in speeches, publications, studies, research undertakings, evaluations and congressional hearings. Its purposes have been examined. Its usefulness and effectiveness have been researched.

Those with an interest in vocational education have never completely agreed about its necessity, its purpose or even its target clients. After almost three-quarters of a century of publicly supported vocational education, even the practitioners within the field do not speak with one voice. As in so many publicly supported enterprises, separate and independent empires are built. Turf must be protected and defended. Billions of public dollars have been invested and still questions continue to be raised. What form should vocational education take? Is it part of a larger education system? Is it an education program at all? Or is it a part of the nation's social welfare system? Can public vocational education's role be defined once and for all? Can its structure and organization be solidified and stabilized?

CURRENT ORGANIZATION AND STRUCTURE

There is not, nor conceivably should there be, a single system of public vocational education, consistent from state to state.

What then must be considered with respect to the future of vocational education? If there is a future for public vocational education it needs to be established within the context of the total publicly supported education system. At the same time, it must be recognized that preparation for employment exists in many other forms. On-the-job training, organized apprenticeships, industry-based training programs, efforts under the Comprehensive Employment and Training Act (CETA), the military and even self-teaching are other structures that prepare people for productive employment. Some of these systems came into being long before publicly supported vocational education and will continue to function usefully for some time to come.

Every state and territory provides vocational education for its youth and adults. The structure, organization and extensiveness vary as does the impact on the respective business and industry communities for which it provides workers.

States Are Not Similar

The commonalities among the states and territories are few. They are found primarily in somewhat similar objectives and in the occupational classifications of programs. Beyond that, the differences are most evident.

There are 10 different state government structures, five different types of state administrative agencies with varying responsibilities for vocational education and five different levels of state authority over institutions that provide vocational education programs. In addition, at the local level there are six types of institutions, 13 kinds of program administrative structures and four different types of single and multi-district services. Beyond these general characteristics of local vocational programs, there exist in systems that are classified as regional in nature, eight types of agencies, five kinds of local boards and six different arrangements for fiscal responsibility.

One might conclude from this description that nationally, vocational education is a disorganized program without any overall system. On the other hand, these are descriptions aggregated from what occurs in the states and territories. It is probably more important to be concerned with the extent of consistency within states themselves, rather than the fact that a single system does not exist nationwide.

However, even within states, governance and organization are not consistent with respect to the various institutions and level of programs operated by local agencies. The structure of vocational education in states range from the few that have a single state board responsible for all education to those with four separate boards and state agencies responsible for various segments of the program. At the local level, the range of institutions is diverse and numerous. In many cases, two or three different kinds of institutions compete for the same clientele.

FUNCTIONS OF VOCATIONAL EDUCATION

The declarations of purpose contained in the Vocational Education Act of 1963 espoused the idea that public vocational education should be able to prepare all people for all kinds of occupations. No longer would vocational education be confined to a few narrow occupational classes. To an extent, this broad statement opened the door to significant criticism of vocational education for not being responsive to *all* the employment requirements of the nation's businesses and industries or to *all* the needs of a constantly changing labor force.

Skill Training and General Education

In any attempt to clearly justify vocational education as an education program, that portion of preparation for employment that can be provided institutionally needs to be defined. However, in addition to specific skill training, other aspects of education are important for entering the labor market. An educated work force must function not only within the specifics of a job, but must also be able to move easily from one level of work responsibility to another, to adapt to increasing knowledge requirements of the work place and to function well as citizens and members of the community. To be economically self-sufficient requires much more than a vocational education. However, preparation for employment should be a major component in assisting each person to achieve economic well-being.

Separation of vocational education from general education is not a viable alternative for most persons entering the labor force. There are points in time, for some individuals, when vocational education is considered a separate element in preparation to entering the labor market. Such a program, isolated from academic or supporting elements, could be specific skill training for adults who are unemployed or seeking new or upgraded skills in order to remain in the labor market. In such cases, the declaration of purpose in the Vocational Education Act of 1963 is more applicable than when considered for those who have not yet left school.

A Distinction Between Functions

Vocational education, within the context of an educational program, should be an available resource in dealing with constantly changing societal requirements. In other words, a distinction exists between the functions of vocational education. The measure of its effectiveness must be distinguishable according to the function it is performing at any single point in time, or where it is serving specific groups of people or purposes. Vocational education can exist as one component of an educational program with goals compatible with those of the larger system. It can also take responsibility separately and independently to meet clearly identified social and economic outcomes.

Drawing a distinction between functions of vocational education does not imply that education in general does not have broad social goals, but rather that vocational education's broad goals are those of the larger education system. In addition, vocational education can be responsive to conditions outside the generally accepted responsibilities of education. The implications are particularly significant with respect to the organization and institutional structure of vocational education.

FORCES AT WORK ON VOCATIONAL EDUCATION

During its long history, vocational education has been moved in one direction or another by many forces and factors. Initially, it was influenced by individuals who saw a need for young people to be prepared to enter the labor market and believed that good training offered the best chances for success. Their early debates helped establish a foundation and direction for vocational education and much of this emphasis has been retained throughout the years.

Since 1917, the federal presence has been felt in vocational education and its influence has ranged from significant to minimal. In more recent years, particularly since 1963, the effect has probably been greater than in all of the previous 45 years. Federal legislation and federal dollars have influenced the structure of vocational education and, in many ways, the clientele to be served.

Economic and Social Problems

At the same time, federal legislation itself has been influenced by a number of forces or episodes of the past 15 years. Primary among these were economic factors, such as high rates of unemployment, first among mid-career workers and then, in an overwhelming way, the unemployment of youth. An awareness of the number of educationally disadvantaged persons increased to the point where it became a significant force in directing the efforts of vocational education.

The belief was that preparation for employment was a solution to the problems of undereducated individuals. Social changes and awareness of the problems of special groups, such as handicapped persons and women, created adjustments and new initiatives in vocational education.

In the past the influences and resulting changes came about as a reaction to conditions or circumstances that reached a point of high impact on the economy, the social system and on public education. Yet these problems, for which solutions had to be found, did not develop so rapidly that they could not have been anticipated. Policymakers were aware of the issues, but in one way or another the systems were slow to react to needs as they developed. Instead, when a problem became an absolute pressure, then action was taken to develop solutions.

Factors to Consider

In terms of specific influences on the future of vocational education, a number of factors may be considered. In fact, if vocational education is to be responsive to the requirements of the labor force and business and industry in the period ahead, it is essential that the most predictable factors be identified and considered early by policy-makers. However, it must be remembered that vocational education is but one of many resources available for helping to resolve current and future problems.

For example, vocational education itself cannot solve the youth unemployment problem of today or the possible unemployment problems that older workers will face in the future as jobs require more knowledge than manipulative skill. The cause of youth unemployment is not totally the lack of vocational education. The large number of young persons now entering the labor market, college graduates taking jobs for which their education was not required and the increasing number of illegal aliens working at low-level jobs all contribute to the competitiveness for jobs once taken by young people just out of high school.

While there are many causes related to youth unemployment, a case also can be made that vocational education can be a positive influence on reducing youth unemployment or at least assisting in preparing high school age persons to meet competition from other workers.

Technology

Technological change relating to types of occupations and the levels of skill and knowledge required will affect the future of vocational education in several ways. Increases in the complexity of occupations will increase the emphasis on vocational education beyond the high school level and lessen the emphasis at the secondary level of specific skill training. However, technological change's greatest influence will be on the *content* of programs provided, rather than on the way vocational education is organized.

Federal vs. State Role

Federal policy, as reflected in legislation, has addressed major concerns about the delivery of vocational education in terms of people and their needs for occupational preparation. It has set priorities in a manner that assumed specific population categories were served. But it has not tampered with the way states and localities deliver vocational education. Perhaps it was an oversight or perhaps it was intentional. The laws themselves do not prevent any major change in system structure.

One critical issue is whether federal policy and future legislation should tinker with what is considered a function of the states. The way future federal policy is enunciated could have a decided effect on the states, if the past is any reflection of the future.

In view of Congress's considerable influence, it would seem that the way vocational education is structured and organized in the period ahead should take into consideration other factors in addition to the needs of people for occupational training. If the needs of the business and industrial community, the changing technology, the changing nature of employment patterns and the shifts in the structure of the population are considered, the end result could be a more viable and improved system for the delivery of vocational education.

Influence from Outside the Field

The future organization of vocational education may not be determined by the wishes of the diverse entities that exist within the education establishment. Vocational education is an education program first, but its role within the social context of serving people must be considered. Economic, social and demographic changes may all affect how vocational education will be organized and structured in the future. More specifically, even its role as an educational program may be based on its ability to help solve problems outside the education structure.

To help do this policy-makers in vocational education will need the expertise of individuals from other fields. An understanding of emerging consequences of economic policy, taxing policies, social policies and political realities must be used to help shape the future functions of vocational education.

Fairly reliable data and projections exist to demonstrate how interventions external to the education system will create change in the period ahead. These forces illustrate how specific changes over the next several years will need to be considered by policy-makers in order to establish clearly the role and nature of vocational education.

Changing Populations

Population change will be one critical factor. The changing population, in terms of age groups and the movement of people from one part of the country to another, influence the extent of possible enrollments at the several levels of a delivery system for vocational education.

The beginning of a significant decline in the youth population has already begun. It will continue at least through 1990. Any future impact of large numbers of high school age persons on the labor market will not be felt until after the year 2000.

Traditionally, vocational education has, for the most part, been targeted upon the 15-to-18-age group, with varying attention paid to employed workers over the age of 25. Only in the past 10 to 15 years has significant emphasis been placed on the 19-to-24-age group. One of the prime target age groups for vocational education in the future will be those persons between the ages of 25 and 49. This group will represent the largest age group in the labor force and will face constant changes in job market skills. People in this age group will need continuous training and retraining. At the same time there will be fewer young workers to compete for jobs and therefore in need of training.

Women will stay in the labor force for longer periods of time. There will be less early exiting among women workers to marry and raise families. This condition will create a need to provide opportunities for advancement and promotion, as women seek upward mobility and increased incomes.

With a declining younger population, unemployment among youth may get a little better although it still may be a problem in the immediate period ahead. As previously mentioned, with more women and older workers in the market place, jobs that once were the territory for high school completers may be taken by women. In addition, college completers who cannot find jobs that require a college education will also be competing with high school graduates for limited jobs.

Minority youth unemployment may continue to be a significant problem. Even though this group will decline numerically, they will represent a larger proportion of new entrants into the labor market.

Mobility of the population is not as much a national problem for vocational education as it is a state or local condition. However, in terms of some policy areas it should be considered. No longer is mobility the exclusive ritual of retired persons moving from population centers in the northeast to the warmth of the south and southwest. Young singles and young families also are following the sun, perhaps because some industries are moving and so are the jobs.

Movement from major population centers to more rural settings is another emerging trend. In this case people are moving to areas that lie beyond the accepted definition of suburbs. Young people are in the group leaving the cities. Rather than commuting long distances back to city jobs they are finding work or are opening businesses themselves in rural areas. This group seems to be searching for a different life style, certainly not a higher income.

Relating Trends to Planning

From the point of view of vocational education, the trends in employment patterns could be significant in determining the kinds of programs offered by local agencies and planning at the state level. With respect to the nation's vocational education program as a whole, future concerns may need to be given to the relationship among levels of programs and the clientele for whom vocational education would be useful. Skill levels of new jobs and the changing nature of jobs may require increased attention to those already in the labor market whose skills will have to be retooled to maintain their employment, rather than preparing individuals for immediate entrance into the market place.

Vocational education planners and policy-makers may need to examine subtle changes in job requirements, education levels of the labor force and the distribution of jobs among the occupational classifications. In this respect, short-term projections will probably be more useful than long-range guesses. Program deliverers will need to create an ability to change and redirect efforts on short time lines in order to maintain a viable public delivery system.

AVAILABLE FINANCIAL RESOURCES

Another key issue for the future will be how much vocational education will cost and who will pay for it. Ultimate decisions will be concerned with the cost of education in relation to how well it can meet the needs of people and the labor market.

Secondary Enrollments Should Decline

The extent of available public financial resources may have a decided effect on future enrollments, particularly if the rate of inflation continues and possible sources of additional public tax funds have limitations placed upon them. Under the financial pressures that school districts find themselves, enrollments at the secondary level may decline, if for no other reason than the inflationary costs can be absorbed by educating fewer students. It may be possible for school districts and states to hold actual dollar expenses level merely by permitting vocational education enrollments to decline at the same rate as the overall high school population.

But Postsecondary May Increase

At the same time, it is entirely possible that enrollments at the postsecondary level will increase, despite the projected decrease in the number of persons in the age group 19 to 21, since the average age of students in postsecondary institutions is well beyond age 21. Available data indicate there will be a decided increase in the number of new entrants into the work force with one or more years of education beyond high school.

In addition, as the knowledge level requirements of jobs increase, added emphasis will be placed on the need to provide postsecondary vocational education for persons entering the work force.

Adult Level Funding is Limited

Enrollments at the adult level probably have more conditions and possibilities associated with future financing than either of the other two levels. The current role of adult vocational education emphasizes upgrading and retraining for persons already employed. It is not unusual for these programs to be supported with limited public money, including federal funds; however, many educational agencies require adult vocational education to operate on a self-sustaining basis.

The portion of the enrollment at the adult level that targets on preparatory vocational education usually utilizes federal funds and in some cases state and local funds. This money is limited and certainly not sufficient to meet the needs of the target group. Other federal programs, particularly CETA, are involved in the preparation of adults for entrance into new jobs, but most of these programs are identified with educationally or economically disadvantaged persons and may not reach other adults in need of training for new jobs.

Fund Shifts Not Likely

The possibility of local educational agencies shifting the savings developed from declines in secondary school enrollments over to adult programs is not very likely. If it happens at all, it will happen in the area of preparatory programs, as opposed to supplementary activities, where a large portion of the costs can be borne by employed adults seeking increased skills and knowledge to maintain their jobs.

At the same time, increased knowledge requirements of jobs could have the effect of pushing older workers out of their jobs, to be replaced by better educated young workers, particularly those with one or more years of college. If this occurs, there will be a greater pool of adults seeking retraining as well as increasing current skills in order to retain jobs. Vocational education systems will need to be able to serve this potential growth area. Yet, considering the economic conditions of the educational agencies and the probable continuation of special programs operated outside public vocational education systems, significant increases in enrollment of adults will not occur in public vocational education without a dramatic shift in the utilization of federal dollar resources.

If vocational education were to operate as a national system, with one government structure operating and financing a total effort, savings occurring because of decline at one level could be available to finance increases at another level. With the kind of non-system that exists, with the diversity of governance and administrative structures in place and with the many different systems for financing vocational education, it is virtually impossible to assume that funds can be shifted from one element to another. To a greater extent such an action can be taken with respect to federal funds for vocational education and to some degree, a shift can be made with state funds.

The real difficulty comes at the local level where programs operate and are governed by a multitude of arrangements and where the greatest differences exist for raising public money for the support of all education programs. The problem is even more complex under the present system of financing where local vocational education agencies pay 55 percent of the cost.

CONSEQUENCES OF CHANGE

Vocational education in the period ahead will be subject to change. The forces and factors that will influence vocational education in the future primarily will be external to the program itself. The vocational education community needs to recognize and understand both the changes that will occur and how they will affect the program. Some social and economic factors will be national in scope, while others will have greater influence within states, or in some localities, may not be factors at all.

The major concern for policy-makers in particular is that vocational education cannot stand still. It must continue to look ahead. The consequences of a changing environment will, to a great extent, determine the future of a publicly supported, publicly operated program.

Vocational education will need to depend on its ability to establish itself as an educational program first. Its role must be that of providing opportunities for people to prepare for entrance into employment. Once established as an education program, vocational education needs to be able to respond to pressing social needs, particularly as they change. Priorities for special emphasis will not be fixed or rigid. Youth unemployment and the needs of women might be imperatives today, but the consequences of economic and technological influences in the future may result in other imperatives, such as structural unemployment of older workers whose skills will no longer be compatible with labor market requirements. Although some of the influences are not easily predictable, vocational education programs should consider the possibilities of these influences and develop the ability to react quickly.

The issues, forces and factors are real and the consequences will be significant. To overlook them, or to believe they will not occur, can lead to the loss of an educational program that has had a distinguished record of accomplishment, but which has been criticized, primarily for holding on to the past and for viewing the future as no more than the present.

SECTION VII

CREATING A FRAMEWORK FOR HUMAN RESOURCE DEVELOPMENT

There are inherent dilemmas in any effort to fashion a framework for human resource development. First, human resource development policy has never been regarded as a serious concern warranting its expression as a populist movement. On the contrary, it has needed the intervention of interested groups to win even modest attention from political leaders. Winning even more of this attention is a main argument of Merle Strong.

Second, the evidence that illuminates the problems of human resource utilization is not keyed to specific directions of policy development. Despite goals, for example, for the achievement of both equity and excellence, the appropriate policies for the achievement of both cannot be easily matched with the goals. Their necessity is argued by William Conroy. He warns us that how these choices are made will increasingly stratify society or it will begin to reduce the stratification.

Third, the multiplicity of government levels and agencies is an expression of the ideal of free choice, which we value more highly than the neatness and the efficiency that accompanies the dream of single unified human resource policy. The view expressed by Sar Levitan describes much of the present reality. Future prospects are developed by each of the authors.

A POLICY FOR HUMAN RESOURCE DEVELOPMENT

Merle E. Strong

As the United States enters the 1980s the country seems beset by as grave a combination of domestic and foreign ills as troubled the country in the years prior to the Second World War. The nation is faced with an insecure economy, problems of simultaneous inflation and recession and significant unemployment. Productivity is reduced, or at best, making only slight increases in output per hour of all persons in the labor market. Many national companies are suffering severe economic losses and workers are being laid off. We have a balance-of-payments deficit that can be blamed only partly on the energy crisis and large crude oil imports. Many products are being imported from other countries that either have a source of relatively cheap manpower, or else are modern, technologically advanced industries (particularly in the manufacture of automobiles, optics and electronics) using highly automated processes and technically trained, sophisticated workers.

The nation seems unable to compete economically on a level commensurate with past ability, current levels of product quality or assumptions of superiority. This is distressing when compared to our impressive economic progress in the past several decades.

While many citizens enjoy a standard of living never before in their grasp, national economic conditions are less than satisfactory to many others. Poverty has not been eliminated, welfare budgets are high, various segments of the population are alienated from becoming productive members of the work force, the middle class continues to flee the central cities, government services are being cut back and the list goes on and on. As always, social problems become exacerbated in periods of economic difficulty.

The time is ripe for a reevaluation of our economic, social and human development goals to meet these present challenges and to provide a blueprint for the future. Our nation needs consistent policies formulated and carried out by the highest levels of government. At the moment our policies are either incoherent, conflicting or inadequate to the task. The days of undirected growth are over; now we must plan and manage more efficiently than before, keeping in mind that as the times change so must the country's goals and policies.

CHANGING NEEDS OF THE WORK FORCE

Policy considerations for human resource development need to be compatible both with the changing characteristics of the work force, which includes youth, women, minorities, older workers and immigrants, as well as with the changing nature of occupations.

Our civilian labor force has grown substantially. In 1968, according to the U.S. Department of Labor figures, there were fewer than 79 million persons in the civilian labor force. In 1978, there were over 100 million. The participation rate of women reached 51 percent in 1980—an increase from 41.6 percent in 1968. Men participate at about 80 percent.

Policy in human resource development must also reflect the changing occupational mix. White-collar workers now make up approximately 50 percent of the work force. This includes professional, technical, managerial, administrative, sales and clerical workers. During the past several decades the nation experienced an increasing demand for persons with technical skills and knowledge, whereas previously, many more jobs existed that did not require a high level of training.

In any attempt to address human resource development policy, it seems appropriate to identify the important areas upon which an impact could be made.

Unemployment

One of the most important problems is unemployment. Heading the list of questions is whether policy should call for full or nearly full employment. Can we continue to be an international leader if one part of the population must support an increasing percentage of unemployed persons? We have grown accustomed to a high standard of living, but can we maintain it? If we opt for full employment, how can it be accomplished? Can the private sector of the economy be stimulated to provide the jobs required—and productive jobs that will add to the nation's economy — or will we end up with "make-work" jobs, merely another form of welfare?

On the other hand, if we decide that full employment is unrealistic, or should not be our policy, another whole series of questions is raised about who should be in the work force. Some present federal incentives seem contrary to a limited work force strategy, although a policy of full employment currently does not exist. The desire to provide everyone a chance for employment regardless of sex, race, citizenship, age, geographic location, educational level or handicap may not be the most cost-effective approach unless full employment is desired or reached.

At the same time, attention needs to be continually focused on the problems of various minority groups, which suffer from higher-than-normal unemployment rates and congregation at the lower end of the spectrum of employment opportunities. Policy is necessary to assure every effort is made to qualify minorities for jobs and to provide equal opportunity in hiring and advancement.

Youth Unemployment

Youth unemployment is a great national concern because social problems have occurred as a consequence of youth being unoccupied. Part of the problem is the high dropout rate from high school. While statistics are not entirely reliable, we know that at least 20 to 25 percent of our high school age youth are not in school.

Should there be a more concerted effort made to keep this group in school? Since a high school diploma represents a basic credential for success in our society, what efforts should be made to help youth achieve this minimal goal? Could curriculum modifications make education more relevant? Initiatives such as work-study programs in the private sector have little possibility of success as long as workers outnumber the jobs available. What can be done about an already flooded labor market and those unemployed youth?

Any policy must consider the welfare of individuals in addition to the goal of an optimally effective work force. The price of failure with youth apparently is a higher rate of juvenile delinquency, alienation from work and society and increasing crime rates. These are human costs our society can ill afford.

Women

Women have presented a special case in the past decade. Not only are more women working outside the home, but they are entering and advancing in occupations traditionally confined in peacetime to men.

Many women are competing with minorities and youth by entering at the lower end of the job continuum. Any future policy must recognize that women make up a sizeable percentage of the work force; therefore, training, education and experience in all occupations must be provided for women if they are to compete on an equal basis.

Immigration

Immigration will bring new problems to education as well as to the work force. Immediate problems of the immigrants are apparent, and history suggests their problems will persist at least through one additional generation. Most notable at this time are the Cubans, Haitians, Mexicans, Vietnamese and other Southeast Asians. Some have come for better opportunities while others were forced from their homelands.

Despite unemployment problems for our own citizens, we have traditionally welcomed large numbers of aliens to work primarily in agriculture or other jobs that are difficult or impossible to fill with our own citizens. As these immigrant people and their children become exposed to our culture and a higher standard of living, their rising expectations will bring new challenges of assimilation for both our educational systems and work force. Low-level jobs that immigrants once filled may then again beg for candidates.

Handicapped Persons

Another category of individuals federal and state governments have addressed extensively in the past decade is the handicapped. Since work is central to the lives of most people for personal satisfaction and feelings of worth, handicapped individuals should continue to have an opportunity to participate in the labor force and economy. Future policies may be forced to address the question of what investment should be made and under what conditions training will be provided for handicapped persons.

The Aged

Longevity of persons in the work force will also be an important consideration. Should policies encourage early retirement through regulations established by employers in the private sector? Should the government establish and implement policy in the public and private sectors? Should persons be expected or allowed to remain in the work force to an older age than is presently the case? With increasing life spans and an awareness of the potential contributions of the older worker's experience and intellect, it seems that we are losing valuable human resources by eliminating this growing percentage of individuals from the work force.

Another question to be addressed is the willingness of the younger population to support the elderly as the age ratio continues to increase. Obviously, our social security system will have to be evaluated continually for its ability to provide financial aid consistent with the needs of the retired population.

Military

The military services are not only one of the bigger users of manpower but also play an important role in the development of human resources. Questions arise about the ideal size of the military forces, their effectiveness, the manner of obtaining their manpower and the relationship between military and civilian human development efforts. How do we maximize the effectiveness of our human resources potential and best provide benefits to individuals who move from one system to the other?

Productivity

At the present time the nation's productivity is not only slowing down but actually losing ground in some sectors. At one time this country was the international leader in technology in almost every field. That picture is no longer clear. Whole industries have lost out in their ability to compete. Obviously, the field of international trade and finance is complicated; however, one does not have to be too economically sophisticated to realize that if we keep importing more and more finished products requiring a high degree of technology while at the same time suffering unemployment, severe economic problems resulting from imbalance in trade will continue to plague us.

The question of how to increase productivity involves a mix of technology, capital and labor. In this country, the most important of these is labor. Improvement dictates a more highly skilled work force than presently exists. We will either compete with foreign manufacturers or suffer more serious economic problems in the future.

Energy

Economic independence for America requires the development of alternative energy sources. Development of such resources must be guided by a policy that interrelates with policies in a number of other areas, including environmental concerns, finance and taxation. Many workers will be needed with new skills and knowledge.

Environment

Although industrialization and new technology have made possible a more comfortable and higher standard of living for Americans, they have simultaneously played havoc wtih our environment. Great strides have been made in cleaning up our streams, lakes and air, but much more needs to be done. The question is, at what point do the costs of this clean-up become too high? Some industries have already been forced to close down or move. Industrial expansion has been curtailed, for example, in the nuclear energy field. What compromises must be made with the environment in order to have an optimum economy while at the same time protecting natural resources for future generations?

Tax Structure

Consideration of the tax structure in our country leads to the question of who should pay the bills for the types of services we have come to expect from government at the various levels. What share of this burden should business and industry pay? What share should be paid by individuals and how progressive should the taxing schemes be? The level of taxes and the methods through which they are assessed will have profound effects on investments, on the size and nature of the work force needed and on all consumers.

A HUMAN RESOURCES DEVELOPMENT SYSTEM

It has become apparent that this nation does not have a clearly defined human resources development policy. The development of such a policy would be a complex undertaking because of the many varied areas that must be addressed and made responsive to each other. The need for a policy is clear, however, and its development and implementation will provide the challenge for creative and innovative planning for the future.

In the American political system, the development of public policy is ideally the responsibility of all citizens. To a great extent, this responsibility is carried out through elected representatives. In theory, at least, national policy-making is a function of the Congress, which passes all legislation. In actuality, however, the executive branch of the government gets involved extensively in the recommendations and drafting of many bills, along with lobbying efforts to pressure passage of legislation. In addition, departments in the executive branch and independent and regulatory agencies establish rules and regulations designed to interpret and implement legislation passed by

Congress. Rules and regulations are the work of attorneys and professionals in specific fields and it is by this process that much public policy is promulgated.

In addition to the respective departments involved in policy-making, the Office of Management and Budget, an arm of the White House, plays a major role in developing the national budget and the determination of proposed allocations of public funds. The judicial branch has played an increasingly important role through decisions rendered by the federal courts. Decisions are as binding as any law and have far-reaching implications for human resource development and utilization.

As we look at how policy is developed, questions arise about the influences on policy-making and the vehicles through which effective communication takes place. Congressional representatives obviously communicate with constituencies from their home districts, but what is the process by which concerns and possible solutions find their way into policy development?

Campbell (1962), developed a flow chart of policy formulation in education that has served the author well over a number of years in his attempt to understand policy-making. This model (Figure 1)

FIGURE 1
A FLOW CHART ON POLICY FORMATION IN EDUCATION

I Basic Forces	II Antecedent Movements	III Political Action	IV Formal Enactment
Social, economic, political, & technological forces, usually national & worldwide in scope	Usually national in scope such as the National Manpower Commission, Rockefeller Bros., Studies, Conant Studies, etc.	By organizations usually interrelated at local, state & national levels such as U.S. Chamber of Commerce, AFL-CIO, and NEA	May be at local, state, and national levels; and through legislative, judicial and executive agencies

SOURCE: *Introduction to Educational Administration,* Second Edition. By Roald F. Campbell, et. al. Boston: Allyn and Bacon, Inc. 1962.

seems to be just as appropriate to address the larger question of human resources development or a variety of other challenges.

Campbell, in speaking about the model, said:

> We note that educational policy has its genesis in basic social change; its generation in antecedent movements, its promotion by educators and by citizens in and out of government; and its formulation in legal expressions by local, state, or national government (Campbell, p. 246).

Since basic social changes and the antecedent movements are usually nationwide, if not international in scope, many decisions on policy happen at the federal level. The challenge then becomes one of how individuals can influence this process.

Campbell suggested that educators can no longer be concerned chiefly with the formal, legal expressions of policy, but must give more attention to political action and to antecedent movements.

Figure 2 illustrates some of the basic forces, antecedent movements, political action groups and lobbying forces that undoubtedly will be influential in forthcoming human resource development policies, particularly as they affect educational programs and initiatives below the baccalaureate level. Policy development in any area is a continuous process with the basic forces changing over time and antecedent movements shifting in response to the magnitude and direction of the basic forces. Furthermore, various combinations of political action groups produce pressure for policy in the form of legislation, court decisions, and executive branch regulations, orders and pronouncements.

Human resource developers need to be involved at all stages of the Campbell model. Involvement at the Formal Enactment Stage is too late in most cases. Considering the list of Basic Forces in Figure 2, it appears that vocational and technical educators and other human resource developers should become involved extensively in the study and interpretation of these forces to help determine their meaning for policy development. For example, what are the implications of the women's movement for vocational and technical education? What are the implications of the mass immigration of Cubans into our economy? What kinds of educational and training needs will they present to our systems? Questions such as these can be asked about all of the items included in the list of Basic Forces.

It is important for vocational educators and other human resource developers to be involved in analysis of the Basic Forces so they may influence what happens under the category of Antecedent Movements.

FIGURE 2
A FLOW CHART ON POLICY FORMATION IN EDUCATION

I Basic Forces	II Antecedent Movements	III Political Action	IV Formal Enactment
See-saw of Detente—Cold War with Russia	Carnegie Report: *Giving Youth a Better Chance.*	American Vocational Association	CETA
Revolution in Iran	NIE-Evaluation of Voc. Ed. mandated by 1976 Amendments to Vocational Education Act of 1963.	AACJC	Vocational Education Amendments
Unsettled Situation in Near East		NEA	
Russia in Afghanistan		Chief State School Administrators	Youth Employment Act 1980 (Title I)
Energy Crisis	*Youth Employment and Public Policy.* By Anderson and Sawhill—The American Assembly 1980.	National School Builders Association	Registration of 18-19 Year Olds
Balance of Payment Problem		AFL-CIO and other organized labor groups	Youth Education and Training Program (Title II) 1980
High Inflation Rate		Chamber of Commerce	
High Unemployment and High Youth Unemployment		Independent Pressure groups	
Concern for Equal Rights Minorities and Women		State and Federal Educational Agencies	
Concern for Slow Rate of Productivity and Growth			
Formalization of Trade-Reduced Tariffs			

247

This is where the rhetoric develops that influences public opinion, both at the grass-roots level and at the level of the elected and appointed officials who actually develop policy. Public opinion is expressed by the media, which in turn continues to arouse public opinion. These factors exert pressure on professional leaders and politicians to make changes.

It is at this stage that task forces, study committees or other organized efforts are initiated to address problems either identified by professionals associated with the particular problems or by popular citizen demand. Such Antecedent Movements as those identified in Figure 2 may come about as a result of initiatives sponsored by either the government or the private sector, especially foundations. Foundations have had and will continue to have great influence on human resource development policy due to their ability to finance commissions and studies and to generate activities such as conferences and think-tanks directed at particular issues. With their resources, they not only can attract adequate staff for research, publications and activities, but can publicize and receive extensive attention for these issues.

The efforts of foundations in educational policy-making have to be viewed as highly constructive. There is some risk, however, that the selected individuals who make up the policy-recommending groups may be biased because of their particular professional roles, backgrounds, frames of reference or lack of knowledge. Their reports then tend to reflect the biases of foundations or elite groups and are not necessarily reflective of real situations. The recent Carnegie report, *Giving Youth a Better Chance* (1979) is an example of this sort of policy-influencing foundation product.

> The Carnegie Corporation of New York consists of a small group of individuals of similar background who have attained a special privileged position at the helm of a large philanthropic trust, thus allowing them to exert influence and exercise power by awarding grants based upon unknown criteria and vested interests (Weischadle, 1977).

Other foundations having a major educational focus and impact are Ford, Kettering, Danforth, Rockefeller, Dana, Russel Sage, Sloan and Markle. These foundations exert an independent, and perhaps at times, a biased view not necessarily representative of opinions of the citizenry or of practitioners.

Governmental and public policy agencies can be cited to represent this same type of phenomenon. The Mondale Task Force on Youth

Employment was a governmental study group, as was the Annual Conference on the Family, which was established by the White House. Independent organizations, which are sometimes partially government funded and partially privately funded, are also established for the expressed purposes of drafting laws, pressuring existing lobbying organizations, influencing legislators, providing in-service or educational programs for various particular public segments, and in seeking and funding potential law suits to reinforce their viewpoint in decisions rendered on a variety of human resource issues.

It is at the Political Action stage of Campbell's model that larger numbers of human resource developers tend to become involved through organized groups. The effectiveness of any group in the support of a policy idea is dependent not only on the quality of the idea, but on the degree of acceptance and support of the idea among its membership. Obviously, it is very difficult for the leadership of any organization to promote a policy for which there is either a strong difference of opinion among the members of the organization or general disinterest.

Optimum effectiveness of a group would also seem somewhat dependent upon the ability of the group's leaders to set forth policy ideas and support them, rather than merely reacting to proposals of others. It also seems highly desirable to involve—in the early stages of development—all other groups that may be affected by the policy in order to form coalitions of support.

The literature on this topic contains many suggestions about how one can be most influential with members of the Congress. Lawmakers must know how their constituencies feel about a proposal and must decide what they believe the consequences of the particular enactment would be for their geographical area as well as for the nation. Communicating with elected representatives directly is one way to attempt to influence policy. Other ways are through organizations one belongs to and through opinion leaders who have direct access to policy-makers, including the elected representatives, congressional staff members and members of the executive branch.

AN AGENDA FOR ACTION

While the earlier part of this discussion examined human resources development in a generic sense, the remainder includes recommendations addressed more specifically to vocational and manpower educators.

National policies are not clear in many areas at the present. Needless to say, policies relating to the work force are quite dependent on and intertwined with broader national policies. That vocational and other manpower educators must become statesmen in a larger arena of policy-making than has been the practice in the past would seem to be a logical imperative. The oversimplified view that effective communication with national legislators in their home districts will be all that is necessary, important as that may be, is simply naive. Policy is influenced in so many other ways and by so many organized groups.

Recommendations for Action by Vocational Educators:

Vocational educators should do all in their power to have the Department of Education staffed with the most qualified people in the nation to provide leadership in the policy-making and implementation of vocational education.

The new department provides an opportunity and a challenge. It will be only through great statesmanship that the department will gain the respect and recognition it must have to provide leadership to the nation's human resource development. Within this department, the assistant secretary for vocational and adult education must acquire a high level of stature if vocational education is to become an important part of the total educational system. Likewise, the other administrators and staff must be chosen from among the best in the nation if they are to effectively develop and implement policy.

A strong, coordinative effort must be made by all federal agencies involved in human resource development.

In the past, policy relating to human resources has been fragmented among the various federal agencies. Not only is there a lack of communication among agencies involved, but at times, competition exists. The Department of Education should have a mission in human resources policy development that is much broader than the mission under the former Office of Education.

Vocational educators should find means to become involved, particularly with persons of other disciplines, in a continuing analysis of "social events" (as described in the model) that affect human resource development.

Such organizations as the American Vocational Association and the American Association of Junior and Community Colleges should join forces in encouraging participation of their memberships and staff in this endeavor. Such efforts could influence the nature of the resulting antecedent movements, which in turn lead to policy development.

Vocational educators should become involved in formulation and implementation of policy studies (Campbell's Antecedent Movements).

Numerous public policy groups exist both at the national level and at the state level. Vocational educators should be involved in making recommendations, particularly through their professional organizations, for studies and other activities that may serve as the antecedents to policy development. Too often we appear to be sitting on the outside of studies and other activities that have far-reaching implications for us and the youth and adults we serve. Foundations have been a source of funding for policy studies in the past and undoubtedly offer great potential for the future. Vocational educators should become involved in these studies.

Vocational educators working with the American Vocational Association and other formal groups should seek to provide more effective communication with both elected and appointed officials at federal, state and local levels at the formal enactment stage of policy development.

An organization can be no stronger than its membership. We must become actively involved in the professional organizations that represent us. While it is important to communicate as individuals, a greater impact can usually be made through an organized group.

Vocational education should be supportive of additional funding for research and evaluation.

Funds for research to develop and try out new methods, procedures, and innovations have been limited. Substantial investments in this area should support the improvement of program quality. There is also a need for systematic evaluation of programs on both a short and long-term basis, not only for the improvement of quality, but to provide a basis for allocation of resources.

SUMMARY

Vocational education is presently in a state of ferment, since it reflects both the changing needs of society and the changing expectations of individuals. We have assumed a lofty goal of development of a policy whereby all our human resources are utilized. There are no simple answers or panaceas. It is now up to us; the challenge is on. The rewards are obvious.

REFERENCES CITED

Campbell, Roald, F., et al. *Introduction to Educational Administration,* Second Edition. Boston: Allyn and Bacon, Inc., 1962.

Carnegie Council on Policy Studies in Higher Education. *Giving Youth a Better Chance.* San Francisco: Jossey-Bass, Inc., 1979.

Weischadle, David E. "Carnegie: A Case Study in How Foundations Make Decisions." *Delta Kappan,* October, 1977.

ADDITIONAL REFERENCES

Anderson, Bernard E., and Sawhill, Isabel, eds. *Youth Employment and Public Policy.* The American Assembly. New York: Columbia University, 1980.

Foreign Policy Association, *American Foreign Policy for the 80's.* New York: Foreign Policy Association, Inc., 1980.

Foreign Policy Association. *Great Decisions 1980.* New York: Foreign Policy Association, Inc. 1980.

McCage, Ronald D., et. al. "Vocational Education Programs of State and National Improvement: Major Legislative Policy Issues." Unpublished copy of a report prepared by the American Vocational Association Policy Task Force, 1980.

Strong, Merle E., editor. *Developing the Nation's Work Force.* Washington, D.C.: American Vocational Association, 1975.

The National Center for Research in Vocational Education. *Current Projects in Vocational Education—FY 1978, Federally Administered Projects.* Columbus, Ohio: The Ohio State University, 1979.

The Vice President's Task Force on Youth Employment. "The Youth Employment Problem: Causes and Dimensions." In *A Review of Youth Employment Problems, Programs and Policies, Volume 1,* January, 1980.

The Vice President's Task Force on Youth Employment. "Special Needs and Concentrated Problems." In *A Review of Youth Employment Problems, Programs and Policies, Volume 2,* January, 1980.

The Vice President's Task Force on Youth Employment. "Program Experience." In *A Review of Youth Employment Problems, Programs and Policies. Volume 3,* January, 1980.

The Vice President's Task Force on Youth Employment. *Private Sector/Education Roundtables.* Summary Report. (1979)

U.S. Department of Health, Education and Welfare (HEW). *Toward a Federal Policy on Education and Work*. By Barry E. Stern. Washington, D.C.: HEW, March 1977.

U.S. Department of Health, Education and Welfare (HEW). *Unemployed Youth: A Postsecondary Response*. Washington, D.C.: HEW, 1979.

U.S. Department of Labor (DOL). *Completing the Youth Agenda: A Plan for Knowledge Development, Dissemination and Application for Fiscal 1980*. Washington, D.C.: DOL, 1979.

U.S. Department of Labor (DOL). *Research and Development Projects*. 1979 Edition. Washington, D.C.: DOL, 1979.

U.S. Department of Labor (DOL). *The Awarding of Academic Credit Under the Youth Employment and Demonstration Projects Act of 1977*. Washington, D.C.: November, 1977.

U.S. Department of Labor (DOL). *Training Information for Policy Guidance*. R&D Monograph 76. By Marcia Freeman and Anna Dutka. Washington, D.C.: Government Printing Office, 1980.

Youth Employment Education Unit. "CETA Education Youth." *Partners,* February, 1979.

"Youth Employment Prospects for the 1980's." *County Employment Reporters,* February, 1980.

Youthwork, Inc. "Public Forum on the Education and Employment of High-Risk Youth." An unpublished report of the minutes of a Youthwork meeting in Washington, D.C., February 2, 1979.

VOCATIONAL EDUCATION'S DUAL ROLE: EQUITY AND EXCELLENCE

William G. Conroy, Jr.

For over three years now I have been attempting to win support to develop and implement a computer simulation model called the Transition to Work Simulator (TWS). The TWS would be used for testing the economic and life style effects of policy recommendations for all human resource development programs (Conroy, 1979, pp. 85-90).

The principal rationale for developing such a tool is simply that there are too many variables in human resource development and utilization for an observer to take into account. Because the human mind is severely constrained by size to store and process information, policy decisions are usually the result of simple heuristics. Computer simulation models are a way of helping persons solve problems and better predict the consequences of a policy recommendation than are otherwise possible.

One of the more interesting ironies of my career is to have been asked to develop this essay without being able to consult an operational TWS. At very minimum, this heuristically grounded discussion should be a convincing argument on behalf of a more sophisticated approach to examining future trends for policy understanding.

LIFE WITHOUT VOCATIONAL EDUCATION

An operational TWS would allow one to back up time and estimate in great detail current social and economic conditions without the historical influence of vocational education over the last decade. A sensible estimation of the historical absence of vocational education must take into account the pronounced differences among vocational education programs at secondary, postsecondary and adult levels.

Such an assessment must consider the impact of vocational education as a compensatory program on unique target groups of students, for instance, center-city black females of above average scholastic ability. Contributions of vocational education to economic growth and productivity would be a part of such an evaluation.

The differences in the practice of vocational education among states are substantial. Although common threads exist among all vocational education programs, a reasonable evaluation must consider differences within states. Unfortunately, the information to evaluate the historical effects of vocational education at the state level is limited. National information is quite good and getting better, but the sample sizes are small and tend to wash out the effects of vocational education within individual states. This topic has been treated in some detail elsewhere (Conroy, 1980, pp. 39-41; 61).

An examination of current conditions in the United States without vocational education as a program option for the last 10 years would focus on the economic and social consequences of target groups of students who would not have been able to elect vocational education as an option. Would the same proportion of students (by target group) have completed high school without a vocational education program alternative? What might be the differences in wage rates, annual earnings and family life patterns of target groups of students if they had not taken vocational education? Since workers are paid at the margin, and persons are paid more because they produce more, what would be the relationship between shutting down vocational education in 1972 and national productivity? Would the elimination of vocational education during the last 10 years have created shortages in sectors of the labor force? Would the total public transfer bill be greater or less with no vocational education during the last decade?

It has long been my view that much more attention needs to be paid to establishing a capability to learn about the historical impact of vocational education (Conroy, 1975, pp. 1656-1676). The limited and mixed literature on the historical effects of vocational education at all levels makes it difficult to represent the influence various funding thrusts for vocational education will have during the next several years.

VOCATIONAL EDUCATION TODAY

Although it is not the purpose of this essay to focus on the past, a few facts about vocational education seem necessary to establish a perspective for a futures discussion. Table 1 suggests that education has been a growth industry during the last 30 years.

Real expenditures for all education have increased by a factor of over five. Education expenditures have risen from a little of over 3 percent of the Gross National Product (GNP) to over 7 percent in the last 30 years. Per pupil expenditures have tripled. The proportion of

TABLE 1
SOME DIMENSIONS OF EDUCATION IN THE
UNITED STATES

	Expenditures			Per Pupil Expenditures	Percent of 5-24 Year-olds
	Current Dollars	1967 Dollars	Percent of GNP	1967 Dollars	Enrolled in School
1950	$ 8.8 Bil	$12.2 Bil	3.3%	$ 389	67%
1960	24.7 Bil	27.8 Bil	5.0%	615	75%
1970	70.4 Bil	60.5 Bil	7.3%	1,032	76%
1977	131 Bil	72 Bil	7.3%	1,218	76%

Sources: Statistical Abstracts of the United States, 1979, U.S. Department of Commerce, Bureau of the Census, Washington, D.C.

Economic Report of the President, 1980 Council of Economic Advisors Washington, D.C.

youth between the ages of 5 to 24 enrolled in school has not increased quite as rapidly as one might expect.

During the last several years investments in compensatory education programs have soared. For example, according to the Department of Commerce (1979, p. 137), the projected public expenditures for all elementary and secondary education in 1979 were 87 billion dollars. The Office of Education (HEW, 1979, p. 113) reported that "although the (federal) funding level for P.L. 94-142 (The Education for All Handicapped Children Act) totals $804 million for FY 1979, the states report that they are projecting outlays for that period that would exceed the federal contribution by a ratio as great as 30 to 1." That is over 24 billion dollars, nearly 28 percent of the total invested in all elementary and secondary education. Only about 10 percent of the handicapped are physically handicapped; the balance are speech impaired, learning disabled, emotionally disturbed or mentally retarded (HEW).

On the federal level compensatory education expenditures are well over three billion dollars per year. Clearly, much of the increased investment in education has been targeted on goals of equality of opportunity for persons who are physically, psychologically, emotionally or economically disadvantaged.

Federal Investment Has Fallen

Total expenditures for vocational eduation in 1978 were about $5.6 billion; that is only about 4 percent of all expenditures for education or 5 percent of all public education expenditures. Federal appropriations for vocational education were $396 million in 1972; they were only $313.5 million in 1979 (in 1967 dollars). Real federal investments in vocational education have tailed off during the last decade.

Table 2 presents expenditures for vocational education during the last several years.

TABLE 2
EXPENDITURES FOR VOCATIONAL EDUCATION*

	Federal	State/local	Total	Total (1967 dollars)
1972	$466,030	2,194,729	2,660,758	2,123,510
1973	482,391	2,551,267	3,033,657	2,279,231
1974	468,197	2,965,623	3,433,819	2,324,861
1975	536,140	3,501,137	4,037,276	2,504,514
1976	543,211	4,607,014	5,150,225	3,020,660
1977	533,611	4,428,945	4,962,555	2,734,190
1978	495,405	5,080,365	5,575,769	2,853,515

Source: Bureau of Occupational and
Adult Education
United States Office of Education
Washington, D.C.

*(In thousands of dollars)

Real growth in annual expenditures for vocational education from 1972 to 1978 is about 700 million dollars per year. This is accounted for by the increase in spending at the state and local level. As previously noted, real federal expenditures for vocational education have fallen during this decade. It is difficult to escape the conclusion that the United States Congress has a diminished concern for vocational education as an intervention program of promise to meet the socioeconomic problems of the 1980s.

As a conclusion to this gross characterization of vocational education, it would be helpful to be able to specify the additional number of students served with the increased annual investment of about 700 million dollars. Unfortunately, the "head count" data of the U.S. Office of Education during the 1970s are too error ridden to be trustworthy. Still, it is possible to estimate the increased enrollment.

In 1972 the National Longitudinal Study estimated that 23 percent of high school seniors were enrolled in vocational education; Grasso and Shea (1979, p. xxii) have estimated that the net migration within the high school years is toward vocational education. Thus, a fairly reasonable estimate of the number of students served by vocational education at the secondary level in 1972 was 23 percent of the approximately 15 million students enrolled in grades 9-12 or about 3.5 million students. (The U.S. Office of Education reported that during 1972 over 7 million students were served by vocational education at the secondary level).

Table 3 shows the enrollments reported by the Office of Education in 1972 and 1978.

TABLE 3
VOCATIONAL EDUCATION ENROLLMENTS

	Total	Secondary	Post-secondary	Adult
1972	11,602,144	7,231,648	1,304,092	3,066,404
1978	16,704,926	10,236,117	2,089,170	4,379,639

Source: Bureau of Occupational and Adult Education
United States Office of Education
Washington, D.C.

If one assumes that the Office of Education over-estimates secondary vocational education enrollments by about 50 percent but is fairly correct in postsecondary and adult enrollment estimations, the real growth has been from about 8 million students in 1972 to 11.5 million in 1978 or about 3.5 million students at all levels. Put another way, the

United States seems to be spending an extra 700 million dollars in 1978 compared to 1972 to service an additional 3.5 million students; that is about $200 per extra student served. Indeed, based on this rough estimate of vocational education enrollments and an annual expenditure of about 5.6 billion dollars for vocational education in the United States in 1978, the expenditure for vocational education is a little less than $500 per student.

SOME THOUGHTS ABOUT THE FUTURE OF VOCATIONAL EDUCATION

If vocational education is going to continue to represent an important investment by government in the future, it is going to have to demonstrate its effectiveness. John F. Jennings (1979, pp. 22-24), staff director for the House Subcommittee on Elementary, Secondary and Vocational Education, made it magnificently clear that the Congress supports programs that are perceived to be responsive to pressing concerns of the country. Funding decisions at state and local levels are considerably less responsive to national concerns and more tradition oriented; they respond to socioeconomic issues on a delayed basis.

On might reasonably argue that without the establishment of new directions for vocational education at the federal level, local and state levels of support might follow the federal lead and begin to drop off. Since there is very little independent information to describe the impact of vocational education at state and local levels, it is not unreasonable to expect local and state governments to follow "informed" federal funding decisions.

Straight-line extrapolation of constant enrollment ratios to projected population growth is not a reliable guide to the future scope of vocational education programs. Table 4 presents the projected population from which it is easy to estimate such ratios from previously presented information.

Declining Enrollments

The pool of students at secondary and postsecondary levels from which vocational education can draw will be reduced nationally by about seven million between 1980 and 1990. The population between the ages of 25-55 will increase by 18 million during this period. These raw data would suggest that vocational education should target increased services on the adult population. More fundamental questions must be considered to generate future policy options for vocational education. Indeed, to base policy on gross population estimates alone is absurd. Yet, it is important not to dismiss the demographic fact that

TABLE 4
POPULATION OF THE UNITED STATES IN 1970, 1980, AND 1990
IN 000'S

Ages	1970	1980	1990
0-4	17,156	17,259	20,096
5-13	36,636	30,246	34,643
14-17	15,910	15,753	12,941
18-24	24,683	29,441	25,162
25-34	25,293	36,157	41,062
35-54	46,452	48,342	61,758
55+	38,749	45,570	49,412
Total	204,879	222,769	245,075

Source: *Declining Enrollments: The Challenge of the Coming Decade**

National Institute of Education
Washington, D.C.
1978

*Another good source for such projection information is *Projections of Education Statistics to 1985-86,* National Center for Education Statistics, Washington, D.C., 1977

the "aging population" will exert an independent effect on vocational education. As Jennings (1979, p. 23) points out, society simply will have a reduced stake in education for youth in the future.

Excellence and Equity
The two issues that seem destined to play a central role in future funding policies for vocational education programs are excellence and equity. It seems obvious that a limited growth economy reduces the possibility of increasing numbers of citizens participating in a fulfilling life. This is true not only for the United States, but for every country in the world. The extension of this argument is that growth in world GNP is critical to improving the lot of people everywhere; it represents the only real hope against continued aggression among people.

Future public policy within the United States is bound to focus on issues associated with economic growth. Planning and managing efficient human resource development program options will be an area of principal concern for public policy during the 1980s.

The labor force in the United States is organized in a way that enormous inequalities exist in job distributions among the population as a result of race, sex and socioeconomic status of parents. Indeed, the basis of support for compensatory programs is to provide a more equal opportunity for target groups to participate in the full range of important activities, not the least of which are opportunities for jobs. Vocational education, particularly at the secondary level, can be viewed as an investment in compensatory education that actually improves a person's chances to succeed in the labor force in terms of increased earnings (Conroy, "Some Historical Effects," 1979, p. 270).

Vocational education at any level is not just a compensatory program; it represents investment in the excellence of future work forces. Although much more evidence is required to sort out the relative contribution of vocational education to excellence, it is accepted that a goal of vocational education is to provide students with occupational-specific skills and generalizable work attitudes so that they will be more productive workers than they otherwise would be. These potential gains may be washed out by conditions in the "real world" labor force; that is beside the point for the purpose of this essay. Much evidence suggests such gains persist for many target groups of students (Conroy, "Some Historical Effects," 1979; Grasso, 1979, pp. xvii-xxxiii).

Vocational education is going to have to become increasingly clear about its equity and excellence goals to the Congress, as well as to state legislatures, local trustees and boards of education. Is vocational education just a compensatory program to increase the probability of the disinfranchised to participate in the lower sectors of the labor market? Or is vocational educational to be regarded as an indispensable investment in the economic growth of the United States?

Difficult public policy choices must be made in the coming years between supporting programs that attempt to achieve equity for target groups and those that support excellence. As the consequences of relatively slowed real economic growth in the United States become apparent, public policy increasingly will become concerned with excellence in the work force.

The Need to Communicate with Congress
Vocational education would appear to describe itself as a contributor

to both excellence and equity goals. Yet it seems to have failed to convince the United States Congress of its potential in any real way. One measure of that failure is the annual federal investment in the Comprehensive Employment and Training Act (CETA) programs of 9.5 billion dollars, almost twice as much as the federal, state and local investment in all vocational education combined. Indeed, many assert that investments in general education, compensatory (non-vocational) education and CETA programs are a sufficient investment in human resource development. Firm-specific training will be provided by business and industry; occupational-specific education is unnecessary (Brenner, 1979).

Vocational education leadership is hiding its head in the sand if it thinks it represents a significant proportion of the national investment in either compensatory programs or human resource development programs concerned with future excellence of the work force. That should be self-evident from the expenditure information presented in this essay.

If vocational education is to present itself to the Congress as part of the solution to the need for equality of occupational opportunity, it must persuade the Congress it can make a significant and consistent difference to the minority population of the great cities in the United States. Table 5 presents the alarming unemployment percentages by sex and race in the United States.

TABLE 5
UNEMPLOYMENT BY RACE AND SEX

	16 to 19 Yrs		20 Yrs +	
	Male	**Female**	**Male**	**Female**
White	13.7%	14.1%	3.7%	5.0%
Black & Other	33.2%	35.4%	8.9%	10.0%

Source: Economic Report of the President,
January, 1980
Washington, D.C.

The proportion of blacks and races other than white between the ages of 5 and 24 will grow from less than 14 percent of the total in 1970 to over 18 percent in 1990 (*Economic Report,* 1980, p. 238).

Table 6 makes clear the location of a substantial fraction of the minority population for vocational education if it is to address the significant compensatory challenges of the 1980s.

TABLE 6
MINORITY PERCENTAGE OF TOTAL ENROLLMENT
IN GREAT CITY SCHOOL SYSTEMS

Atlanta	85%
Baltimore	75
Boston*	48
Buffalo	48
Chicago	73
Cleveland	61
Dade County*	54
Dallas*	56
Denver*	46
Detroit	70
Long Beach*	26
Los Angeles*	58
Memphis	70
Milwaukee	38
New Orleans	81
New York City*	66
Oakland*	78
Philadelphia	67
Pittsburgh	43
St. Louis	70
San Diego*	30
San Francisco*	69
Toledo	34
Washington	97

*Substantial Hispanic population

Source: Office of Civil Rights
   U.S. Department of Health,
    Education and Welfare
   1974

The prevailing wisdom that guides federal funding is not convinced that vocational education offers much of a solution to the problems of unemployed youth in the present or in the future. This is clear by previously cited expenditure statistics. The arguments advanced by the Employment and Training Administration (ETA) have persuaded the Congress that the "aging vat" work experience programs are the principal vehicle for meeting the compensatory needs of poor urban youth (DOL, 1979, pp. 31-57).

The irony is that a strong case can be made on behalf of vocational education at the secondary level as an "aging vat" that allows students to acquire occupational-specific skills and good work habits. Yet, it will take an enormous effort to mount a convincing argument that vocational education is a meaningful program alternative for a substantial number of poor urban youth. Such an argument must be supported by a carefully developed body of policy research on the same level as the program research being completed by ETA.

(It is this author's view that the policy research capability of ETA is far superior to that of vocational education. It is difficult to know if that is a function of hiring practices, the concentration of vocational education research funds in a single university or the background of labor economists compared to vocational educators. The differences in the quantity and quality of research is evident to anyone who takes the time to make a comparison.)

Multi-Agency Coordination Is Needed

In point of fact, the range of target populations requiring compensatory programs in the United States is too varied to be accommodated by a single program solution. If vocational education is to make a contribution in helping large numbers of disadvantaged youth attain a fair employment opportunity, leadership must provide coordinated services with other agencies, most notably Title IV of CETA. The private sector must not be left out of such planning, though its track record in providing opportunities for the disadvantaged is quite poor (DOL, 1979, p. 41).

Multi-agency planning for a wide range of target groups is complex. Persons not salaried by vocational education institutions are unlikely to play a role in determining a significant future for vocational education in addressing the compensatory education problems of the 1980s. It would be less than candid not to raise some questions about the capability of vocational education leadership to mount a sustained effort to compete in the complex policy planning process at state and national levels.

The concerns of equity and excellence cannot be separated. Excellence is critical everywhere in the labor force. Programs of intervention that efficiently contribute to the development of excellence in all sectors of the labor market are important to the nation's economic future. It seems axiomatic that programs that prepare target groups for productive jobs in the labor force, reducing the need for expensive training or public service employment "slots," are important to the future of the United States. Vocational education needs to organize a clear description of its potential contribution to both equity and excellence. Simulation can be a very powerful policy tool for such planning.

Focus on Selected Areas

A unique and surprising policy strategy for vocational education leadership would be to focus its attention on excellence within selected occupations, say computer programming, drafting or machine trades. Such a policy would lead to establishing entrance criteria that predict post-program success in selected occupations.

Excellence, as measured by post-program performance, would become the driving objective of vocational education programs. Such planning might be supported by the wide variety of "aging vat" alternatives developed by the ETA, ranging from Job Corps (an intensive remedial experience) to work experience on low head dams. The selective concentration of resources on target populations most likely to succeed could make a valuable contribution to economic growth in certain sectors of the economy.

Students who were found unlikely to be successful in existing secondary vocational education programs would simply pick an alternative CETA "aging vat" program. Such students could eventually enroll in an occupational-specific educational program or enter the labor force through an on-the-job training alternative.

Based on the supporting and critical literature, vocational education leadership has not developed a well-structured and documented position about its historical or potential support to the goals of excellence and equity. Such a structure must consider relationships between vocational education at secondary, postsecondary and adult levels, target populations and the very real existence of competing programs. Planning must anticipate various strategies under various occupational demand conditions by various segments of the labor market. It is difficult to imagine how this complex planning can be done in any meaningful way without simulation.

A FEW CONCLUDING REMARKS

The future of vocational education is in the hands of vocational education leadership. There are no forces that are going to sweep it into the mainstream of critically essential social intervention programs or shipwreck it on the shores of formerly useful educational alternatives.

Jennings seems absolutely right when he identifies the most likely socioeconomic issues of the future as economic growth, equality of occupational opportunity for minority poor in urban areas and the needs of an aging population. Within each of these major topics is a stream of component problems.

Vocational education is not a single solution to any of these current issues; it can play a part helping solve some of the national concerns within each current problem area.

Investments in human resource development programs have long been acknowledged as critical to economic growth (Denison, 1971). The argument for investments in occupational-specific programs needs to be carefully examined and advanced. Vocational education research needs to learn more about the historical consequences on vocational education, including the relationship between industrial discipline and future labor force behavior.

Vocational education must be more responsive to labor market needs, consistent with the capabilities of students, and considerably more concerned with the economic growth of neighborhoods, cities, states and the nation. No longer is it appropriate to avoid an examination of the effectiveness of existing programs. Vocational education must be prepared to institute major changes based on the results of such investigations.

At the secondary level, a principal policy concern is to develop a comprehensive plan with general education and CETA prime sponsors, so the impact of vocational education is maximized on behalf of poor youth and the needs of the labor force. This might mean focusing occupational-specific education on students who demonstrate a readiness to learn in a public school setting. At any rate, it is clear vocational education planners are going to have to enter into complex planning with other agencies, with planning on a target-group basis. Vocational educators are going to need to be forceful to represent vocational education as a meaningful part of the solution to the problems of the urban poor. "Placement in the field for which trained" expectations at the secondary level must be realistically presented. It benefits no one to raise false hopes.

The aging population provides a new target audience for vocational education. They will most likely be served through postsecondary schools. The focus of postsecondary and adult vocational education must be clearly differentiated from secondary vocational education. This must result from a unique body of research and be reflected in state and federal legislation. One might construct an argument that as long as postsecondary and adult vocational opportunities remain open to all on an "equal support basis," postsecondary and adult vocational education should become increasingly concerned with excellence.

Vocational education can either play an important role in stratifying American society as it does in Great Britain (Halsey, 1979) or it can facilitate career development for a wide variety of individuals within a complex economy. If vocational education is to provide occupational-specific learning opportunities for significant target groups and contribute to future excellence of the work force, coordinated planning among secondary, postsecondary and adult levels is critical. This coordinated strategy must be explicitly represented in human resource development planning for the entire economy. The future of vocational education depends on such planning.

The needs of economic growth in a society just awakening to the reality of its changing position in the world economic order, the challenges of helping the poor become productive and participating citizens and the occupational-specific challenges of an aging population represent the major challenges of the future to vocational education. This future depends on how well leadership can convince legislatures that it can contribute to the efficient solution of these problems.

Whether vocational education can mount the effort required to become a major part of the significant social programs in the 1980s is not yet clear. In general, the trends seem to be in directions quite opposite from significant growth in public support for vocational education. In fact, there is some question if vocational education can hold on to the real gains it has achieved during the last 20 years.

From my perspective, an erosion of support for vocational education would be unfortunate. It is my belief, based on experience as a policy analyst for vocational education and a former vocational education high school principal, that 10 years from now the world will not be a better place if vocational education does not become a more significant part of human resource development. I fear it will not; fault must be borne, in part, by salaried persons of vocational education who are now in a position to affect policy in an important way at this critical time.

REFERENCES

Brenner, Patricia D. *Vocational, Career and Compensatory Education: A Review of the Experience,* Fifth Annual Report to the President. Washington, D.C.: National Commission for Employment Policy, 1979.

Conroy, William G., Jr. "The Earning Power of Vocational Education." *VocEd,* September, 1980.

Conroy, William G., Jr. "Some Historical Effects of Vocational Education at the Secondary Level." *KAPPAN,* December, 1979.

Conroy, William G., Jr. Testimony for Vocational Amendments of 1976 before the Subcommittee on Elementary, Secondary and Vocational Education of the Committee on Education and Labor. Washington, D.C.: House of Representatives, 94th Congress, May 22, 1975.

Conroy, William G., Jr. "The Transition to Work Simulator." *The International Review of Education,* USESCO Institute for Education (Hamburg), 1979, 25(1).

Denison, Edward D. "The Sources of Past and Future Growth," in *Human Capital Formulation and Manpower Development.* New York: The Free Press, 1971.

Economic Report of the President. Washington, D.C.: U.S. Government Printing Office, 1980.

Grasso, John T., and Shea, John R. *Vocational Education and Training: Impact on Youth.* Berkeley, Calif.: Carnegie Council on Policy Studies in Higher Education, 1979.

Halsey, A.H. *Origins and Destinations: Family, Class and Education in Modern Britain.* London: Clarendon Press, 1979.

Jennings, John F. "What the Future Holds: A View from the Hill." *VocEd,* September, 1979.

U.S. Department of Commerce, Bureau of the Census. *Statistical Abstracts of the United States.* Washington, D.C.: U.S. Government Printing Office, 1979.

U.S. Department of Health, Education and Welfare (HEW), Office of Education. *Progress Toward a Free and Appropriate Public Education: A Report to Congress on the Implementation of Public Law 94-142: The Education for All Handicapped Children.* Washington, D.C.: HEW, Office of Education, 1979.

U.S. Department of Labor (DOL), Office of Youth Programs, Employment Training Administration (ETA). *Youth Employment Policies and Programs for the 1980's: Analysis and Proposals of the Department of Labor.* Washington, D.C.: DOL, 1979.

DOING THE IMPOSSIBLE— PLANNING A HUMAN RESOURCE POLICY

Sar A. Levitan

To evaluate the United States' human resource policy involves, first of all, making the assumption that such a policy exists. The evidence is not supportive. Instead of a comprehensive design, American efforts in this area are more a collection of diverse policies dealing with a variety of issues. A cogent policy requires a combination of comprehending the overall picture, setting realistic goals and coordinating action.

In many specific areas a basic understanding of all the issues involved is still lacking. Policy-makers and analysts have not identified general and consistent goals across areas, and coordinated action, therefore, is missing. A few examples will illustrate.

DOES AN OVERALL POLICY EXIST?

If a clear and unified American human resource policy existed, then it would seem logical that one office in the federal government would be responsible for keeping tabs on how much—and where—the federal government invests in human resources. A perusal of the federal budget discloses that various human resource efforts are administered under different agencies and managements, isolated from each other, and sometimes operating at cross purposes. Since 1975 the government has ceased even to collect and publish the total funds it allocates to aid of the poor.

Welfare reform, minimum wages, programs geared to fight unemployment and labor productivity remain vital human resource topics. Yet, policy-makers and researchers often fail to consider the interrelationship between these various issues. How much attention do minimum wages receive when efforts to reform the welfare system are proposed? The two are not isolated policy issues, but the tendency is consistently to treat one without as much as a mention of the other.

And what of such grand policy pronouncements as the Employment Act of 1946, the Full Employment and Balanced Growth Act of 1978 or even the Comprehensive Employment and Training Act (CETA)? These acts may sound cogent and clear, but a comprehensive policy requires much more than lofty preambles expressing noble sentiments written to placate various groups.

Instead of a unified policy, what this nation has are diversified human resource programs, which individually were often created as a reaction to one burning issue of the day. Given the political realities of this country, it is doubtful whether a comprehensive human resource policy could be created. As long as we remain a vast and diverse country—with the ideal of free choice and a semblance of free markets—a single unified human resource policy is not a distinct possibility and perhaps not even desirable.

That we are not very good at planning overall economic and social activity and anticipating future developments does not mean we cannot examine parts of the animal. Accordingly, instead of addressing a human resource policy, the best that can be done is to discuss various aspects of what is intended to be a rounded policy. The reader may put the pieces together, but should be warned that the result may be a logical order that never was intended—nor in fact even exists.

INVESTMENT IN EDUCATION

When economists talk about human resource policy, the first thing that comes to mind is investment in education. Presumably this can be easily investigated since we can add up numbers and come up with totals. The results are impressive indeed. In 1980, the government at all levels invested some $170 billion in education. But this is only the proverbial tip of the iceberg. Total investment is much higher because government outlays do not include the total societal investment, and they hide foregone earnings of students who could have produced goods and services and added to the Gross National Product (GNP) instead of filling their heads with additional book learning—which they may never use.

If one could make a clear-cut case that longer education—or higher education, as some call it—adds to total well-being, then the high expenditures and foregone earnings would be well justified. But making a persuasive case for this proposition is becoming increasingly difficult. Other advanced countries get along with much less formal education. Indeed, it is only recently that we have expanded our educational institutions to keep roughly nine out of every 10 youngsters in the schools until age 18, and then have more than half of them continue into college.

Granting that we are living in an increasingly complex society with advancing technology, it still is not at all clear how many workers need more than mastery of the three Rs to perform effectively in their occupations. Additional education increasingly seems to be utilized as a screening device rather than as preparation for work. Added education may be good for the soul, but it is doubtful that it adds to total production. Diminishing returns hold here, and beyond a certain level the added return from more education is quite small—if it exists at all.

In the 1970s the nation kept adding to the total outlays for education, but the growth rate of our productivity declined. While other factors must also be considered, nevertheless, there apparently is very little relationship between investment in education and productivity—at least not at this country's stage of educational development.

What is true for the society as a whole, however, does not apply to individuals. Education has paid off very handsomely for certain individuals, giving credence that it is heavily used as a screening device. Adapting estimates made in 1972 by the U.S. Census Bureau, lifetime earnings based on years of schooling completed are as follows (in 1980 dollars):

8 years:	$ 788,000
12 years:	1,130,000
16 years:	1,580,000
17+ years:	1,910,000

Similarly, what is true of the past is not necessarily true for the future. It is difficult to project these earning differentials into the future, for if the supply of college graduates exceeds demand—as the Bureau of Labor Statistics projects—then the relative price for college graduates is likely to decline. Moreover, there apparently is a limit to the number of jobs requiring college degrees that can be generated. If this is correct, it is reasonable to conclude that the fat years for the educational system are over and that investment in education is about to face some lean years.

As suggested at the outset, education is only one aspect of human resource policy. A more rounded review requires further exploration. At the present, inflation and unemployment, declining growth of productivity, work time, the presumed demise of the work ethic, the growth of the welfare state and discrimination in the labor market are all relevant to any discussion of human resource policy. This list is, quite obviously, selective, and others will no doubt want to add their favorite items.

INFLATION AND UNEMPLOYMENT

Considering the conventionally accepted trade-off between unemployment and inflation, we are now living in the worst of all possible economic worlds. Unemployment is rising, while at the same time the country is experiencing double-digit inflation. Some pessimists also predict double-digit unemployment. Here there is neither space nor purpose in discussing the debate among economists as to whether there continues to be a trade-off between unemployment and inflation.

What is indisputable about the current inflationary pressures is that this nation is paying increasingly more to the Organization of Petroleum Exporting Countries (OPEC) and to others who sell raw materials. It has been called blackmail, but it is also the inevitable operation of the law of supply and demand. A pervasive challenge to the American economy is to overcome its dependence on imported sources of energy.

Such a transformation will affect occupational distribution and skill training during the 1980s and mandates, thus, an examination of human resource policies. Until we sharply reduce our dependence on Middle East sources of energy, it is quite clear we will not escape continued rising inflation and may face as well a reduced standard of living.

Two scenarios about the outcome of this challenge are apparent. We can turn to the prophets of gloom and doom and anticipate continuing higher prices of oil and even worse—a breakdown in relations with supplying countries might portend disaster for the American economy. In the other scenario we will take the necessary steps to reduce our dependence on Middle East oil, whether through conservation, expansion of nuclear or solar energy, or coal. To gain economic independence, the chances are we will have to resort to a combination of all these measures. While we have made very slow progress, it is possible we are now on the road to reaching an energy policy. Implementing the policy will remain a major challenge of the 1980s.

The changes accompanying any liberation from Middle East energy sources will have a significant impact on the development of human resources since new emphasis on sources of energy will involve changing technology. In turn, this will require more training in some occupations and probably obsolescence in others.

Beyond energy, there will be the requirement of restrained fiscal and monetary policies for at least a few years. But the economic burdens must be equitably distributed within society. No quick fix that places the majority of the burden on the poor will work in the long run. Human resource efforts and aid to the poor have not been the prime causes of inflation.

PRODUCTIVITY AND WORK TIME

Dependence on oil and other foreign raw materials shows clearly that we are not a self-contained economy. However, the decline in productivity during recent years would have presented considerable problems, even if we were not dependent on foreign supplies or markets.

Considering the loose labor markets experienced in the 1970s as well as the social and political upheavals of the late 1960s and the succeeding decade, the decline in our productivity should not have been a surprise. An increase in the number of new entrants in the labor market, including youth and women, has resulted in a less experienced labor force. Coupled with the entry of females and blacks into new occupations from which they were effectively barred earlier might, in itself, account for a decline in the growth rate of productivity.

Lest this be misunderstood, it should be emphasized that the entry of minorities and females into traditional white male occupations is a wholesome development and one that should have occurred many, many years ago. But given past discrimination, the entry of these groups into the traditional white male occupations has created frictions in the work place and an accompanying decline of productivity. This should be regarded as a small price to pay to redress discrimination. But we have to recognize that there is no free lunch and that corrections require a transition pricetag.

In the 1970s it was also decided to boost capital investment by expenditures on pollution abatement, safety in the work place and general improvement of our physical environment. The result was a decline in the growth rates of productivity as measured by economists and statisticians though, in many cases, the social benefits were great.

Similarly, the growth in the service industries has contributed to a decline in the overall rate of productivity. Service industries do not lend themselves, as easily as manufacturing or other goods producing industries, to measures of productivity. We don't want our surgeons to cut us up on an assembly line in order to increase their productivity and waiters can't increase productivity by smiling twice as fast.

275

Finally, there is persuasive evidence that capital investment has declined in recent years as a result of growing inflation. People have saved less, leaving inadequate funds for capital investment. Some laws have also contributed to questionable investment priorities by providing all sorts of inducements for speculators to invest in land and buildings and few incentives for producers of goods.

The collective projections of most productivity experts indicate we will again witness a growth in productivity in the 1980s, although few anticipate a return to the same growth rates experienced in the 1950s and early 1960s. But as suggested before, there is little basis for claims that either education or additional training is going to have much of an impact upon the growth rate of productivity.

Even if productivity does not increase, total production can be boosted by adding additional hours of work. Since the end of World War II, there has been very litle decline in the work week of full-time workers. While the average number of hours in the work week has declined, the decline is due to the increase in the number of part-time workers. Full-time workers have continued to work roughly the same number of hours—an average of 43 hours a week. Unions may have preached the gospel of shorter hours, but when it comes to the moment of truth—to strike or to sign a new collective bargaining agreement—union representatives, reflecting apparently the wishes of their members, bargain for more pay rather than for fewer hours.

Whether this trend will continue is anybody's guess. However, assuming inflation is abated before too long and productivity growth resumed, we can anticipate an increase in demand for shorter work hours and more flexible work schedules. This preference already exists by many women who hold dual careers in the work place and in the home. Whatever improvements women have achieved to change their status in the work place, the traditional role of the woman at the home has changed little. Yet as more and more women work full time, the chances are men will have to share increasingly the household duties. If that happens, men will also value fewer hours, and total hours are likely to decline. But for the time being, this is more a hope than a report of changing conditions.

THE WORK ETHIC

Though labor force participation is on the rise and workers continue to prefer added pay to more leisure, the impression persists that the work ethic is dying in the land and that people will want to work less and less. There is considerable evidence that the fashionable obituaries to the work ethic are premature. The impression that people don't want to work is a misinterpretation of what is actually happening in the work place.

Clearly, we don't work as hard as we once did, but that is a function of the technology rather than an attitude toward work. We are the first or second generation accustomed to pushing buttons to do a great deal of work that was done manually by our ancestors. Most of the repetitive and physical labor has been eliminated by technological change. But old views die slowly, and sweat of the brow is still associated with work.

Productivity during this century alone has quintupled. A few numbers will illustrate. In 1900 a work force of 29 million labored approximately 80 billion hours to produce a gross national product of $197 billion (in 1980 dollars). In 1980 an average of 97.2 million people worked 182 billion hours to advance it to $2.6 trillion. An hour of labor in 1900 that produced the 1980 equivalent of $2.60 in goods and services produced $14.30 in 1980. Though these remarkable gains have tapered off in the last decade, the long-range trend in productivity should still be upward.

Accordingly, if we wished to live at the same standard of living as our grandparents lived at the beginning of the century, we would not need a labor force of 104 million; 20 million could do the job. At the beginning of the century, more than a third of all the labor force worked to produce our food and fiber. Today less than four percent perform the same function, and we produce a surplus of food to export to the four corners of the earth.

As a result, we can afford many jobs once considered unnecessary, or those frequently referred to as overhead. The U.S. armed forces have more generals and admirals now than during World War II. This situation is not unique to the military, where brass is a highly sought and valued commodity, but is also true for other organizations—private enterprises, universities and government agencies. By comparing the number of vice presidents and special assistants to vice presidents that have accumulated in most organizations over the years, it becomes clear we have created a lot of work that society might do without. Yet as long as we have the resources, we can generate additional cushy jobs.

Transfer payments are another factor contributing to the belief that people don't work any more. As long as the option was either to work or to starve, the choice was quite clear. But in today's society where nearly a sixth of the total disposable income comes from transfer payments, we offer some people the opportunity of not

277

working by allowing early retirement, or supporting them because they are disabled, unemployed or just to take care of their children. Again, this is a reflection of an affluent society and not a reflection that the work ethic is dying.

There comes to mind the often-repeated story of the assembly line worker who was berated by his foreman for having skipped work on Friday. The worker's response was he would also be glad to skip work on Mondays, but the company does not pay him enough to miss two days. Only in a society where the pay is sufficiently high are people allowed the choice between working full time or part time. There is very little danger that productivity will rise so much that work will be unnecessary. The futurists' misguided dream (or nightmare, depending upon your point of view) that machines will replace us is a creation of a fat society that pays people for spinning tales about the demise of the work ethic and who fail to understand the value work has to most people.

People need the feeling of performing useful functions in society and for most this means work. It is unlikely machines will replace people simply because no matter what machines can accomplish, they are still not likely to be able to inspire us. A machine might diagnose a patient, but it could hardly reassure him. Sigmund Freud put it as follows, "Man's work at least gives him a secure place in a position of reality in the human community." Bernard Shaw put it more felicitously when he stated, "Perpetual holiday is a good working definition of hell." Those of us who are neither psychologists nor poets simply say, "Thank God there is work to be done."

WORK AND WELFARE GO TOGETHER

If people like to work, the question arises then—why do so many people prefer welfare or other transfer payments to work? The answer is simple. This country has developed a welfare system that is often more remunerative than work. While minimum wages have put a floor on earnings, they are frequently too inadequate to replace welfare. The welfare recipient may also have an advantage over the worker, in that he or she is assured of payment, while the worker, especially in many low-paying or seasonal positions, faces the possibility of periodic layoffs and no income at all.

The challenge this nation faces is to design a system that will pay more for work than for welfare. While this sounds rather elementary, experience has shown its implementation is very difficult. Obviously, it is not a new idea. President Kennedy talked about "rehabilitation but not relief." President Nixon created his own alliteration, "workfare but not welfare." President Carter apparently ran out of alliterations and was satisfied with the slogan, "better jobs and income." President Reagan was elected with a slogan of "putting America back to work."

Whatever the slogans, the goal is clear. For the last 20 years we have sought to create a system that could pay more for work than for welfare. We are, indeed, closer to that goal. Job-creating programs that offer welfare recipients a chance to work seem to offer the most hope. For millions of people in our society the option is not work or welfare; for them work and welfare go together.

DISCRIMINATION IN THE LABOR MARKET

A final important aspect of human resource policy is the need to carry out a vigorous antidiscrimination policy. In the 1960s, the issue was mainly of preventing *de jure* discrimination and opening entry-level jobs to members of minority races and to women. Currently, the implementation of civil rights is becoming more difficult as women and minorities are competing for "white men's jobs." Opening doors for women or minorities to enter colleges or to get jobs as technicians in hospitals was one thing, but many liberals of yesteryear are not as tolerant when women and minorities insist on equal opportunities in competing for the more lucrative positions.

While considerable progress has been made, there is much more left to be done. Eli Ginzburg referred to the influx of females into the labor force as the "most outstanding phenomenon of the century." For the time being, he is maybe only partially right. He will be completely right when minorities and females share fully in all occupational jobs and are not concentrated in low-paying jobs and on the lowest rungs of professional and managerial positions. Vigorous enforcement of civil rights remains a major item on the agenda for the 1980s if the nation is to develop the full potential of its human resources.

AN ELUSIVE ASSIGNMENT

This brief review should suggest that a formulation of human resource policy affects every aspect of life. The discussion was clearly selective. It only touched on demographic considerations and, except for the reference to linking employment with welfare, no mention was made of the developments during the past two decades in providing compensatory education and remedial training. Military manpower policy was completely ignored, and not a word was mentioned about the need for a data system for planning a human resource policy.

A human resource policy can be accomplished by authoritarian ukase or is a fit subject of Humpty Dumpty who decreed that words mean exactly what he said they meant, "No more, no less." But the reality is we have many policies that are not linked and cannot be combined into a unified system. Even if we continue to have a variety of policies, instead of a central human resource system, we should strive to gain insights and to illuminate how these diverse programs react within the context of a mature welfare state. General and consistent goals must be maintained. The right hand should know what the left hand is doing and how they both can coordinate their efforts. Even this modest step would improve our highly diverse human resource efforts.

YEARBOOK AUTHORS

Roy Amara, is president and senior research fellow at the Institute for the Future in Menlo Park, California. His research activities have included work on the future corporate environment, emerging societal issues, methodologies for long-range planning and forecasting, decision analysis and the social impact of information generating, processing and dissemination systems. Before joining the staff of the Institute in 1970, Dr. Amara held a variety of positions, including senior research engineer at Stanford Research Institute.

Melvin L. Barlow is emeritus professor, Graduate School of Education at the University of California, Los Angeles, and emeritus director of the Division of Vocational Education for the statewide University of California. Dr. Barlow's fascination with the historical foundations of vocational education has led him to devote many years to research and writing in this area. He has been AVA historian since 1965.

Robert Beck is regent's professor of history and philosophy of education at the University of Minnesota in Minneapolis, where he has taught since 1947. His special areas of interest and research include development of manpower in international education, with an emphasis on Western Europe and the Soviet Union, educational planning and education in the ancient West. Dr. Beck's works in this latter area include *Aeschylus: Playwright, Educator* and *Homer: Poet, Educator.*

Theodore Buila is assistant professor of vocational education studies in the Occupational Education Program at Southern Illinois University at Carbondale. Dr. Buila has a particular interest in education in developing nations and at press time was working in Pakistan with the Third Education Project of the United Nations Development Program.

William G. Conroy, Jr., was an associate professor at the College of Management Science, University of Lowell, Massachusetts, until December, 1980, when an automobile accident took his life.

George H. Copa is professor and director of the Minnesota Research and Development Center for Vocational Education, Department of Vocational and Technical Education at the University of Minnesota in Minneapolis.

Lawrence F. Davenport is provost of the San Diego Community College District. Dr. Davenport has also served as adjunct professor in education at California State University, Long Beach, visiting lecturer in counseling and guidance at the University of Michigan and currently serves as a member of the adjunct faculty at Pepperdine University. He has been a consultant to many organizations including the U.S. Office of Education and Systems Development Corporation.

Marvin Feldman is president of the Fashion Institute of Technology in New York City, a specialized college under the program of the State University of New York, which prepares students for creative and management careers in the fashion industries. Dr. Feldman has held positions with the Office of Economic Opportunity in the U.S. government, the Ford Foundation and served for 12 years in the field of university and secondary school administration and education with the state of California.

Joel D. Galloway is dean of the School of Technical and Applied Arts at Ferris State College in Big Rapids, Michigan. A vocational-technical educator for 19 years, he was head of the Industrial Education Department at Oregon State University before his appointment at Ferris State in 1979.

Katy Greenwood is assistant professor and project director of the Education-for-Work Linkage Project, Interdisciplinary Education at Texas A&M University, where she has also served as coordinator of graduate vocational education and as the director of the Project to Provide In-Service Training to Vocational Counselor Educators. Dr. Greenwood's major research emphasis has been in the history and philosophy of vocational education.

Samuel Halperin is director of The George Washington University's Institute for Educational Leadership, a coalition of professional development programs designed to strengthen and improve policymaking in American education, particularly at the federal and state levels of educational governance. Prior to joining the University in 1969 he was deputy assistant secretary of HEW for legislation, assistant U.S. commissioner of education for legislation, and a legislative aid in several executive and legislative branch posts.

Paul L. Hammar is professor at the Colgate Rochester/Bexley Hall/Crozer Divinity Schools and a regular visiting professor at the University of Rochester. Dr. Hammar received his higher education at the Naval Academy, Nebraska Wesleyan, Yale and Heidelberg (Germany), with post-doctoral study at Harvard and St. Andrews (Scotland). A native of Nebraska, Dr. Hammar was a student of vocational education in high school and he served as the state president of the Future Farmers of America.

Warren A. Johnson is professor of geography at San Diego State University with special interest in the fields of natural resources, resource economics, and resource planning and conservation. His book *Muddling Toward Frugality* (Sierra Club Press, 1978) offers a view of the future where, in spite of scarcities, people will be better off in many ways than they are today.

Lowell P. Lerwick has spent the last four years in vocational education research. Most recently Dr. Lerwick served as manager of the Small Farm Curriculum Project at Pine City, Minnesota. He also conducted several projects while associated with the Minnesota Research and Development Center for Vocational Education (MRDC) at the University of Minnesota. His involvement in the MRDC project "Alternative Concepts of Vocational Education," and his graduate participation in the University's "Vocational Educational Tutorial," has earned him recognition for his influence on educational thought.

Sar A. Levitan has been research professor of economics and director of the Center for Social Policy Studies at The George Washington University since 1967. His career has combined research and teaching with government service centered in the fields of labor economics and social policy. He is chairman of the executive committee of the National Council on Employment and Unemployment Statistics and on the Federal Mediation and Conciliation Service, the American Arbitration Association labor panels.

The Future of Vocational Education

Richard Ruff is a senior researcher at the National Center for Research in Vocational Education at The Ohio State University, where he is currently directing work in futures research and policy analysis. Dr. Ruff is an organizational psychologist who first worked in futures research with Litton Industries. He has spent the last 10 years at the national and state level managing and directing research and evaluation projects in career and vocational education.

William E. Schoonmaker is a faculty member of the School of Technology, Kent State University. His teaching activities include courses in industrial design, manufacturing processes and educational research. Mr. Schoonmaker has presented topics related to educational forecasting at Kent State University and the University of Minnesota, where he is presently completing his doctoral studies in vocational and technical education.

Robert S. Seckendorf is associate professor of education and director of vocational education research at the University of Nevada, Las Vegas. Dr. Seckendorf has had extensive state administrative experience in vocational education, including 12 years as assistant commissioner for occupational and continuing education in the New York State Education Department. He was a national fellow of the Advanced Study Center at the National Center for Research in Vocational Education at The Ohio State University, where he studied various influences on the future organization, structure and financing of vocational education.

Bruce J. Shylo is currently at the National Center for Research in Vocational Education at The Ohio State University. His academic background is in vocational-technical education. He has most recently been engaged in futures research in vocational education; prior to that he worked on projects that sought to identify vocational education research and development priorities and to upgrade the capabilities of large city vocational education administrative and supervisory personnel in critical performance areas.

David Pearce Snyder is life-styles editor of the *Futurist* magazine and an independent consulting futurist. Mr. Snyder is also the co-author/editor of *The Family in Post-Industrial America* (1979, Westview Press). Much of the material in his yearbook article is based on information that will appear in his forthcoming book *Watersheds: The Next Ten Years in America,* which will be published in the spring of 1982 by Macmillan.

Merle E. Strong is professor in the Department of Educational Administration and the Department of Continuing and Vocational Education, at the University of Wisconsin-Madison. He is also the director of the University's Vocational Studies Center. Dr. Strong has served as a high school teacher, a local school administrator of vocational education, head of an instructional materials laboratory and with the U.S. Office of Education on the staff of the vocational-technical division.

INDEX

Index

F

Families, 5, 26, 32, 53, 82, 96, 132, 134-135, 138, 140, 156, 161, 180, 202, 232
Family in Post-Industrial America, The (Snyder), 284
Family in Renaissance Florence, The (Alberti), 65
Farmers, 59, 66, 130, 172-173
Fashion Institute of Technology, 39, 282
Federal aid, 57, 67, 216-221, 228-234, 247, 250, 258-263, 271
Federal Mediation and Conciliation Services, 283
Feedback, 125, 141, 148
Feldman, Marvin, 5, 35-39, 282
Feminism, 86, *see also* Women
Fertility, 136-137
Financial resources, 6, 65, 232-234
Fischer, R. G., 49-50
Fishing, 10, 17
Five Year Plan, 91
Flexibility, 110, 113, 191, 218, 276
Florida, 166, 173
Food, 132-133, 141-142, 152, 171-173
Ford Foundation, 248, 282
Forecasting, 5, 33, 41-52, 95
Foreign manufacture, 20, 145
Foundations, 248
Four-year colleges, 31, 189
Francke, August Herman, 10, 12
Frank (Judge), 66
Freedom, 5, 7, 65, 87, 91, 93-96, 104, 175
Free markets, 38, 76, 272
Free Religion movement, 86
Free societies, 74
Freud, Sigmund, 278
Frictional unemployment, 197
Friere, Paul, 66
Fulfillment, 78
Full employment, 75-76
Full Employment and Balanced Growth Act of 1978, 271
Future, 1-7, 13, 33, 41-42, 50-51, 72, 82, 107, 114
Future circles, 45-48
Future shock, 35, 71, 88
Futurist, 111, 284
Futurists, 35, 51, 111, 151, 278

G

Galbraith, John Kenneth, 221
Galloway, Joel D., 6, 177, 187-193, 282
Gaming, 48
Garden of Eden, 15
General education, 11, 16, 19-20, 193, 202-204, 208-209, 227
General Electric, 185
Genetics, 111, 147, 153
Geographical relocation, 197, 200, 207
Geography, 26, 124, 172
Germany, 35, 77, 135
G.I. Bill of Rights, 56, 195
Gilbert, Fontelle, 188-189, 192
Giving Youth a Better Chance (Carnegie Corporation of New York), 247-248
Gnostic Gospels, The (Pagel), 65
Goal-oriented forecasting, 45
Goals, 91, 272
God, 101, 103
"God the Father/God the Mother" (Pagel), 65
Gompers, Samuel, 28
Good life, 74-75, 183

Goods, 80-81, 130
Government, 57, 138, 148, 155, 185, 239, 244
Government training programs, 55
Grasso, John T., 116, 259, 262
Great man theory of history, 10
Greece, 74
Greek Commonwealth (Zimmern), 64
Greek philosophy, 79
Greeks of classical times, 13-19, 22
Greene, Theodore M., 26-27
Greening, 74
Greenwood, Katy, 5, 67, 71-83, 282
Gross National Product (GNP), 127, 133, 137, 157-158, 256-257, 261, 273
Growth, 2-3, 35, 37, 77, 81, 110, 113-116, 136-137, 154-156, 247, 274, 276
Guidance, career, 118, 201-203, 209
Guilds, 64-65
Guzzardi, Walter, Jr., 189-190

H

Habitats, 133-134, 142
Haitians, 242
Halperin, Samuel, 6, 213, 215-223, 283
Hammar, Paul L., 5, 101-106, 283
Handicrafts, 12, 18, *see also* Crafts
Handicapped persons, 117, 187-188, 229, 242, 257
Have We Kept the Faith (Prosser), 25
Hawthorne, Nathaniel, 85
Health, 104, 117, 132, 141-142, 147, 158, 202
Health maintenance organizations (HMOs), 141-142
Heritage, 21, 27, 101-106
Hesoid, 10, 13
Hewlett Packard, 37
Hierarchies, 75
Higher education, 79, 81, 148, 179, 183, 268
High School Longitudinal Study (1972), 60, 259
High schools, 19, 25, 31, 60, 81, 116-117, 148, 158-159, 190, 202, 231, 233, 241, 256, 267
Hispanics, 188
History, 5, 9-32, 71-73, 76, 101, 139-140
Homer, 13, 16
Homo Faber—Work through the Ages (Tilgher), 63
Horatio Alger, 5, 74
Households, 132, 135-137, 142-144, 180, 232
Hudson Institute, 35
Hull House, 28
Human capital, 77, 139
Humanitarianism, 86
Human resources, 6, 29, 123, 151, 154-155, 196, 213, 237-253, 255, 271-280
Humphrey, Hubert H., 195
Hunting, 10, 17

I

Ideals, 16, 78, 88
Ideology, 71-72, 85-88, 93
Illiad (Homer), 16
Illich, Ivan, 64
Images, public, 57-58
Immigration, 4, 156, 177, 182, 229, 240, 242
Incentives, work, 75
Income, 2, 75, 78, 82, 180-181, 189, 277
Indians, 91-92
Indiana State Commission on Industry and Agricultural Education, 28
Individual education plans, 218
Individualism, 87

290

Index

Index

Index